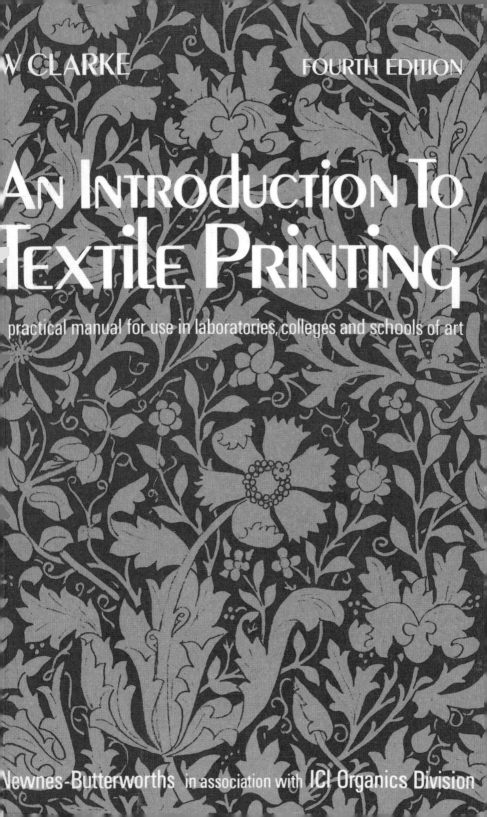

W CLARKE   FOURTH EDITION

An Introduction To
Textile Printing

practical manual for use in laboratories, colleges and schools of art

Newnes-Butterworths in association with ICI Organics Division

An Introduction to

Textile Printing

Other books on Textiles

Man–made Fibres
Principles of Textile Testing
Standard Handbook of Textiles
Watson's Advanced Textile Design
Watson's Textile Design and Colour
Further details are included at the end of this book

An Introduction to
Textile Printing

A Practical Manual for Use in Laboratories,
Colleges and Schools of Art

W. Clarke, B.Sc.Tech., A.M.C.T.

TEXTILE
BOOK The book company
for the textile world
SERVICE

1447 E. Second St.
P.O. Box 907
Plainfield,
New Jersey 07061
U. S. A.

THE BUTTERWORTH GROUP

UNITED KINGDOM Butterworth & Co (Publishers) Ltd
London: 88 Kingsway, WC2B 6AB

AUSTRALIA Butterworths Pty Ltd
Sydney: 586 Pacific Highway, Chatswood, NSW 2067
Also at Melbourne, Brisbane, Adelaide and Perth

CANADA Butterworth & Co (Canada) Ltd
Toronto: 2265 Midland Avenue, Scarborough,
Ontario, M1P 4S1

NEW ZEALAND Butterworths of New Zealand Ltd
Wellington: 26–28 Waring Taylor Street, 1

SOUTH AFRICA Butterworth & Co (South Africa) (Pty) Ltd
Durban: 152–154 Gale Street

USA Butterworth (Publishers) Inc
Boston: 19 Cummings Park, Woburn, Mass. 01801

First published in 1964
Second edition 1967
Third edition 1971
Fourth edition 1974
Reprinted (with revision) 1977

© Butterworth & Co (Publishers) Ltd, 1974

ISBN 0 408 00141 0

Printed in England by Billing & Sons Limited,
Guildford, London and Worcester

Preface

This publication originated many years ago as a collection of typed notes prepared by the Dyestuffs Division of Imperial Chemical Industries Limited for the guidance of students in colleges and schools of art. Published under the title *The Printing of Textile Fabrics by Block and Screen*, it was considerably extended in scope and five editions were issued. The current title is considered to be more appropriate to its present contents and aims. Considerable revision has taken place since the second edition, much new material has been added and the chapters put into a more logical sequence.

In a publication of this size only an outline of the subject can be provided. Detailed chemistry of both fibres and dyestuffs has been avoided, since this requires a considerable background in organic chemistry. The terminology used more and more in the technical press to distinguish between fibres has been introduced and related to a number of fibremakers' trademarks. Dyestuff classes and fastness properties of dyes on a given fibre have been described. These have been illustrated by listing the important fastness properties of recommended dyestuffs.

Before printing is attempted, one should be certain as to which fibre or fibres compose the fabric. For this reason fibres and fibre blends are now dealt with in Chapter 1. Dye and fibre suitabilities have been tabulated and the classification of dyestuffs has been described in Chapter 2. A chapter on thickening agents then follows in which emphasis is made on the convenience of modern cold-dissolving thickeners, which are so much easier to use than traditional gums.

A survey of printing methods and the equipment required covers block, screen and roller printing. The latter refers to the laboratory type of machines. All the equipment and print pastes in the world are of little value if the fabric to be printed has not been scoured. Preparation of fabrics therefore receives a separate chapter which is followed by one on the various stages of printing procedure. Information sources for further details on processing machinery are listed.

The printing of individual or related fibres is dealt with over the next six chapters. Readers familiar with the first or second edition will note

4128

the disappearance of detailed recipes for mordant dyes. Reasons for this withdrawal are, however, given in the text.

The recipes given in the various chapters on printing different fibres have been taken from practice, but students in particular are reminded that they may need to work out modifications under their own conditions. In general, modification of viscosity will be the most frequently needed adjustment and this is easily carried out.

The descriptions of discharge and resist printing which are more difficult to carry out, although more rewarding, have been left until later in the book. Resist printing is confined to Indonesian Batik and West African Wax printing. Batik printing has long been of interest as a handicraft study and pastime.

Special methods of textile printing form a short chapter, and these range from carpet printing to transfer printing with several diverse methods in between.

In this book reference is occasionally made to 'Technical Information Notes' by number, and these can be obtained through the Sales Offices of ICI if required. In such cases, readers should request the latest information on the subject of interest to them and not rely only on quoting the number of the Technical Information Note.

In this, the fourth edition, an extra chapter has been added on transfer printing which is the fastest-growing area in modern textile printing. Recent major changes in dyestuff nomenclature would have necessitated extensive revision of the text. To avoid this a glossary has been compiled in the form of an additional appendix that provides a guide to both the original and the latest dye names. Appendix 2 on suppliers of screen printing equipment has also been completely revised.

W.C.

Contents

1
Fibres and Fibre Blends

Before attempting to print any textile fabric it is important to know from which textile fibres it has been produced. This determines which classes of dyestuff are potentially suitable to colour the fabric. Equally important, it becomes clear which classes of dye must not be used. Convenient main and subdivisions of fibres are given below.

NATURAL FIBRES

This class includes cotton and linen; both are cellulosic fibres (i.e. cellulose is the fibre forming material). Wool and silk contain peptide links in their fibre molecules and the term *polypeptides* has been applied to them. They have also been called protein fibres. While there are other natural fibres they are only very rarely encountered in a form requiring printing.

MAN-MADE FIBRES

There are now a very large number of fibres which come under this category. While these fibres fall into relatively few chemical types, many trademarks are used by the manufacturers to describe their individual products. It is proposed to give a few examples of trademarks under each chemical type. Comprehensive dictionaries relating trademarks to chemical types have been compiled and are revised at regular intervals [1-9]

Physical Modifications

When a man-made fibre is produced it is extruded continuously either into hot air or a chemical coagulating bath. Filament yarns are produced from these extruded fibres in which each filament is more or less continuous. Another method consists of extruding a much larger number

1

of individual threads called a *tow* collectively. The tow is subsequently cut into short lengths, which are determined by the type of machinery on which the yarns are to be spun, either wholly from the cut fibre or in admixture with a natural fibre. Once the tow has been cut it is termed *staple fibre* and yarns prepared from it are called *staple yarns*.

Two terms frequently encountered nowadays in connection with man-made fibres and yarns made from them are *texturised* and *bulked* yarns. These yarns have been physically modified, and while this does not alter their chemical type, they are frequently sold under a trademark which differs from that used for the parent fibre. The bulking process, which may be achieved by a variety of methods depending on the fibre, produces a series of coils, loops or crimps along the fibre length. While most bulked yarns are very stable there is a danger that if the fabric is treated at temperatures above those recommended by the manufacturer loss of bulk will occur. This is accompanied by fabric stretching and a loss of the attractive fabric handle produced by bulking.

Chemical Types of Man-Made Fibre

Regenerated Cellulose Fibres: Cuprammonium and Viscose Rayons

Since cellulose has not been synthesised it is necessary to use a natural source for fibre making. Normally, bleached wood pulp is used. In some instances cotton *linters* (i.e. fibres too short for spinning) are also employed but generally inadequate supplies are available.

The name of the dissolving process used to produce a solution of cellulose for extrusion through the spinarettes is often associated with the end product. Thus cuprammonium rayon described a product sold under the trademark 'Bemberg' by a company with German and American interests. Cuprammonium rayon is today of far less importance than viscose rayon. The viscose process is cheaper to operate and successive improvements in technique have enabled a wide variety of viscose rayon qualities to be marketed throughout the world. A group of physically modified viscose rayons are termed *polynosic* fibres. One measure of the fineness of a yarn is the *denier*. This is defined as the weight in grammes of 9 000 m of a continuous filament yarn, hence the lower the denier the finer the yarn. The system is applied to all man-made fibres. Industrial qualities are defined by denier and, where necessary, staple length.

Cellulose Acetate and Cellulose Triacetate

While these are classified as regenerated cellulose fibres they differ from cuprammonium and viscose rayons in one important aspect. Cellulose is converted to its acetate derivative to enable it to be dissolved in an appropriate solvent from which it is spun. The spinning operation does not remove the acetate groups and so the cellulose is regenerated in a chemically modified form. In the manufacture of cellulose acetate the solvent used is acetone and this necessitates the removal by hydrolysis of a proportion of the acetate groups. The resulting product is often called the *secondary acetate,* the *2½-acetate,* or simply *diacetate.* Such terms are understood to mean that the product is a cellulose derivative.

Cellulose triacetate is a much more recently marketed fibre than the diacetate. For a long time the problem had been to find an economical solvent to dissolve the triacetate. Chloroform had the solvent power required but possessed other defects as well as economic ones. By using methylene dichloride a suitably priced and otherwise satisfactory product was evolved. The fibre is marketed by Courtaulds under the trademark 'Tricel' and by the Celanese Corporation of America as 'Arnel'.

Polyamide Fibres

The term *polyamide* indicates that the fibre molecules contain many CONH − groups. These have been formed from intermediates which are not themselves of a fibrous nature.

Because the starting material for one type of nylon is caprolactam, fibres derived from it may be designated *polycaprolactam* rather than *polyamide,* in some literature references. Such products are always called nylon 6, using a number classification which will shortly be explained.

Nylon was the first commercially available product of this type and the first wholly synthetic fibre. It was first marketed by Du Pont in the USA in 1939. A classification system has come into use among fibre and dyestuff chemists which indicates the type of nylon. This is important, since the dyeing properties and other properties differ depending on the starting material. Nylon 66 and nylon 6 are the two types most commonly encountered. Nylon 11 is marketed in very much smaller amounts. The number refers to the number of carbon atoms in the repeating unit of the molecule. When confronted by a trademark relating to nylon the first step should be to find out which type is meant. Trademarks and the companies who own them (parent company first) include:

Nylon 66:   'Bri-nylon' (ICI Fibres), 'Banlon' (Bancroft, USA).
Nylon 6 :   'Celon' (Courtaulds), 'Enkalon' (AKU, Holland; American Enka Corp., USA), 'Perlon' (Hoechst, W. Germany).
Nylon 11:   'Rilsan' (Snia Viscosa, Italy; Organico, France).

Positive identification of nylon 66 or 6 depends on the fact that nylon 66 melts at 250°C, while nylon 6 melts at 210°C. Without a suitable melting point apparatus no reliable sorting procedure can be recommended.

3

Other varieties of nylon, particularly in carpet yarns, are the *differential dyeing* type. These are produced at the fibre manufacturing stage by incorporating small amounts of special chemicals. The resulting nylons, while still essentially of the 66 or 6 type, will absorb greater or lesser quantities of acid dyes than normal. Alternatively, such modified nylons may be designed to be dyeable with dyes of a class not normally used on nylon (e.g. basic dyes). The three most common types of differential dyeing nylon are termed *deep-dyeing, regular dyeing* and *basic-dyeable-acid-dye resist**.

Polyester Fibres

The name is derived from the fact that the molecules of the starting materials join together by ester links to form the long fibre molecules. Although the original patents were filed in 1941, commercial develop-ment was delayed by war-time conditions. 'Terylene' polyester fibre was first marketed by ICI in 1952. The Du Pont Company, operating under a licence from the original UK patentees marketed 'Dacron' in the USA. Subsequently, other manufacturers obtained licences and know-how from ICI and produced the polyester fibre under names which include:

> 'Trevira' (Farbwerke Hoechst, Germany)
> 'Tergal' (Soc. Rhodiaceta, France)
> 'Terital' (Montecatini, Italy)
> 'Terlenka' (AKU, Holland)
> 'Tetoron' (Toyo Rayon, Japan)
> 'Fortrel' (Fibre Industries, USA).

When a polyester fibre has been processed by one of the bulking processes the resulting yarns and fabrics produced from them are sometimes marketed under a trademark which differs from the parent fibre, e.g. 'Crimplene' (ICI) is a bulked variety of 'Terylene' and hence both remain classed as polyester fibres.

Acrylic Fibres

The name for fibres in this group is derived from the major starting material which is acrylonitrile. Research to convert this chemically simple substance to a polymer with useful fibre properties commenced in both USA and Germany in the early 1940's. The major problem was that of dyeing the resulting fibres. By incorporating quantities of other polymerisable materials with the acrylonitrile, co-polymers were produced containing dye-receptive sites. These are termed *modified*

---

*Some carpet yarns may be spun to include all three types and hence give three shade depths in one dying operation.

4

acrylics or *modacrylics* and largely constitute the now commercially available fibres in this group. Because the nature and degree of co-polymerisation vary it cannot be assumed that one manufacturer's acrylic fibre will behave in an identical fashion to another in all respects. There are sufficient general properties, however, which are close enough to enable the group to be discussed as a whole. Acrylic fabrics are very often produced from bulked yarns and this need not be indicated by a change in trademark. A short selection of acrylic fibre trademarks are as follows:

> 'Acrilan' (Chemstrand Corp, USA)
> 'Courtelle' (Courtaulds, UK)
> 'Dralon' (F. Bayer, W. Germany)
> 'Orlon' (Du Pont, USA).

Elastomeric Fibres

These, as the name suggests, are elastic fibres. They are intended to replace rubber in those outlets where it is used with other fibres to produce elastic fabrics. The generic name 'Spandex' has been approved in the USA by the Federal Trade Commission for fibres containing a defined minimum of a segmented polyurethane. The first elastomeric fibre, called 'Lycra' was introduced by Du Pont in the USA, in 1959. Dyeing and printing fabrics containing 'Lycra' require processes which do not affect the unique properties of the fibre.

Blended Fibres and Union Fabrics

It is possible to blend two or more different fibres at the spinning stage provided they are of the appropriate length. A synthetic fibre must be in staple form and if two synthetic fibres are being blended then naturally they will be cut to equal length. The resulting yarns are termed *blended* yarns.

Fabrics which are woven from at least one blended yarn, whether this forms the warp or the weft, are called *union* fabrics. The term also includes fabrics which are woven from two different yarns on the warp and weft, even if each of these is composed of only one fibre.

Fibre and/or fabric blends in current use are often coupled with an indication of the proportion of each fibre in the blend, e.g. *Terylene/ cotton 67/33* indicate that 'Terylene' forms $\frac{2}{3}$ of the total fibres present and cotton the remaining $\frac{1}{3}$. Typically, this blend would be composed of both warp and weft yarns in which the two fibres were present in the same proportion.

5

Blends may be encountered which are being promoted under a separate trademark, e.g. 'Tricelon' (Courtaulds) which is a blend of 'Tricel' (cellulose triacetate) and 'Celon' (a nylon 6 polyamide fibre). The presence of two or more fibres in a fabric may call for the use of different classes of dye to colour each fibre.

Fabric Terms Related to Methods of Production

The method by which a fabric has been produced is sometimes used to complete its description. Thus a woven fabric is one which has been produced on a loom. Weft and warp knitted fabrics represent much more recent developments designed to accelerate the rate at which yarn is converted to fabric. By omitting the spinning and weaving stages *non-woven* fabrics are produced. This is a field where extensive research and development is proceeding. The primary question which must follow any request to print non-woven fabrics remains the same as for the woven or knitted fabrics, viz. What fibre type or types comprise the fabric?

When a fabric is described as, for example, a poplin, twill, haircord, waffle or honeycomb, this refers to a special appearance achieved by varying the yarns and weaving or knitting mechanisms. These are only a very small sample of the vast number of possibilities. The best source of information when an unknown term of this type is encountered is a textile dictionary, of which some examples are given in the list of references.

Identification of Fibres

If the fabric has a commercial trademark, or has been ordered on the basis of one, it can usually be assigned to one of the main groups already mentioned. Where an unknown fabric is to be printed this must be identified so that an appropriate class of dye may be chosen. Several simple tests are available and a combination of them may enable a positive identification to be made. While fibre cross-sections are often illustrated and are indeed characteristic of many fibres, their preparation requires skill, experience and sophisticated equipment. The burning test which will be described often gives a preliminary indication of the fibre present. Fuller information requires the use of Shirlastains *A, C* and *D*. These products are dyestuff mixtures compiled so that different fibres are dyed selectively with their components. See Appendix 2 (page 258) for their supplier.

Burning Test

A thread of the fibre is placed in contact with a naked flame and the behaviour of the fibre noted.

Protein fibres (wool and natural silk) do not burn readily, and burning ceases as soon as the fibre is removed from the neighbourhood of the flame. These fibres burn forming a black bead and give off a characteristic smell of burning feathers.

Cellulosic fibres (cotton, viscose rayon, linen) burn readily and burning continues even after the flame has been removed. These fibres burn without forming a bead and give off a smell of charred paper.

Cellulose acetate fibres burn less readily than cellulosic fibres, forming a bead which shrinks away from the flame. The bead formed is black in colour and can easily be crushed between the fingers; a smell of acetic acid can be noted during the burning of cellulose acetate. Cellulose 'secondary acetate' is identified by being soluble in a mixture of 70% acetone and 30% water. Cellulose 'triacetate' is insoluble in this mixture.

Nylon and 'Terylene' do not burn, but shrink from the flame, giving a hard round bead which cannot be crushed between the fingers. Nylon gives off a smell similar to that of celery, whereas 'Terylene' gives off an aromatic odour.

It should be noted that in many fabrics the warp (that is, the threads running parallel to the selvedge) and the weft (threads running perpendicular to the selvedge) are composed of different fibres and it is, therefore, suggested that the warp and the weft be examined separately. Furthermore, the yarns themselves are sometimes composed of two or more different fibres. In this case identification is more difficult but should be possible by the use of Shirlastains *A, C* and *D*.

REFERENCES

1. *Textile Terms and Definitions,* 5th edn., Textile Institute, Manchester, 1963
2. HATHORNE, A. L., *Woven, Stretch and Textured Fabrics,* Interscience, New York, 1964
3. MARK, H. L. *et al., Man-Made Fibres Science and Technology,* Interscience, New York, 1967, 3 vols
4. MONCRIEFF, R. W., *Man-Made Fibres,* 5th edn., Butterworths, London, 1970
5. LINTON, G.E., *The Modern Textile Dictionary,* 2nd edn., Duell, Sloan and Pierce, New York, 1963.
6. WINGATE, I. B., *Fairchild's Dictionary of Textiles,* 2nd edn., Fairchild Publications, New York, 1967
7. BLACKSHAW, H. and BRIGHTMAN, R., *Dictionary of Dyeing and Printing,* Newnes, London, 1961
8. *Guidebook to Man-Made Textile Fibres and Textured Yarns of the World,* 3rd edn., The United Piece Dyeworks, New York, 1969
9. *Index to Man-Made Fibres of the World,* 3rd edn., Harlequin Press, Manchester, 1967

2

The Various Dyestuff Classes and Their Fibre Suitability

Dyestuffs classified according to their chemical structure would form at least 30 classes. The alternative method of classification relies on trade usage. Since dyemakers sell the majority of their products under a trademark it is important to be able to recognise to which class of dye this trademark refers. The major reference work in this field is the Colour Index[1] which has the additional advantage of allowing dyestuff equivalents to be looked up. An equivalent is the same dye made by two or more makers. Such dyes would have the same Colour Index (CI) number within a given application group (i.e. based on trade usage).

CLASSIFICATION OF DYESTUFFS

Acid Dyes

This is a large class characterised by their substantivity for protein fibres (wool, silk). They are normally applied from an acid dyebath, and hence the name. They are also used for nylon dyeing and printing. ICI trademarks are 'Lissamine', 'Coomassie', 'Carbolan' and 'Nylomine'Acid. Acid dyes are anionic, i.e. the dye molecule is negatively charged.

Azoic Dyes

These are used in printing, mainly for cellulosic fibres (predominantly cotton). The characteristic feature of these dyes is that they are formed *in situ* within the fibre by the reaction of two components, i.e. the diazo component and the coupling component. These components are applied separately, i.e. the coupling component first, followed by the diazo component. A variety of chemical modifications to diazo compounds have enabled them to be mixed with coupling compounds without

8

immediately generating the dyestuff. The dye is formed in a subsequent steaming operation. Trade names are 'Brenthol' (coupling component) and 'Brentamine' (diazo component). The former Brentogen range was based on stabilised 'Brentamine' and 'Brenthol' mixtures, acid steaming being needed to form the dye. Ordinary steaming suffices to develop the 'Neutrogen' (CFMC) and 'Rapidogen' N (FH) brands.

Basic Dyes

These dyes are cationic, i.e. the dye molecule is positively charged. To apply them to cotton it proved necessary to give a tannin mordanting treatment. The resulting fastness of the dyes was still only moderate and the style is now virtually obsolete. Basic dyes may be applied to wool and silk without mordant, but again the results are characterised more by brightness than fastness. Specially developed basic dyes are widely used on acrylic fibres, upon which they are quite fast. The ICI trademark is 'Synacril'.

Direct Dyes

The name arose from the fact that the dyes possessed direct substantivity for cotton, i.e. without the necessity for a pre-mordanting treatment. A wide range is available both in colour and in fastness. The limiting factor for these dyes in printing is their lack of washing fastness even when given one of the various aftertreatments available. ICI trademarks are 'Chlorazol' and 'Durazol'.

Disperse Dyes

These are water insoluble dyes sold as aqueous dispersions or as redispersible powders or grains. They were originally introduced for the dyeing of cellulose acetate. Modern disperse dyes are printed on 'Terylene' polyester fibre, cellulose acetate and cellulose triacetate. ICI trademarks are 'Dispersol', 'Duranol' and 'Procinyl' (disperse reactive type).

Mordant Dyes

These are dyes which are applied to the fibre in conjunction with a metal salt. The dye-metal complex possesses greater fastness than the dye alone.

In spite of the fact that basic dyes were applied to cotton by means of a tannin-antimony mordant it is conventional to exclude such dyes from the mordant group. Similarly excluded are direct dyes requiring a metallic salt treatment to obtain full fastness. Some mordant dyes are of great antiquity and many used even fifty years ago were of natural origin. Turkey reds, madder and alizarin reds all relied on an aluminium mordant while logwood blacks were based on iron. Chromium acetate was widely used in admixture with mordant dyes for cotton printing. These dyes are only very rarely encountered in modern textile printing.

Premetallised Dyes

These may be regarded as a later development of mordant dyes. Prior to their discovery wool had been mordant dyed by three processes:

(i) Applying a chromium salt to the wool before the dye (chrome mordant method).
(ii) Applying the dye first and aftertreating with a chromium salt (the afterchrome method).
(iii) Applying the dye and chromium salt simultaneously (the metachrome method).

The difficulty especially in the afterchrome method was due to colour matching in the presence of an appreciable shade change. This led to research on preformed dye-metal complexes. Swiss and German manufacturers achieved the first real success on wool in 1915, and introduced ranges of 1:1 chrome complex dyes. The strong acid necessary to dye these products led to further work. By linking chromium with two molecules of dye, the 1:2 chromium complexes were formed. These were easier to apply and are widely used in dyeing and to a lesser extent in printing. Trademarks are 'Irgalan' (Geigy) and 'Cibalan' (CIBA).

Onium Dyes

A small range of dyes which owe their name to the fact that they are either ammonium or sulphonium compounds. They are water soluble cationic dyes and hence must not be mixed with anionic dyes, otherwise they will precipitate each other. In the presence of heat and alkali the solubilising groups split up to give a very fast dye on the fibre. This is an example of a temporarily solubilised dye. Cotton is the most important fibre for onium dyes. The ICI trademark is 'Alcian'.

Pigment Dyes

These products are insoluble in water and are preferably also insoluble in white spirit and in chlorinated solvents used in dry cleaning. In admixture with a suitable resin binder they may be printed on the majority of textile fabrics. In recent years extensive research especially in USA and in Germany has produced greatly improved binders. This has resulted in prints of much softer handle (drape) as well as better wet and dry rubbing (crocking) fastness. The trademarks are 'Aridye' and 'Hifast' (Inmont, USA), 'Acramin' (F.Bayer), 'Helizarin' (BASF, W. Germany) and 'Monolite' and 'Monastral' (ICI).

Oxidation Dyes

In principle, a small molecular weight intermediate is treated under acid oxidation conditions to form a much larger coloured molecule. These products have been most widely developed as hair and fur dyes. In printing, aniline black is still of importance, while diphenyl black is now little used although a solubilised derivative of the starting intermediate 'Solonile' black (CFMC) is of value in certain styles. Paramine brown, one of the few other oxidation colours formerly employed in textile printing, fell out of general use on fastness grounds.

Reactive Dyes

First marketed by ICI in 1956, this group of dyes owe their name to their ability to undergo a chemical reaction with cellulose fibres. This produces a covalent dye-fibre bond which gives dyeings and prints of excellent washing fastness. Reaction with wool and silk is also possible, while on nylon, although some of the dyes fix well, the molecular size of some of the others is too large to penetrate the nylon efficiently. Reactivity and hence dye stability may vary widely. It is usual to indicate differences in reactivity either by using two trademarks or by using two different letters and a single trademark, e.g. 'Procion' *M* (more reactive) and 'Procion' *H* (less reactive) dyes.

Soluble Vat Dyes

These must be distinguished from conventional vat dyes, which will be described shortly. The most important difference is that to make a soluble vat dye the dye maker reduces the parent vat dye and forms the

11

sodium salt of the sulphuric acid ester. The resulting water soluble product is converted by an acid oxidation process back to the parent vat dye on the fibre. The dyes are applicable to cotton, viscose rayon, natural silk and wool. The ICI trademark is 'Soledon'.

Sulphur Dyes

These products may be dyed to give fabrics of good washing fastness at low cost. As a range they have never been successful in textile printing owing to erratic fixation. An exception is the sulphur black 'Indocarbon' *CL* (Casella) and its equivalents. These are printed alongside the cheaper members of the vat range where all-round fastness requirements are not excessively stringent, e.g. dress goods, but not furnishings.

Vat Dyes

These dyes are insoluble in water and contain keto groups. In alkaline solution a reducing agent, e.g. sodium hydrosulphite will produce a soluble leuco compound. It is the sodium salt of the leuco compound which dyes into the fibre. To obtain the vat dye back in its original form an oxidation treatment is necessary. Indigo is a vat dye and synthetic sulphur-containing derivatives are termed *thioindigoid* vat dyes. The other and larger vat dye groups are termed *anthraquinonoid* vats. This broad classification is often used as the basis of dividing the dyes into two ranges by using two trademarks, e.g. 'Durindone' (for indigoid and thioindigoid vat dyes) and 'Caledon' (for anthraquinonoid vat dyes).

Dyestuffs Chemistry

Dyestuff chemistry is a specialised branch of organic chemistry but students with a good grounding in organic chemistry will profit from a study of the books listed at the end of this chapter[2-7]

Choice of Dyestuffs for a Particular Fibre

Table 2.1 gives a preliminary indication of whether a particular dyestuff class is potentially suitable for a class of fibres using the groupings given in Chapter 1. More specific recommendations are given in succeeding chapters. Within a particular range of dyes which are potentially suitable

Table 2.1. APPLICABILITY OF VARIOUS DYESTUFF CLASSES TO DIFFERENT FIBRES IN TEXTILE PRINTING

| Class of Dyestuff | Natural Fibres | | | | Regenerated Cellulosic | | | | Man-Made Fibres | | | | | Fibre Blends |
| | Cellulosic | | Protein | | | | | | | | | | | |
	Cotton	Linen	Wool	Silk	Viscose Rayon. e.g. Fibro	Cuprammonium Rayon. e.g. Bemberg	Cellulose Acetate, e.g. Dicel	Cellulose Triacetate e.g. Tricel	Polyamide Nylon 6 Nylon 6.6 e.g. Bri-nylon Celon	Polyester e.g. Terylene Crimplene	Acrylic e.g. Courtelle Acrilan	Elastomeric e.g. Spandex, Lycra	Fibre Glass	
Acid Dyes, e.g. Carbolan, Coomassie, Nylomine	NS	NS	SI	SI	SLFO	NS	SUD	SUD	SI	NS	NS	SI	NS	
Azoic Dyes, e.g. Brenthol-Brentamine	SI	SI	NS	NS	SI	SI	NS	NS	NS	NS	NS	NS	NS	
Basic Dyes, e.g. Synacril	SLFO	SLFO	SUD	SUD	SLFO	SLFO	NS	NS	NS	NS	SI	NS	NS	
Direct Dyes, e.g. Chlorazol, Durazol	SUD	SUD	SUD	SUD	SUD	SUD	NS	NS	NS	NS	NS	NS	NS	
Disperse Dyes, e.g. Dispersol, Duranol	NS	NS	NS	NS	NS	NS	SI	SI	SUD	SI	SUD	SUD	NS	
Mordant Dyes, e.g Alizarin	SO	SO	SUD	SUD	SO	SO	NS	NS	NS	NS	NS	NS	NS	
Onium Dyes, e.g. Alcian	SI	SO	NS	NS	NS	NS	NS	NS	NS	NS	NS	NS	NS	
Pigment Dyes (+ Binder) e.g. Monolite, Monastral	SI	SI	SI	SI	SI	SI	SI	SI	SI	SI	SI	SLF	SI	
Oxidation Dyes e.g. Solanile black	SI	SI	NS	NS	SI	SI	NS	NS	NS	NS	NS	NS	NS	
Reactive Dyes, e.g. Procion *M* and *H*	SI	SI	SI	SI	SI	SI	NS	NS	NS	NS	NS	NS	NS	
Soluble Vat Dyes, e.g. Soledons	SUD	SUD	SUD	SUD	SUD	SUD	NS	NS	SUD	NS	SUD	NS	NS	
Sulphur Dyes, e.g. Indocarbon (CFM)	SI	SI	NS	NS	SI	SI	NS	NS	NS	NS	NS	NS	NS	
Vat Dyes, e.g. Durindone, Caledon	SI	SI	SUD	SUD	SI	SI	NS	NSE	NS	NS	NS	NS	NS	

Assuming the fibres forming the blend and their relative proportions are known, proceed as follows:

(1) Check if one class of dye is suitable for both fibres. If none are, note which two classes of dye are potentially suitable for both fibres. If still none, note which two classes of dye are potentially suitable for each fibre.

(2) Where more than one choice of dye class is possible the final choice will be determined by ease of application and subsequent after-processing.

SI   = Suitable and of interest
SLF   = Suitable but lacks fastness
SLFO = Suitable but lacks fastness and is now obsolescent

SUD = Suitable but usage declining
SO = Suitable but obsolescent

NS = Not suitable
NSE = Not suitable except in fibre blends

for colouring more than one fibre, individual members of the range may be eliminated on one fibre for reasons of yield or fastness.

REFERENCES

1. *The Colour Index,* 2nd edn., The Society of Dyers and Colourists, Bradford, 1957–1958, 4 vols
2. *An Outline of the Chemistry and Technology of the Dyestuffs Industry,* ICI Dyestuffs Div., 1968
3. FIERZ DAVID, H. E. and BLANGEY, L., *Fundamental Processes of Dye Chemistry,* London and New York Interscience Publications, 1949
4. VENKATARAMAN, K., *Chemistry of Synthetic Dyes,* Academic Press, 1952, 2 vols
5. ABRAHART, E. N., *Dyes and Their Intermediates,* Pergamon Press, London, 1968
6. ALLEN, R. L. M., *Colour Chemistry*, Nelson, 1971.
7. BEECH, W. F., *Fibre Reactive Dyes,* Logos Press, London, 1970.

3

The Types and Properties of Thickening Agents

The prime function of a thickening agent in textile printing is to enable the dyestuff or pigment to be transferred to the fabric at the printing stage. Immediately following printing the thickening must contain the dye within the printed area during drying. Furthermore, the thickening agent must not break down during steaming or any other fixation process to such an extent that colour 'bleeding' occurs. Finally, the thickening agent must be completely removed from the fabric during the washing-off treatment given to the dyestuffs. One further requirement is that the thickening agent must be compatible with all the other components in the print paste, and it must not be too expensive.

Textile thickening agents were at one time divided into gums and mucilages according to whether they were of a sticky or slimy nature. Now the chemical nature of these products is better understood, so too are the chemical reactions capable of modifying their properties on a commercially worthwhile basis. Thickening agents, like fibres, are long chain polymers and are classified as polysaccharides because the individual building units (monomers) of the polymer are simple sugars. Commonly encountered sugars in thickening agents include glucose, mannose and galactose (hexoses) as well as xylose and arabinose (pentoses). A given thickening may be composed entirely of one sugar unit (monosaccharide) present in long chains forming a homopolysaccharide. When the molecular chain is composed of two or more different monosaccharides it is termed a *heteropolysaccharide*. The molecular chains may be linear or branched and this is important in determining the properties of the thickening agent[1].

Natural Gums Used in Textile Printing

These are summarised in *Table 3.1.* which lists various natural gums and indicates their extraction sources.

Table 3.1. NATURAL GUMS USED IN TEXTILE PRINTING

Extraction Source	Gum Name	Trade Name
Trees and shrubs	Gum Arabic, Gum Senegal Gum Tragacanth and Gum Karaya	
Plant or tree seeds	Locust Bean gum	Gum Gatto and Cesalpiniagum (Cesalpina, Italy)
	Guar gum and starches	
Seaweed	Sodium alginate	Manutex (Alginate Inds.) and Lamitex (Protan, Norway)
	Carragheenan	Irish Moss (Blandola, UK)

NOTE. Gums based on solvent emulsions. Emulsion thickenings usually incorporate small amounts of a conventional thickening.

Modified Natural Gums Used in Textile Printing

By means of chemical and/or physical modification of a number of the gums listed in *Table 3.1* improved products result. These are sold under a number of trademarks by firms specialising in this work. The various brands available represent differing degrees of modification and make the product suitable for different outlets. Cellulose, which is normally very insoluble in water, will, by chemical modification, produce valuable thickeners. Typical products and the original source material (where published) are given in *Table 3.2*.

Table 3.2. TYPICAL PRODUCTS AND ORIGINAL SOURCE MATERIAL

Product	Source
British gums (various suppliers)	Starches
Nafka Crystal Gum (Scholtens, Holland)	Gum Karaya
Indalca series (Cesalpina, Milan)	Locust Bean gum (a mannogalactan gum)
Polyprint series (Polygal, W. Germany)	Probably Locust Bean derivatives
Meyprogum series (Meyhall Chemical, Switzerland)	Probably Guar gum derivatives
Solvitex and Solvitose series (Scholtens, Holland)	Starch derivatives such as ethers

The weight of dry thickening agent required to make a print paste of the correct viscosity varies from product to product. This depends essentially on the chain length and degree of chain branching in the thickening agent

16

molecules. Where relatively large weights of dry thickener are required, say 8% and upwards, the resulting thickening is described as being of *medium* or *high* solids content. Conversely, thickenings made with less dry agent are of *low* solids content. Thickening agents must possess satisfactory mechanical properties under printing conditions, otherwise an even print will not result. In addition, they must be fully compatible with the other components in the print paste. The viscosity of a print paste is most important, but an added complication is that with the majority of thickenings available, the viscosity falls at increasing rates of shear. The shear rate is determined by the mechanical stresses to which the paste is subjected at the printing stage. In effect it is a measure of the rate at which adjacent layers of thickening are being forced along relative to each other. For a long time there has been a tendency to refer

Table 3.3. THE INTERRELATIONSHIP BETWEEN LOW AND
HIGH SOLID THICKENING PROPERTIES

| *Characteristic Property* | *Type of Thickening* | |
	Low Solids	High Solids
Flow	*Short*	*Long*
Effect of increasing shear on viscosity	Viscosity falls off rapidly	Little or no falling off of viscosity
Yield of dye	Generally high	Usually of a lower order than low solids thickenings
Levelness of print	More difficult to achieve than with high solids thickenings	Generally good
Viscosity	High	Medium-low
Handling of dried or baked print	Flexible film giving moderate-good handle	Film tends to be hard, brittle and may crack off fabric
Nature of polysaccharide chains	Very long and straight with little or no side branching	Shorter than low solids types. Heavily branched, coiled in solution
Price of made-up thickening (i.e. price of dry thickener x% necessary to make a satisfactory paste)	Relatively low	More expensive than low solids type
Chemical resistance	There is no clear demarcation between the two types (see text)	

17

to thickenings as being either *short* or *long*. This describes their behaviour when a stirring rod is dipped into the thickening, raised out again and the adhering paste allowed to fall back into the container. A *long* thickening flows readily to form long streamers in the same way as syrups. The *short* type of thickening either stays on the rod or falls off in lumps, leaving no streamers. The interrelationship between these various properties is summarised in *Table 3.3*.

The manufacturers of chemically modified locust bean and guar gums usually offer a series of products with the same trademark sub-classified by brand letters or numbers, e.g. 'Indalca' *PA3*, 'Meypro' Gum *CRX*, 'Polyprint' *S–145*. The makers' literature should be consulted for the detailed properties of individual brands. Resistance to acid, alkali and salts of metals such as copper, chromium and aluminium is normally specified. Where a brand is lacking in resistance to one or other of these reagents there is invariably a suitable alternative brand offered by the same manufacturer.

SELECTION OF THICKENING AGENTS

An extremely useful feature of modern thickening agents is their ability to be dissolved in cold water with the aid of a high-speed stirrer. Natural gums of the exudate type, sold in lump form, require soaking in cold water for up to 24 h. This is followed by boiling the swollen lumps in a double-jacketed steam heated pan, with constant stirring. The boiling and cooling routine, albeit without preliminary soaking, is necessary for powdered gums such as locust bean gum and starches.

In the preparation of a thickening agent for use with a particular range of dyestuffs it is often advantageous to incorporate assistants and other chemicals necessary to fix the dyestuff. This is termed a *stock thickening*. A *reduction thickening* normally containing reduced amounts of chemicals may also be required. Using this technique a large number of printing colours are prepared very rapidly because the number of individual weighings is considerably reduced.

An emulsion thickening derives its viscosity from the dispersion of a large number of extremely tiny droplets of one liquid in another by means of a suitable dispersing agent. The two liquids must not mix or be soluble in each other, otherwise an emulsion will not form. It is conventional when describing emulsions to state, first, the substance existing in droplets and then the substance in which the droplets are dispersed (termed the *continuous phase*). Thus a water-in-oil (w/o) emulsion is one which owes its viscosity to water droplets dispersed in oil. In textile printing the 'oil' is supplied under names such as White

Spirit, Distillate, Safety Solvent, etc., by most oil companies. The specifications with regard to toxicity, flash-point, boiling range, specific gravity and KB (Kauri-butanol) value have been defined. Recommendations for ventilation conditions are available. These solvents are equally suitable for the preparation of oil-in-water (o/w) emulsions as for the w/o type. It is necessary to change to dispersing agent and often convenient to thicken the water phase with a small amount of conventional thickening agent (often called a *film former*). When rather more thickening is added the term *half-emulsion* is applied. After dyestuffs have been printed on the fabric and dried they must be fixed by steaming, baking or some other suitable process. This is usually followed by washing-off which serves to remove both unfixed dye and thickening agent plus any added chemicals. The ease with which a thickening agent may be removed is most important and manufacturers of thickeners have paid much attention to this property.

An additional property of some thickenings is their ability to be coagulated by alkaline solutions particularly where borax is also present. This is used to aid dyestuff fixation in two-stage processes and prevent dyestuff bleeding or spreading.

A prime requirement is that the thickener functions satisfactorily by the printing method chosen, e.g. screen blockages should not occur in screen printing or 'sticking-in' (i.e. blocking up the engraving) in roller printing. Since starchy thickenings are difficult to remove during washing-off their use with dyes of poor washing fastness would be unwise. A compromise is often possible by using mixed thickenings. The greater ease of cleaning-down equipment, rollers, screens, printing blankets and containers often results in oil-in-water emulsions being used in preference to water-in-oil systems. Available equipment is often decisive in determining which thickening is chosen from those available. Thus, if gum boiling pans such as the ones that are required for the preparation of British Gum Thickening are not available, an alternative cold-dissolving thickening agent may be used. The cold-dissolving thickenings are also convenient for small scale operation. Polythene containers, preferably with lids, are ideal for storing made-up thickenings. They must be washed out thoroughly before re-use to minimise bacterial decomposition. Most chemically modified thickeners already contain a preservative but natural gums do not. The addition of 0·5 parts 'Proxel' *PM* (ICI) per 1000 parts is often beneficial in such cases. To improve the lubrication properties of thickening agents, especially under commercial conditions, a printing oil may be added. Mineral oil Grade SAE 10 at the rate of 10–20 parts per 1000 parts usually effects an improvement in, for example, starch-gum tragacanth and thickenings containing relatively large amounts of electrolytes.

THE PREPARATION OF SELECTED THICKENING AGENTS

British Gum D and British Gum No. 5

These are used for printing vat dyestuffs and discharges. Gum *No. 5* is less dextrinised than Gum *D* and hence the same proportion of gum yields a more viscous paste. By mixing the two a thickening of the required consistency and total solids content can be obtained.

   Recipe:

British Gum D	British Gum No. 5	
500 parts	250 parts	powder are stirred with
500 "	750 "	water and bulked to
1 000 parts	1 000 parts.	

The paste so obtained is boiled with constant stirring for 20–30 min and cooled. The volume is adjusted to 1 000 parts and the thickening is finally strained.

Locust Bean Gums (Gums Gatto)

These gums are coagulated by alkali, and this property is utilised in the Flash-Age process for vat dyestuffs. They are also employed for general purposes where alkaline conditions are not encountered.

   Recipe:

0·5 parts	borax dissolved in
1 000 "	water. Then gradually, stirring constantly,
20 "	of the gum powder are added.

The paste is made slightly acid with acetic acid and is then heated to 80°–90°C (175°–195°F). It is finally cooled, bulked to 1 000 parts and strained. This thickening has poor keeping properties and only a sufficient quantity for immediate use should be prepared at any one time. An addition of 0·5 parts of 'Proxel' *PM* will extend the storage life to several days.

Gum Tragacanth

This thickening is widely used, both on its own and in mixtures with starch. It is particularly useful where the goods are not to be washed well and for blotches.

Recipe:

| 70 parts | Gum Tragacanth are mixed with |
| 1 000　" | cold water and allowed to stand for 2–3 days, with occasional stirring. |

The mixture is then raised to the boil and maintained thus until the gum is dissolved. A steam or water-jacketed pan should be used and the operation usually takes 8–12 h. Further boiling results in a thinner paste. After cooling, the thickening is bulked to 1 000 parts and strained.

Wheat Starch-Tragacanth

Recipe:

140 parts	wheat starch are stirred into
400　"	cold water. Then
600　"	Gum Tragacanth thickening (7%),

made as before, are stirred into the paste, which is brought to the boil and maintained thus for 30–40 min with constant stirring. It is then cooled, bulked to 1 000 parts and strained.

Gum Senegal (Gum Arabic)

This is a high-solids content thickening which can easily be removed and which is used specially for silk.

Recipe:

600 parts	Gum Senegal lumps are stirred into
500　"	water. The mass is bulked to
1 000　"	

and then brought to the boil and maintained thus with constant stirring for about 3h. It is then cooled, bulked to 1 000 parts and strained.

'Indalca' U

'Indalca' U is a useful general thickening, giving good level prints.

Recipe:

| 45 parts | 'Indalca' U are added gradually with constant stirring to |
| 1 000　" | cold water. |

The mixture is brought to the boil and maintained thus for 30 min. After cooling, it is bulked to 1 000 parts. Straining is not normally necessary.

'Nafka' Crystal Gum Supra

This thickening is widely used for printing cellulose acetate, nylon and 'Terylene'.

Recipe:

200 parts	'Nafka' Crystal Gum Supra are stirred quickly into
1 000 ,,	cold water and the paste is allowed to stand overnight.

After straining, the thickening is ready for use. If required for use quickly the suspension of the gum may be heated to the boil, boiled for a few minutes, cooled and strained.

'Celacol' MM10

This thickening may be used for the printing of 'Procion' dyestuffs on wool and silk.

Recipe:

150 parts	'Celacol' *MM10* are sprinkled into
850 ,,	boiling water. The mixture is allowed to cool without stirring and bulked to
1 000 parts.	

It is then stirred to produce a smooth paste. Straining is not normally necessary.

'Meypro' Gum CRX

This is a general-purpose thickening that is stable to acids and alkalis.

Recipe:

50 parts	'Meypro' Gum *CRX* are sprinkled slowly into
950 ,,	cold water and the mass is stirred for 15 min.

It is then boiled for 15–20 min and cooled to 50°C (120°F), and bulked to 1 000 parts. In order to avoid bubbles the thickening is then allowed to cool by standing without stirring. Straining is not normally required.

'Meypro' Gum KN

This thickening is not alkali-resistant. It yields a suitable thickening at 25 parts per 1 000 parts and is made up in a similar manner to 'Meypro' Gum *CRX*.

'Meypro' Gum AC

This thickening is recommended for printing on synthetic fibres.
  Recipe:

80 parts	'Meypro' Gum *AC* are sprinkled slowly into
900 "	cold water and the mass is stirred for 15 min.

It is then boiled for 5 min and cooled to 50°C (120°F) and bulked with cold water to 1 000 parts.

'Solvitose' C5

This thickening is used for printing vat dyestuffs and Soledons and for discharge printing. It gives a high colour yield.
  Recipe:

100 parts	'Solvitose' *C5* are added rapidly, with stirring to
1 000 "	cold water.

Stirring is continued until a homogeneous smooth mass is obtained. Straining is not normally necessary.

'Manutex' RS and 'Lamitex' L

These thickenings are based on sodium alginate and are suitable for printing 'Procion' dyestuffs, as well as direct and acid dyestuffs.
  Recipe:

12·5 parts	*'Calgon' S are dissolved in
137·5 "	water at 60°C (140°F) and
800 "	cold water are added;
50 "	thickening are sprinkled on the solution and stirring is continued for 5–10 min to break down any lumps. Finally, the mixture is bulked to
1 000 parts.	

*sodium hexametaphosphate

After standing overnight the thickening is ready for use; straining is not normally necessary.

'Manutex' F

A sodium alginate thickening of high solid content especially suitable for printing 'Procion' dyestuffs, where very good definition is required, e.g. in 'wet-on-wet' fall-on patterns on all fabrics or when printing 'Procion' dyes on wool or natural silk.

Recipe:

12·5 parts	*'Calgon' S are dissolved in
137·5 ,,	water at 60°C (140°F) and
700 ,,	cold water are added;
150 ,,	thickening are sprinkled on the
	solution and stirring is continued
	for 5—10 min to break down any
	lumps. Finally, the mixture is
	bulked to
1 000 parts.	

After standing overnight the thickening is ready for use; straining is not normally necessary.

EMULSION THICKENINGS

'Dispersol' *PR* is a concentrated product marketed in the form of light coloured flakes which are readily soluble in hot water. It is particularly recommended as the emulsifying agent in the preparation of oil-in-water emulsion thickenings suitable for printing all 'Procion' *M*, 'Procion' Supra and 'Procion' *H* dyes.

In the recipes for the preparation of 'Procion' print pastes based on a 'stock emulsion thickening' technique there is an appreciable quantity of hydrocarbon solvent present having a specific gravity of less than 1·00. The specific gravity of the final print paste is influenced by the specific gravity of the hydrocarbon solvent. Thus, the preparation of an emulsion thickening on a weight/volume basis could lead to variation in

*sodium hexametaphosphate

the effective percentages of the components of the emulsion thickening. In order to avoid discrepancy and involved calculation, the recipes are presented on a weight/weight basis.

Preparation of Stock Emulsion Thickening

Recipe:

8– 15 parts	'Dispersol' *PR* are dissolved in
192–185 "	water at 60°–70°C (140°–160°F); then after cooling
800 "	white spirit or distillate etc., are added with high-speed stirring, which is continued until the mixture is thoroughly emulsified.
1000 parts	(all parts by weight).

Notes
(1) This stock emulsion thickening is most easily prepared using a high-speed stirrer (1 000 rev/min or higher). A suitable stirrer is the Greaves High-speed Stirrer (Joshua Greaves and Sons Ltd., Ramsbottom, Nr. Manchester, England).With an effective stirrer the minimum quantity of 'Dispersol' *PR* shown in the recipe will prove sufficient.
(2) The stock emulsion thickening is very stable under normal colour shop conditions. On prolonged storage, however, some separation of the oil phase may occur. Stirring or rehomogenising of the emulsion will produce a thickening of unimpaired performance. Heating tends to break down emulsion thickenings, and storage should normally be in a cool place, preferably in non-porous containers fitted with lids.

General Information

Anti-frothing Agent

Should frothing of the emulsion thickening prove troublesome at any stage an addition of 'Silcolapse' 5 000* (0·5–1 part per 1 000 parts of print paste) is recommended.

*Manufactured by ICI Nobel Division.

25

Aftertreatment of Prints

Replacement of a conventional thickening by an emulsion thickening does not necessitate any modification of the normally recommended aftertreatment procedure.

Advantages of Emulsion Thickenings with 'Procion' Dyes

'Procion' dyes printed from an emulsion system produce a good sharp mark, revealed to full advantage in roller or screen-printed patterns involving 'wet-on-wet' fall-on effects. The prints using the emulsion system show less tendency to mark-off during processing, and are more readily washed-off, compared with prints produced with a conventional thickening. When using an emulsion thickening an increase in visual yield is obtained with many 'Procion' dyes, and this is particularly noticeable on viscose rayon fabrics.

Possibility of Fire and Explosion Hazards during Baking (Dry-Heat) Treatment

The handling in bulk of relatively large quantities of inflammable solvents of the white spirit or 'distillate' type naturally calls for precautions to ensure that potentially explosive air-solvent mixtures are not formed in practice.

It is considered advisable to remind users or potential users of emulsion thickenings that, although these products may be handled with safety under conditions of adequate ventilation, there have been isolated cases of fires or explosions attributable to the use of solvent-based emulsions. Investigations have indicated that the operation usually likely to give rise to potentially explosive conditions is the baking treatment given to fix the dye.

Within the United Kingdom a recognised authority on hazards of this type and on the best methods for minimising them is H.M. Inspectorate of Factories. In the U.K. users should, in their own interest, avail themselves of the advice and facilities offered on this matter by their local branch of H.M. Inspectorate of Factories. Much of their information has been accumulated by a detailed study of specific cases of air-solvent explosions in textile factories.

In the majority of overseas markets, bodies corresponding to H.M. Inspectorate of Factories exist and overseas users are recommended to consult them.

REFERENCE

1. WHISTLER and BEMILLER, *Industrial Gums,* Academic Press, New York and London, 1959

4

An Introductory Survey of Printing Methods

A printed textile fabric can be produced by a wide variety of methods. Some of these require expensive equipment but others need only a very modest outlay. All methods represent the means of transferring the creative talent of the designer to the fabric. They differ basically in the speed with which reproduction of the original design may be effected.

Historical Development

To present the various known forms of printing on a simple basis it is convenient to envisage arbitrary stages in the historical development of textile printing. Three such stages may be distinguished:

(1) The artist transfers his own design to the fabric. This stage includes simple hand painting of dyestuffs* to form the design, or alternatively, painting on a substance that forms a mechanical barrier to dyestuff subsequently applied all over the cloth from solution ('resist printing'). The reason why early users of hand painting often tended to use the resist method, especially for garments, was that practically no dyes existed that were capable of giving satisfactory fixation by direct hand painting. On the other hand, many dyes applied by a dyebath technique had moderate to good fastness. In addition to painting a mechanical resist on the fabric, designs can be constructed by sewing or tying the fabric locally prior to dyeing. Examples of this stage of development still survive today and include 'tie and dip' styles, some forms of batik printing, styles involving the painting of mordants, and others involving the use of resist pastes based on such widely differing substances as Cassava starch and clay.

*For example, using 'Procion' designers colours.

27

(2)   This stage embraces a wide variety of techniques evolved for the purpose of taking the artist's original design and reproducing it more rapidly. The artist now draws the original design on some convenient medium, not necessarily a textile material, and a craftsman uses this as a working diagram. The craftsmen then have to separate out the various colours in the design since practically all printing processes apply colours to the cloth individually. All the colours must fall into their correct places at the application stage, i.e. the pattern must be 'in fit' or in 'correct register'. Three main possibilities exist and represent quite different forms of printing on textiles:

    (i) to raise the design in relief on a flat (usually wooden) surface — block making

    (ii) to cut the design below a flat metal surface — flate plate engraving

    (iii) to cut the design through a flat metal or paper sheet — stencil cutting.

(3)   The most advanced stage of development involves a progressive increase in the degree of mechanisation introduced. Although reciprocating actions formed the basis of early mechanisation attempts these were in turn replaced by machines based on a rotary action. Success came at different times to each development for the following reasons.

Hand Block Printing

Hand block printing is a slow operation. The size of the block is limited by the weight that the printer can handle for long periods without undue fatigue. The pattern must invariably be fitted both across and along the cloth. Early mechanisation devices increased the block size to print a full fabric width and two or even three pattern repeats. Both the perrotine printing machine and the flat press block printing machines were of this type. Practically no working examples survive, the reciprocating system having given way to a rotary one. This involved the replacement of the flat block by a cylindrical roller. Furnishing this printing roller was an endless felt blanket to which print paste was applied and excess scraped off. These machines were frequently called *surface printing machines* and were used with great success for printing high quality furnishing fabrics. They have only restricted use on textiles today, but are more widely employed for printing wallpaper. The printing method involves relatively light pressures and machines based on these principles have been evolved for 'duplex printing', i.e. printing the fabric simultaneously on both sides. Another variation is one in which the print paste uptake of the raised parts of the wooden printing roller has been greatly increased by using polyurethane foam. A machine modified in this way is used for printing carpets.

Printing from Engraved Metal Surfaces

Textile printing from flat engraved surfaces was relatively short lived although a very high level of craftsmanship was achieved. By engraving designs on a copper cylinder, rapid reproduction of the design becomes possible. Although each individual colour requires a separate roller, multicolour effects are possible but all the rollers must be used collectively. To prolong the life of copper printing rollers it is usual to chromium plate them after engraving. Apart from accidental damage the rollers are subjected to a wearing action by the 'doctor blade'. This is an accurately set and sharpened steel or stainless steel blade, which presses on the printing roller and scrapes off all printing paste except that filling the engraving. The 'doctored' portion of the roller then comes in contact with the cloth at the 'nip' between the individual roller and the central printing cylinder. The colour paste is transferred to the cloth by the high pressure on the roller and the resiliency of the coverings on the central cylinder.

The machinery necessary for roller printing is both complicated and expensive. It is seldom installed for purposes other than full scale commercial production, although some colleges have a laboratory roller printing machine for demonstration purposes. When the term *machine printing* is used in the textile industry it invariably refers to printing from engraved rollers.

Stencil and Screen Printing

A stencil is a flat sheet of paper or metal out of which a design has been cut. The stencil suffers from the defect that complete rings or circles fall out of the pattern and some form of 'tie' is necessary to link such shapes to the main stencil. Most authorities credit the Japanese with the ingenious adaptation that led to the development of screen printing. Stencils were cut from paper and hair was used to hold to the main design those areas that would otherwise fall out. These fine lines did not show on the final pattern because the dyestuff diffused sufficiently to cover the thin unprinted line originally protected by the hair.

The next step was to stretch a silk gauze over a light wooden frame and attach the stencil to it. The fine threads of gauze are not visible in the final print and few limitations are imposed on the design. Gauzes of various materials and a wide variety of different techniques for putting designs on them exist; these are discussed in detail in a later section.

In screen printing, mechanisation has followed two lines, as with block and roller printing. Again, expensive machinery is required and this usually limits the use of such devices to the industrial printer. Screen printing today employs both flat and rotary techniques. Fully automatic and semi-automatic devices exist which utilise normal-type flat screens and mechanise the movements of screen, squeegee and cloth to varying extents. In addition, ingenious hollow circular screens have been produced which are fitted into a machine bearing a marked resemblance to a roller printing machine, but of lighter construction. This is known as the Aljaba machine, the name being derived from the initial letters of the Portuguese inventor's name, Almerindo J. Barros. It has proved possible to develop the Aljaba machine into a duplex form, i.e. to print both sides of the fabric simultaneously. Because of the relatively light printing pressures involved both rollers apply a single colour simultaneously from opposite sides of the cloth. The cloth then passes vertically upwards to the next pair of printing rollers. Such equipment is in complete contrast to the large and complex machines needed to carry out duplex printing using engraved copper rollers. Among the makers of flat-bed automatic-screen printing machinery the Dutch firm of Stork pioneered the rotary-screen printing machine. A model was exhibited first in Hanover in 1963 and since that time large numbers of these Stork Rotary machines have been installed all over the world. Other firms active in this field include J. Zimmer (Austria), P. Zimmer (Austria), Buser (Switzerland) and Meccanotessile (Italy). From time-to-time other variations of printing techniques appear but these rarely introduce a radically different idea. One of the exceptions seen in recent years uses a photogravure technique to print a design on paper, where in a separate operation the design is transferred from the paper to the cloth, e.g. by heat. This method enables the art of photogravure – not normally capable of successful direct application to textiles – to be exploited. The total length of fabric printed in this manner is, however, small at present but is growing rapidly.

The equipment normally available to Colleges and Schools of Art will be such that screen printing, and to a lesser extent block printing, is practical. It is for this reason that most details are given on these two methods. Roller printing and rotary-screen printing machinery impose two main limitations, firstly, their high cost, and secondly, the complex ancillary equipment needed to produce printing rollers for them. Not all industrial operators of such machinery possess their own engraving equipment and they therefore have to have this process done by specialised commission engravers.

Although methods of screen preparation are given in some detail it is worth remembering that some firms will undertake flat screen engraving on a commission basis.

BLOCK PRINTING

Details of Construction

A separate block is required for each different colour in the finished design. The majority of blocks are made largely of wood, but metal may be used to reinforce parts of the design. Such blocks are used to apply thickened dyestuff pastes at normal room temperatures. A completely different type of block fashioned from copper strips soldered into a copper lattice is used to apply hot waxes in the traditional Javanese batik industry (see Chapter 15).

Distinct differences in block construction are distinguishable between those used in Europe (largely for factory production) and those evolved in the East, particularly in India. In Europe supplies of wood suitable for cutting into blocks are scarce and expensive. Although a block may be about 40 mm (1·5 in) thick the cutting necessary to raise the design in relief seldom penetrates deeper than 5 mm (0·2 in). By bonding together a layer of carefully selected, fairly hard, close-grained wood (e.g. sycamore, pear or lime) with cheaper woods, economies are possible. The layers in the bonded wood are arranged so that the grain runs in directions at right angles to each other. The size of block may vary slightly to allow for a design to be fitted in and have an irregular outline to encompass the pattern area. Because the block must be lifted and transferred to the cloth repeatedly during the printing operation, its weight, and therefore its average size, must be restricted. Dimensions greatly in excess of 500 mm x 500 mm x 40 mm (18 in x 18 in x 1·5 in) are unusual but may be required for special designs.

A block intended for commercial use must be constructed robustly and requires craftsmanship of a high order to produce it, whether European or Eastern techniques are used.

Multilayer blocks are common in Europe, but in India blocks are more often fashioned from a single piece of wood and are smaller in size. The type of design and fabric to be printed determines the method of block making, particularly the area of a given colour required. It is difficult to apply printing paste evenly over large areas from a wooden surface; therefore any large, plain areas of the design are usually recessed, leaving a wooden outline wall, the cut-out portions then being filled in with a hard wool felt pad. Again, very fine lines in the design are fragile if left in wood, and these are therefore built-up with copper strip. Double copper strip outlines interleaved with felt are also widely

31

employed. For some kinds of pattern, modern blocks are often cast in type metal and then mounted on a wooden back. A large proportion of the blocks in use in the main centres in north India rely solely on the use of raised wooden areas.

For craft studies in colleges the block may not be required to print large areas of fabric. Under these conditions a piece of linoleum is often attached to a suitably sized piece of wool and the pattern cut into the linoleum surface. To assist the transfer of printing paste from this type of surface, it may be coated with a suitable adhesive and then dusted with specially prepared fibrous material to produce a 'flocked block'. These very simple blocks often prove quite adequate for preliminary exercises in fabric printing, and with patience and acquired skill they are capable of producing excellent results.

To enable the printer to fit his block lays in correct register on the cloth, 'pitch pins' are often fixed round the block sides. These pins are arranged so as to coincide with certain well defined points in the pattern printed during the previous lay.

Printing is generally carried out on very heavily built tables, preferably with stone or concrete tops. The printer may work in a standing position, but in the East sitting cross-legged on the floor may be a preferred alternative. The height of table varies accordingly, but it is usual to cover the rigid surface with a resilient material. First, several thicknesses of blanket are carefully laid on the table, and the whole is then covered with a sheet of waterproof fabric. The cloth to be printed is spread out on the table and kept in place either by pinning it on to a 'backgrey' (i.e. back cloth), or by gumming it down directly on to the waterproof cover. It is essential that no movement of the cloth occurs during the printing operation.

Gumming Down

The cloth is wound round a wooden tube, called a *shell*. Some British Gum or Gum Senegal paste is then placed at the end of the table and spread along it in as thin a film as possible, using a rubber squeegee. The roll of cloth is unrolled along the table so gummed, and lightly pressed into place either by hand or by careful ironing. As an alternative to gumming, plasticised resin preparations are available. Their use avoids the need to wash the table each time a fresh length of cloth is to be printed.

The Tiering Table

The method adopted for applying printing paste to the block is practically universal. A typical arrangement where fairly long printing

tables are in use consists of a shallow box of dimensions
0·6 m x 0·9 m (2 ft x 3 ft) fitted on a table that can be wheeled up and
down alongside the printing table. In the box, which is known as the
swimming tub, is placed some old semi-fluid starch paste or other
thickening paste, and upon this floats a wooden-sided tray, the bottom
of which consists of a sheet of waterproof fabric. On this is placed a
piece of blanket or a sieve impregnated with the colour paste to be
printed (the sieve is simply the blanket stretched in a light wooden
frame).

The Printing Operation

The block is carefully placed on the blanket so that it picks up an even
layer of paste, which is then transferred to the cloth, the block being
struck by the handle of a small but heavy mallet or maul to effect
even and thorough penetration. After each transfer of printing paste in
the manner just described, the sieve is resupplied evenly with colour by
means of a small whitewash brush called a *tiering brush*. By repeated
transfers of the colour paste to the cloth the whole piece is therefore
gradually printed with one colour. The sieve is then removed, replaced
by a clean one, and the second colour is applied in the same way, the
process being repeated until all the different colours have been separately
applied. The cloth is then removed from the table, dried and treated in
the manner appropriate to the particular dyestuffs used.

SCREEN PRINTING

Screen printing is a relatively simple method of printing which can be
carried out without the use of complicated and expensive equipment.
Details of the manufacture and use of the necessary equipment are
discussed under the headings *Methods of Preparation of Screens, Screen
Printing Tables, Squeegees, Methods of Fixing the Material to be Printed
to the Table* and *the Printing Operation.*

Methods of Preparation of Screens

The Photographic (or Photochemical) Method

This method uses a silk, nylon or polyester gauze and has become the
most important method for the preparation of screens. For some of the
more intricate designs considerable experience and skill are required.

This method will now be discussed in detail, and references to alternative methods will be found later.

General Procedure. The silk gauze, stretched on the frame, is painted with a sensitising solution such as gelatine dichromate, and dried in the dark. The pattern to be produced is painted on transparent paper with a dense opaque ink, a separate painting and screen being necessary for each colour of the design. The coated screen may be regarded as a piece of daylight photographic printing paper and the painted pattern as a negative or as it is more generally known, a positive. The positive is now placed in contact with the sensitised screen and exposed to light. The length of exposure will vary according to the actual distance from the source of light and the type of light used (electric or daylight). The exposed screen is now well washed, first in cold water to harden the insolubilised gelatine and then in warm water to remove the soluble gelatine. The screen is allowed to dry slowly. The layer of gelatine must be reinforced by the application of a lacquer which should be reasonably resistant to acids, alkalis and organic solvents.

Details of Construction

The Screen Frame. Screen frames are usually made of either wood or metal. The wood must be smooth and well seasoned and only a soft wood with a low water absorbency, resistant to warping and to varying degrees of humidity and heat, is suitable. The types of wood that satisfy these requirements are coniferous, and the most important are the following: Western Red Cedar, Yellow Pine, Kenya or other Cedars. Hard woods such as Teak are not recommended for the making of screen frames.

Metal frames are made of rigid lightweight materials and will not warp or twist. They are expensive and are usually used in conjunction with metal gauze. Screen frames vary in size and may be as large as 2·4 m x 1·8 m (9 ft x 6 ft) and are used mainly for the printing of flags, bunting, etc. They are usually prepared from wood of approximately 35—50 mm (1·5—2 in) in depth and 60 mm (2·5 in) in width. The frames must be made very rigid and the corner joints can be strengthened with angle brackets. The side pieces of the frames are bevelled at a slight angle so that when the screen is laid flat on the table only the minimum area of the frame makes contact with the table. This helps to prevent marking-off on the following repeat. The outer edge of the wood is slightly rounded all round the frame to prevent the gauze from being cut when stretched over the frame.

34

The Screen Gauze. There are various screen gauzes used for covering the frames, e.g. silk bolting cloth, cotton organdie, nylon, 'Terylene' polyester fibre and phosphor bronze. The main factors which decide the choice of gauze are accuracy of fitting in a design, fineness of lines and size of motifs. Where extremely accurate fitting is required the metal frame fitted with phosphor bronze may be preferred, although it is rather more expensive than a screen made with a wooden frame.

A phosphor bronze screen has little elasticity and is easily dented and damaged on the printing table by any projections such as nails, pins, registration stops, etc. A dent in a metal screen cannot easily be rectified, whereas a silk screen with its greater elasticity is less prone to damage in this way, and can in the majority of cases be repaired. Moreover, a wire gauze screen, when extensively used, has a tendency to stretch with the friction and pressure of the squeeges and so become slack. Organdie is a cheap form of gauze that can be used for the printing of designs with small areas of colours which will not show slight irregularities in the printing. In large areas, because the mesh and threads of organdie are somewhat uneven, variations in depth are observed. If the screens are used for long runs there is a tendency for the threads of the organdie to become 'fluffy' and to choke the mesh slightly. Organdie will not stand rough handling and tears easily. Nylon, 'Terylene' and other synthetic fibres are also used for screen making, but more skill and a modification of normal technique may be required when using them. Silk bolting is widely used for screen making because of its strength and elasticity. The mesh is very regular and it can be obtained in various widths and sizes. The mesh size is represented by numbers, and the lower the number the coarser the mesh.

The mesh numbers normally used for screen making are 8 (a coarse mesh) to 14 (a fine mesh) depending on the fabric and the design being printed. Thus for fine, smooth fabric, where an excess of paste should be avoided a finer mesh is used, whereas for linen, where good print paste coverage is required, a coarser mesh is preferred. For outline work a mesh finer than that used for large motifs is advised.

Stretching of the Silk. The screen gauze can be stretched over the frames either by hand or machine. To cover a screen by hand needs a great deal of care to enable the correct and even tension to be obtained. This is best achieved by ensuring that the warp and weft of the fabric are, throughout, parallel to the sides of the screen. Screens that have been loosely stretched or screens too tightly stretched give rise to inaccurate printing.

Stretching the gauze by hand is carried out in the following manner. For illustration purposes the four corners on the screen frame can be labelled *A, B, C, D,* in a clockwise order. The fabric is cut larger than the frame to allow for gripping. Corner *A* is fastened either at the side or on the upper surface of the frame. On the upper surface the staples or tacks are placed about 20 mm (0·8 in) from the outside edge of the frame. The fabric is stretched from *A* to *B,* ensuring that the threads of the gauze run parallel with the sides of the frame and keeping the gauze under tension, and it is fastened to the frame. The staples or tacks must be close together. The fabric is then fastened at *C,* and again kept under tension with the threads parallel to the frame, while the whole side is attached. Pulling diagonally from *B* to *D,* the fabric is fastened at *D.* It is stretched tightly over the rounded edge of the frame between *A* and *D* and fastened along this side, the same procedure being followed for the last side from *D* to *C.*

The surplus fabric is trimmed and extra staples or tacks are inserted at each corner. The edges of the gauze, etc., may be covered with tape which is stuck down with glue, preferably of a waterproof type. The whole frame is painted with a lacquer to render it waterproof and easily washable. The screen is then washed thoroughly on both sides of the silk with warm water. This wetting out equalises any latent tension in the gauze and removes impurities in the silk. After drying, the screen is ready for coating with the light-sensitive film.

Sensitising the Screen. The majority of sensitising solutions are based on gelatine or polyvinyl alcohol, sensitised with either ammonium or potassium dichromate, or a mixture of these dichromates. Any one of the following sensitising solutions may be employed:

Sensitising solution 1 (Gelatine-dichromate)

A	125 parts	gelatine	dissolved at 50°–60°C (120°–140°F) with the minimum of stirring
	552·5 "	water	
B	50 parts	zinc oxide	
	200 "	water	
C	13·5 parts	ammonium dichromate	
	6·5 "	potassium dichromate	

36

D	50 parts	ammonia (sp. gr. 0·880)
	2·5 "	'Calsolene' Oil *HS*

Add B to A, then C, and finally D, and bulk to 1000 parts. Strain the mixture and treat the screen with this solution at 50°C (120°F) and allow to dry at room temperature in the dark or in an orange safe light.

Sensitising solution 2 (Gelatine-dichromate)

95 parts	gelatine	dissolved at 50°–60°C (120°–140°F) with the minimum of stirring, and to this are added
865 "	water	
13·5 "	ammonium dichromate	
20 "	ammonia (sp. gr. 0·880) and finally	
3·5 "	vegetable oil	

Bulk to 1000 parts. Strain the mixture and treat the screen with this solution at 50°C (120°F) and allow to dry at room temperature in the dark or in an orange safe light.

Sensitising solution 3 (Polyvinyl alcohol-dichromate)

A	475 parts	polyvinyl alcohol emulsion are slowly stirred into
	375 "	water at 60°–70°C (140°–160°F)

B	30 parts	ammonium dichromate
	125 "	water

B is added gradually to A with stirring. An addition of 3% of titanium dioxide may be made to the above solution to render the film more visible during washing after exposure. The solution is bulked to 1000 parts and

strained before use. Coating of the screen should be carried out at
35°–40°C (95°–105°F).

Notes
(1)   These sensitising solutions can be applied by a scraper or brush
technique, but where the addition of a pigment such as zinc oxide
or titanium dioxide is recommended, application by brush should
be avoided.
(2)   Coating of the screen can be carried out in daylight but not in
direct sunlight. The coated and dried screen should only be
examined and stored in an orange safe light.

Preparing the Positive Design. The original drawing is first examined to
assess its suitability for the screen printing process. It may require
adapting to screen printing, or putting into repeat where possible without altering the character of the design. If the artist keeps to a standard
repeat, frames of a standard size can be produced and the stops on the
printing tables will not require frequent adjustment. Some designs,
however, cannot be made to a standard repeat because of their nature.
For every colour in a design, a separate positive is required. These are
produced on tracing paper which must be stable to moisture and
temperature changes (if the material is unstable, distortions of the
design occur, resulting in inaccurate fitting). For this purpose a smooth
acetate film, frosted on one side and very stable, is suitable. Examples
are 'Kodatrace' and 'Ethulon'. The design is drawn or painted on to the
tracing media and while it is essential that the design must be opaque, it
need not necessarily be black, though most opaque inks are. The
following are suitable for use as opaque inks:
    (i)   'Photopake'
   (ii)   'Albavar' Durable Varnish No. 9 (ICI) to which 'Drop Black'
         is added to make it opaque
  (iii)   'Bedacryl' *L* Ink. Prepared by mixing 80 parts 'Bedacryl' *L*
         and 20 parts Carbon Black *VS* paste.
The intensity of the black may be increased by raising the percentage of
the Carbon Black *VS* to 30–40% at the expense of the 'Bedacryl' *L*.
'Photopake' may readily be removed from the tracing film, but the
other two opaque inks are much more durable, and positives made from
them can be stored without risk of scratching or flaking.

Transferring the Positive Design to the Silk. The positive is laid flat on
the dry sensitised silk and secured to the screen frame by, for example,
adhesive tape. A glass plate of suitable dimensions is then laid on top of

the positive and securely clamped to the screen frame by means of suitable clamps. To ensure good contact between the positive and the silk the hollow underside of the silk screen should be supported by means of a wooden block of such a size as to fit comfortably in the silk frame. This operation must be carried out in an orange safe light. Next, the positive, clamped on to the frame as described previously, requires to be exposed to a suitable light source. Exposure may be carried out in either daylight or artificial light, and the following table gives suggested times of exposure required for light of different intensities and from different sources.

	Distance from light source	*Time of exposure required*
Strong sunlight	–	5 min
Bright daylight	–	10 min
Dull daylight	–	up to 2 h
Mercury vapour lamp	450 mm (18 in)	15 min
150 W lamp	450 mm (18 in)	3 h
300 W lamp	600 mm (24 in)	up to 2 h

Exposure under the mercury vapour lamp gives the most satisfactory results. An important point that must be remembered, however, is that the temperature at the face of the glass must in no case exceed 30°C (85°F). After exposure the positive design and the glass plate are removed and the silk screen immersed for 2 min in cold water. This initial wash is followed by a second treatment in a fresh bath of water at 35°–40°C (95°–105°F) until the soluble gelatine or PVA (polyvinyl alcohol) is completely removed.

Hardening of the Exposed Design. Screens based on a gelatine-dichromate sensitising solution are often given a hardening treatment, although this is not absolutely necessary. The screens are treated in the cold for 10–15 min in the following solution:

25 parts	ammonium dichromate
50 ″	chrome alum crystals
50 ″	formaldehyde (40%) solution

bulked to 1 000 parts.

The screens are washed well in cold water and allowed to dry slowly.

Screens based on a polyvinyl alcohol-dichromate sensitising solution require a hardening treatment, and this is carried out by immersing the screen for 45–60 min in the following solution:

	50 parts	acetaldehyde
	50 "	isobutyraldehyde or normal butyraldehyde
	20 "	sulphuric acid 66° Bé (168°Tw)
bulked to	1 000 parts	at a temperature of 15°–20°C (60°–70°F).

After rinsing and drying, the screen is ready for use. If, after inspecting the screen, it is found that certain parts of the motif are blocked, they can be cleared by brushing lightly over the screen with a 1:1 solution of lactic acid 80%.

The screen is tested by treating for 1 min in a solution of 1 part of 'Chlorazol' Sky Blue *FFS* per 1 000 parts of water. If the exposure and hardening are satisfactory, no staining of the screen, except the silk itself, will take place; if, however, a screen is insufficiently hardened, it will be stained. In this case the screen is given a second hardening treatment.

Reinforcement of the Screen. In the case of screens prepared from polyvinyl alcohol the hardening treatment just described is sufficient protection, and further reinforcement of the screen is not absolutely essential. With screens prepared from gelatine, protection of the gelatine is obtained by application of a lacquer. The gelatine-coated screens are coated with lacquer from the inside of the screen by either brushing or scraping. While the lacquer is still wet, the outside of the screen is rubbed with a dry cloth, in order to remove the lacquer from the open places of the screen. If it is considered necessary to coat both sides of the screen with lacquer, this is carried out after drying by applying the lacquer from the reverse side of the screen and removing by suction or by wiping with a cloth from the inside of the screen. If the lacquer used is viscous, it may also be necessary to wipe out with a solvent. A screen lacquered on both sides, such as the one just mentioned, should be satisfactory for the normal wear and tear of screen printing provided the lacquer used is resistant to acids, alkalis and such organic solvents as are used in printing pastes.

As an alternative to this lacquer, 'Bedafin' *2001* or 'Bedafin' *2101* (ICI) may be used. 'Bedafin' *2001* or *2101*, when used as a screen lacquer, gives protection against alkalis and solvents. Before use, the 'Bedafin' is diluted to brushing consistency with 'Cellosolve' or a mixture of equal parts of butanol and xylene, and applied to the dry coated screen by brush, scraper or squeegee. The open parts of the screen are cleared in the manner just described using 'Cellosolve' or a butanol-xylene mixture as the solvent. The treated screen is dried and subsequently baked at a temperature of 120°–150°C (250°–300°F) for 3–5 min, the higher temperature requiring the shorter time. The baked screen is coated in a similar manner on the reverse side, any excess being removed as before. After drying and rebaking, the screen is ready for use.

Notes

1. *Possible sources of trouble in screen making*

   (*a*) Pin-holes (porous places) in the gelatine or PVA/dichromate film

   Cause:
   (i) Frothing of the sensitising solution
   (ii) The sensitising solution applied unevenly
   (iii) Very humid atmospheric conditions during application of the sensitising solution
   (iv) The sensitising solution incompletely mixed
   (v) Dust on the screen before coating.

   (*b*) *Exposed gelatine film is partly or completely washed out*

   Cause:
   (i) Under-exposed
   (ii) Very humid atmospheric conditions during application of sensitising solution
   (iii) Sensitising solution heated to too high a temperature, causing decomposition.

   (*c*) *Gelatine or PVA/dichromate coating not completely removed from unexposed places*

   Cause:
   (i) Over-exposed
   (ii) Temperature too high during exposure
   (iii) Screens kept too long at a high temperature before exposure
   (iv) The positive not completely opaque.

   (*d*) *The designs have poor edges and the lines have closed up in places*

   Cause:
   (i) The screen has not been in perfect contact with the positive
   (ii) The coating is too thick.

   (*e*) *Complete absence of coating in certain places of the screen*
   Cause:
   Impurities or grease on the screen before coating.

41

Alternative Methods for the Production of Screens

The *Direct Painting* method is the simplest of all, and as the name implies, the paint or lacquer is painted by hand directly on to the silk, blocking out the portions not required to be printed.

The *'Profilm'* method has been developed by Selectasine Silk Screens Ltd. 'Profilm' is a cellulose acetate film coated with plasticised shellac supported on a backing sheet of glazed transparent paper by means of gutta-percha coating. In carrying out this process the 'Profilm' is placed over the design to be produced, and the necessary motifs are cut out with a stencil knife, making sure that the top of the film is removed, the unwanted portions being stripped away. The stencil is subsequently ironed on to the silk screen, which, after peeling off the backing paper, is ready for printing.

In the *Resist* method the silk is painted with the following solution:

600 parts		sodium silicate, 52° Bé (112°Tw)
200	"	china clay
50	"	cold water
100	"	glycerine
50	"	Gum Tragacanth thickening (7%)
Bulk to	1 000 parts.	

To get the best results after painting with this solution, the screen is dried and painted with a fairly quick-drying lacquer, dried and washed in lukewarm water. The design is seen as the paint washes away from the portions where it fell on the sodium silicate.

Screen Printing Tables

The length of the table for works practice varies between 50–100 m (55–110 yd) in length. It is usually 0·75 m (30 in) high and approximately 1·2–1·6 m (48–62 in) in width. The table is made of well seasoned wood, reinforced concrete or a combination of iron frames and iron stands with wooden tops. It is usually covered with a woollen felt about 6 mm (0·25 in) in thickness. If the goods to be printed are to be fastened with pins, then the felt is covered with a cotton backgrey, but if the goods are to be stuck down to the table with an adhesive, then a waterproof cover is used. Suitable waterproof coverings for table tops of screen tables are:

(i) rubber-coated materials

(ii) coatings based on synthetic rubbers such as 'Alloprene' (chlorinated rubber) or 'Neoprene'

(iii) ICI (Hyde) Ltd., Newton Works, Hyde, Cheshire, UK may be able to supply nitrocellulose coated materials suitable for covering screen printing tables.

Registration of the design is ensured by means of a guide rail, which is fitted along the side of the screen printing table. Adjustable metal stops are attached to this rail, and are screwed in place to fit the width of each repeat. Adjustable screws or bolts fastened to the base of the screen frame make contact with the guide rail. A bracket or angle iron is fitted on the end of the screen frame and makes contact with stops fastened on the guide rail. It is most important that the guide rail attached to the side of the screen printing table be aligned correctly.

Squeegees

Various types of squeegees are available. Some are made entirely of wood while others have wooden handles with rubber or metal plates inserted. The length of the squeegee is approximately 40 mm (1·5 in) shorter than the internal dimensions of the screen.

The type of squeegee required varies according to the material being printed and the type of table covering. For large designs, and for fabrics that absorb a good deal of colour paste, a soft rounded blade is required. Patterns with fine detail that are to be printed on a flat, silk-like fabric require a sharp hard blade. Furthermore, a hard table covering requires a soft rubber squeegee, while a table with a soft underlay requires a harder blade. If the squeegee is held near the upright position, less paste will be applied than when a shallower angle is used. A more rapid movement of the squeegee or lighter pressure also results in less paste being applied. The edge of the blade must be perfectly level and clean. The edge of the squeegee must always be kept uniform and sharpened when necessary by sandpapering or other suitable means. Even if the squeegee is perfect some skill is required to produce sharp, level prints, especially when fine lines are printed. The printer must draw the squeegee over the screen at the correct angle with an evenly distributed pressure. If the pressure is unevenly distributed and the stroke of the squeegee over the screen is fitful, the resulting print will be unlevel and have poor definition. In order to make the printing independent of the varying pressure of different printers, squeegees are often weighted and provided with long handles.

Methods of Fixing the Material to be Printed to the Table

There are three methods that can be used for fixing the cloth to the screen table. One is by pinning, the second by direct adhesion to the waterproof table top, and the third is by combining the material to a backgrey with a special combining machine.

If the material to be printed is fastened to the table with pins the waterproof cover may be omitted and the undercover felt covered with a backgrey. Pinning is a slow process, but for certain materials, such as cellulose acetate, nylon, 'Terylene', etc., it is still used. The material is first laid on the printing table, dampened slightly with a fine spray of water and then stretched with tensioning devices which are fixed on the ends of the table. When stretched the material is pinned by the selvedges to the underfelt (that is, pinning through the backgrey to the underfelt). The cloth during printing has a tendency to move owing to expansion or contraction, and close-fitting designs are difficult to keep in register.

The second method is to fix the material to the waterproof table top with adhesives such as dextrine, British gum or Gum Arabic. In addition, semi-permanent adhesives such as 'Mobilcer' A, 'Lankro' table adhesive and 'Lankro' Permanent Adhesive H are available. Some of the natural gums used for sticking down are not compatible with the thickening or the dyestuff in the print paste, and will give flushing of the printed edge, or will fix permanently on the cloth to produce a harsh handle on it. For example, Gum Tragacanth when used as a thickening in the print paste loses its viscosity when printed on material that is stuck down with Gum Arabic or Gum Senegal, and the print loses its definition. The adhesive is spread evenly over the table either by the use of a rubber squeegee or by machine. If too much adhesive is used, it penetrates the fabric and has a resisting action on the applied print paste, giving irregular prints.

The material to be printed is pressed gently on to the adhesive. If a gum is used as adhesive, the fabric is fixed by ironing with a warm iron, but with semi-permanent adhesives ironing is unnecessary. Semi-permanent adhesives do not absorb aqueous printing pastes very readily and when the printed material is removed, the tables are easily washed. As soon as the table has dried, another piece of material may be stuck down without regumming and up to 20 lays may be put down without further application.

The third method used is the sticking of the material on to backgreys by a combining machine whereby material to be printed can be combined in advance with the backgrey. It is then only necessary to roll the cloth down the table and fasten the edges of the backgrey on to hooks at the side of the table or to gum down the edges of the cloth. When printed, the material is removed, the greys are taken away and another roll of combined material is rolled down without any inter-mediate washing and drying of the table.

The Printing Operation

In using the screen, a suitable amount of print paste is poured into the well of the screen frame and transferred through on to the cloth underneath, by drawing it to and fro across the screen with the squeegee, two to four passages generally being given. Before beginning to print with a screen it is advisable to 'wet out' the screen first, by printing on to a piece of spare fabric or absorbent paper. A properly 'wet-out' screen ensures a good transfer of dyestuff paste to the fabric being printed in bulk. To avoid marking-off, the screen printer does not carry out his printing in a continuous order, but prints in alternative positions, that is, position 1, then misses a position to position 3, and on to position 5 and so on until the whole table length has been completed. The drying of the printed material is assisted by blowing hot air over the table or by heated tables, so that provided the printing pastes are not too hygroscopic and the material is not too light in weight (and consequently limited in absorbency), the material should then be dry; otherwise it is necessary to wait until the print is dry enough to avoid picking-up and marking-off. Printing is then continued in positions 2, 4, 6, etc., until the whole table is printed with the first colour. The same procedure is followed for the second and subsequent colours in the pattern.

It is important that each screen should be washed as soon as possible after use. A screen that is left to dry with print paste on it is difficult to clean, and in extreme cases this may lead to blocking of the screen mesh, so rendering the screen useless for future printing. Screens are usually cleaned by using a jet of water, and drying is carried out by wiping them with an absorbent cloth and keeping them in a warm place. Too much heat will warp a screen frame. After printing, the table should be washed if the fabric has been stuck down. The printed fabric is either allowed to dry on the table or is dried by hanging in a drying chamber before further processing, which will depend on the type of fabric and the dyestuffs used.

SEMI-AUTOMATIC SCREEN PRINTING

Before the advent of fully automatic flat bed screen printing machines a number of attempts had been made to partially mechanise some of the operations and so increase output. The screen carriage was one such device and it was produced by a number of firms. As the name suggests, the screen carriage ran along two rails, one fitted at each side of the table. Instead of positioning the screen by hand in each printing position, raised slots were used. While still on the rails the carriage could be lifted over and lowered into these slots. The squeegee was pushed to and fro across the table in guide slots by a single operator, who was aided by a long handle which was attached to it. Later models were developed in which the squeegee was driven in both directions across the table using a chain mechanism. The number of strokes could be pre-set and the pressure applied varied within appropriate limits until the optimum was achieved and then set for the remainder of the run. With a fully automatic flat-bed machine the cloth moves a repeat at a time while all the fixed screens are lowered to print and raised again. By utilising a modified printing unit from, say, a Buser machine a printing carriage suitable for use on a conventional table may be made. Such devices are sometimes used industrially for sampling purposes using a short table. By having two such units the effect of 'wet-on-wet' fall-ons may be examined.

Laboratory Roller Printing Machines

These are sometimes available in technical colleges and are most useful for carrying out comparisons between dyestuffs as well as demonstrating the behaviour of various dyes, thickenings and processes. Such machines differ from industrial roller printing machines in a few important details. The laboratory machine is invariably a single colour machine, i.e. it has only one printing roller. This fact means that the special gear wheels or 'box wheels' which must be attached to the end of each printing roller in a multi-colour machine may be dispensed with. The box wheels are necessary in multi-colour printing machines to enable the various rollers to be 'fitted' in the vertical direction. Pattern registration is not complete without 'side fitting' and occasionally 'skew fitting' as well. Screw threaded bolts installed at each side of the industrial machine make such adjustments possible. By restricting the laboratory printing machine to a single roller the necessity to 'fit' the pattern is avoided and a much simpler bearing drive, weighting system and colour furnishing system are employed. In a full scale machine the print paste is contained in a colour box, and in this box revolves either a brush or a plain roller. The function of the brush or roller is to furnish print paste to the printing roller. The excess print paste so applied is removed by the carefully sharpened *'cleaning doctor'*. To prevent contamination of the paste in the colour box a second doctor blade, a *'lint doctor'*, is set against the face of the printing roller. When a very short sampling run was needed the printer would have the colour box removed together with the furnishing roller. The lint doctor was reversed and a small wad of cotton rag inserted at each of its ends. This formed a small trough

46

into which a small amount of print paste was poured. When the machine started, the engraving was filled with print paste and the excess was partially scraped off by the lint doctor. The cleaning doctor completed this operation. The method is known as *printing off the lint* and it forms the basis of single colour laboratory printing.

The laboratory printing roller is fitted into the machine so that it rides freely in both side bearings and the driving cog is locked and in mesh with the driving gear. A stainless steel doctor blade accurately sharpened and firmly fitted into the doctor shears is placed in position in the doctor steps. The doctor blade setting is adjusted so that the face of the doctor blade, i.e. the non-bevelled side, presses evenly across the roller. An equal weight is then hung on each doctor blade arm and cloth or isocyanate foam wads inserted a short way outside the width limits it is required to print. Printing paste is poured into the trough formed between doctor blade and roller. Next, without applying any pressure to the printing roller, the latter is turned a few times to ensure the roller is furnishing properly and the doctor cleaning satisfactorily. If this proves to be the case, the cylinder with its blanket and backgrey covering is brought into contact by screwing the weighting mechanism. Movement of the printing roller now moves simultaneously the cylinder, blanket and backgrey and allows pattern lengths to be printed when they are inserted into the nip at the back of the machine. On large printing machines the centre cylinder is not raised or lowered but the printing rollers are themselves screwed up to or away from it. These larger cylinders are carefully wound with several layers of a special 'lapping' cloth. By using a linen warp and woollen weft, lapping fabrics are produced which are both resilient and hard-wearing. The very small cylinders on laboratory machines are not particularly suitable for lapping. A rubber coating about 10 mm (0·4 in) thick has proved a very satisfactory alternative. The printing blanket should be of the same quality as used in industry, preferably rubber coated on both sides. To join the ends of the blanket it will probably be necessary with most laboratory machines to hand-sew so that the cut edges meet but do not overlap. Backgrey is provided from a roll of cotton fabric at the back which after use is wound on to a similar roll at the top of the machine. To avoid the inconvenience of repeatedly washing backgreys they may be replaced with rolls of paper towelling of suitable quality and absorbency.

Operating Precautions

(1)   A place should be provided for the sharpening of doctor blades as well as space for the storage of the files and oil stones needed.

Doctor blades when not is use are best stored on wall racks. If this is impractical their edge should be protected. A piece of wood of greater width and length than the doctor blade is carefully sawn so that it will slot over the blade. Strings fitted to the edges may be tied round the doctor shears to secure the wooden guard.

(2) If there are only a few engraved rollers forming the complete stock they are conveniently stored in individual wooden boxes. These should be sufficiently sturdy to allow the roller to be sent for re-engraving when necessary and returned without damage.

(3) If the printing machine is hand operated it must always be turned in the correct direction, otherwise the doctor blade will dig in the roller and ruin the engraving. Most machines have a ratchet mechanism which ensures that this does not happen.

(4) At the end of the printing operation the handle used to turn the machine should be left at the bottom of its turning circle. If this precaution is not taken the roller will spin when the printing weight is released and roller damage from the doctor blade will result.

(5) The roller and the doctor blade must be thoroughly washed and dried as soon as possible after printing. A scrubbing brush will ensure that no print paste becomes dried in the engraving.

(6) To minimise the handling of the roller and doctor blade during washing a supply of water should be piped to a small tank in front of the machine. This should be wide enough to hold the doctor shears by their rounded ends, while the blade suspended in the tank is easily cleaned. By placing a coarse mesh sieve below the roller and extending it to cover the inside of the machine frame the roller washings may be disposed of. This technique requires the building of a four-sided funnel and attaching it to the sieve at the top. The delivery end of the funnel is either fed into the exit pipe from the washing tank or direct to drain, as convenient.

5

Preparation of the Fabric for Printing

The importance of knowing which fibre or fibres are present in a fabric has already been stressed. Because the many fibres available differ in their chemical and physical properties the methods used to prepare fabrics made from them for printing also vary. A woven fabric is said to be in the *'loom-state'* if it has received no further processing since it left the loom. The terms *grey-state* and *grey cloth* (in N. America *greige* is synonymous with *grey* in this context) are also used to describe loom-state fabrics. The use of the adjective *'grey'* is more widely applicable since it may be used to describe knitted as well as woven fabrics.

Depending on the origin of their component fibres, fabrics may contain both natural and other non-fibrous impurities. The nature and amount of these impurities varies with different fibres, and so do the methods adopted to remove them. Such impurity-removal operations are known as *scouring* treatments and they are often followed by bleaching. It is important to distinguish between chemical bleaching done with sodium hypochlorite or hydrogen peroxide, and optical bleaching. In chemical bleaching the coloured impurities are destroyed by chemical attack and the material is whitened as a result. Optical bleaching refers to an effect produced by a fluorescent brightening agent. This is generally a colourless dyestuff which is absorbed by the fibre. Such agents cause the reflectance of the fibre to be increased in the visible region of the spectrum by converting ultra-violet radiation into visible light. The overall whiteness of the fabric is thus increased. Because not all fluorescent brightening agents dye equally well on all fibres, it is normal to have a short range of products specially suitable for groups of fibres.

It is generally advisable to have the material supplied scoured and bleached where appropriate, ready for printing, since special equipment is required to do this work satisfactorily. Care must be taken to avoid purchasing, e.g. cotton fabrics which have been 'finished white'. These fabrics could either have been finished with starchy materials which would require removal before printing or by some form of crease-resisting (resin-finishing) process. In the latter case the printing properties of the fabric would be permanently impaired.

If an unexpectedly poor dyestuff yield is obtained when printing already prepared fabric, a piece should be rescoured. A print on the rescoured piece and a further portion of the original often shows an improved yield of dyestuff on the rescoured portion. A quicker but more empirical test is to cut two small pieces of equal area, one from each fabric and place them simultaneously on the surface of water at room temperature. If the rescoured piece wets out and sinks much more rapidly than the other piece then the latter will very often give rise to lower dye yields or other printing difficulties. If, however, the material to be printed is in the grey state and not in sufficient quantity to be despatched to a specialist firm for preparation, satisfactory results may be obtained by adopting the following techniques where applicable.

Cotton

In the case of very light cotton fabrics it is sufficient to boil the material for 30–45 min in a solution containing 2 parts of 'Lissapol' *ND* and 5 parts of soda ash per 1 000 parts of liquor. After this treatment the fabric is rinsed very thoroughly in water and dried.

To obtain the brightest shades on cotton, the material, if in the grey state, is bleached after scouring. This is done by working the material gently in a cold solution of $1\cdot0°-1\cdot4°$ Bé ($1\cdot5°-2°$ Tw) sodium hypochlorite solution for about 30 min and then washing thoroughly in cold water. This should be followed by a treatment in weak acetic acid ($0\cdot1\%$ solution) and, finally, by rinsing completely free of acid in cold water. Heavier cotton fabrics require more severe treatment than this method. Industrially, this could consist of boiling for several hours under pressure in caustic soda in a closed vessel called a *kier*. Alternatively, a shortened continuous operation using J-boxes to get the appropriate dwell times, and hydrogen or sodium peroxide as the active bleaching agent, would be used. These operations are not easily reproduced on a small scale. Sodium peroxide, for example, needs care both in storage and in handling and the granular industrial grade is not normally available in small quantities. Research carried out by ICI Mond Division over recent years has led to the establishment of a solvent scouring system based on the use of trichloroethylene. This gives cotton cloths a very much improved absorbency due to the removal of most of the natural or added fats and waxes, together with a substantial amount of the warp size. With the introduction of small-scale dry cleaning machines into launderettes, which use the same solvent, the possibility of solvent

50

scouring small lengths of grey cloth in this equipment should be borne in mind. Such treatments remove the more tenaciously held impurities from the cotton which constitute the major obstacles to obtaining a satisfactory print. Solvent scouring is followed, if required, by bleaching with sodium hypochlorite as already described. This chemical bleaching may be supplemented or replaced by an optical bleaching treatment. 'Fluolite' *BW* is suitable for cellulosic fibres and is easily applied by padding or by dyeing. The dry weight of the fabric needs to be known for dyeing application because the amount of 'Fluolite' *BW* to be applied may vary from 0·05–0·4% (based on the dry fabric weight) depending on the quality of white required and on the initial fabric shade. The material is entered into the dyebath at pH 6 or higher and at 50°C (120°F). The 'Fluolite' *BW*, previously dissolved in a little warm water, is added slowly. After 5 min of dyeing, 5% of common salt (calculated on the fabric weight) is added. A further 5% of salt is added 15 min later and dyeing is carried out for a total of 20–30 min, after which the material is rinsed and dried.

Two other processes are encountered in the preparation of cotton for printing, viz. *mercerisation* and *causticisation.* Mercerisation involves the treatment of cotton material either prior to, or after bleaching, in a strong solution of caustic soda of 33° Bé (60° Tw). After immersion in the solution the fabric is held sufficiently under tension to prevent it shrinking while the caustic soda is washed out. Mercerisation gives a more lustrous cotton fabric and significantly increases the uptake of many dyestuffs. Causticisation requires less complicated equipment and involves padding in a weaker solution of caustic soda of 12° Bé (18° Tw), allowing to lie for a short while and then washing off. Although causticisation does not give the same degree of lustre as mercerisation the improvement in dyestuff uptake is quite marked. It is unlikely that many colleges will have equipment suitable for carrying out these operations but they should be borne in mind if ordering fabric. Not every fabric is capable of being mercerised satisfactorily, the determining factors are the yarn and fabric constructions. Relatively open weave fabrics with loosely twisted weft yarns are apt to become wiry. In such cases, particularly where heavy shades are to be printed, it is possible that a causticisation treatment will suffice.

Viscose Rayon

Since viscose rayon is a cellulosic fibre regenerated from natural cellulose that has already been purified and bleached, few of the impurities present in grey state cotton are present in grey state viscose.

Woven viscose fabrics, do, however, contain warp size and this must be thoroughly removed, otherwise the absorbency will be poor.

A treatment is given for 30 min at the boil in a solution containing 1·5 parts of 'Lissapol' *ND* and 2 parts of soda ash per 1 000 parts, followed by a thorough rinse in cold water. After this treatment either a chemical bleach or a treatment with 'Fluolite' *BW* may be given if required as described for cotton, or alternatively the material is simply dried.

Linen

In the grey state linen fabrics may contain appreciable quantities of impurities and be relatively dark in shade. Linen is often printed in what is termed a *half-bleached* state. It is important to appreciate that this refers to the amount of natural colour retained and not to an inadequate scouring which would give insufficient absorbency. For a lightweight linen the scouring treatment described under cotton will suffice. A heavier linen, especially in the grey (or loom) state, may require a combined scouring, bleaching and de-sizing operation. In this case the linen, maintained in open width if possible, is treated in a solution containing 1 part sodium silicate (Q79 grade, slightly less alkaline than the J–81 grade which has been withdrawn), 1 part sodium peroxide, 1 part sodium bicarbonate and 1 part of 'Lissapol' *ND* per 1 000 parts of liquor. The treatment is carried out over a period of 45 min with the temperature rising from 40°C (105°F) to 85°C (185°F). Finally, the linen is well rinsed in water and dried.

Cellulose Acetate

The material is treated for 30 min at a temperature of 60°C (140°F) in a solution containing 1·5 parts 'Lissapol' *ND* and 2 parts ammonia (sp. gr. 0·880) per 1 000 parts of liquor, rinsed thoroughly in water and dried. The use of alkalis stronger than ammonia such as soda ash and caustic soda are to be avoided, otherwise some saponification (hydrolysis) of the rayon will occur and the fibre properties will be modified as well as the fabric undergoing some loss in weight. Fluorescent brightening may be carried out, by applying 0·2–1·0% of 'Fluolite' *XMF* paste (calculated on the dry weight of the material) by dyeing for 45 min at 85°C (185°F) using any convenient method.

Cellulose Triacetate ('Tricel', 'Arnel')

When purchasing triacetate fabrics prepared for printing the term
'S'-finished may be encountered. This refers not to the addition of a
finishing agent to the fabric but to a controlled saponification treatment
with caustic soda. 'S'-finishing is widely used to improve the handle
(i.e. 'hand'), antistatic properties and ironing properties of cellulose
triacetate, and is carried out prior to printing together with the other
preparatory processes. This is a specialised process and it is not
recommended that attempts to carry it out on a small scale are made.

The use of high temperature scouring liquors does not impair the
lustre of triacetate which is also very resistant to alkalis in concentrations
normally used in scouring. A bath containing 0·5—1·5 parts 'Lissapol'
ND and 0·2 parts soda ash per 1 000 parts is used, and a treatment of
30 min at 85°C (185°F) is given. This normal type of scour usually gives
triacetate fabrics with a slightly yellow white. Excellent whites may be
readily obtained by means of any of the usual bleaching agents. Acid
and alkaline hypochlorites, sodium chlorite, hydrogen peroxide and
peracetic acid may all be used under the correct conditions of pH,
temperature and strength of reagent (without adverse effect on the
tensile strength of the fibre). An alkaline hypochlorite bleach consists
of 4·0 parts sodium hypochlorite (18% available chlorine) 0·3 parts soda
ash and 0·1 part 'Lissapol' *ND* per 1 000 parts. This is used at 50°C
(122°F) for 30—45 min and is followed by a wash-off and a treatment
in 2 parts sodium sulphite per 100 parts for 20 min at 65°C (150°F).
A thorough wash completes the treatment. As an alternative, or to
supplement the chemical bleach, an optical bleach may be given
consisting of applying 0·5% 'Fluolite' *XMF* paste (calculated on the dry
weight of the material) by any convenient dyeing method and treating
at the boil for 45 min. The fabric is then rinsed and dried in the normal
manner.

Nylon and 'Terylene' Polyester Fibre

A simple scour to remove yarn lubricants is given. The material is treated
for 30 min at 70°C (160°F) in a solution containing 1·5 parts 'Lissapol'
ND and 2 parts of soda ash per 1 000 parts of liquor, well rinsed in water
and dried. If required, an optical bleach may be given for nylon by
applying 'Fluolite' *XMF* paste at the rate of 0·1—0·5% (calculated on
the dry weight of material) at a temperature of 95°C (200°F) for 45 min.
This is followed by rinsing and drying in the normal manner. Two
different types of optical bleaching agent are applicable to nylon and
behave in a manner analogous to either acid or disperse dyes. The acid

53

dye type of fluorescent bleaching agent occupies the same dyeing site
on the nylon as coloured acid dyes used in printing this fibre. An excess
of optical bleach present on the nylon may give lowered dye yields in
printing. 'Fluolite' *XMF* behaves analogously to a disperse dye and thus
does not affect the yield obtained from acid dyes.

To use an optical bleaching agent on 'Terylene' under normal dyeing
conditions it is necessary to employ a carrier such as 'Tumescal' *D*. From
0·1—0·5% 'Fluolite' *XMF* paste (calculated on the dry weight of the
fabric) is applied by dyeing together with an addition of 'Tumescal' *D*
at the rate of 1 part per 1 000 parts of dyebath. Dyeing is carried out for
45 min at the boil and followed by rinsing and drying in the normal
manner.

Wool

Wool fabrics that have not been scoured have poor wettability and
consequently poor absorption properties for print pastes. The removal
of the natural and added oil and grease needs a treatment with an
efficient detergent, but the use of alkali should be avoided. A scouring
bath is prepared containing 1% of 'Lissapol' *ND* (calculated on the dry
weight of the wool). The material is treated for 30 min at 40°C (105°F),
being gently turned during the process. The wool should not be worked
vigorously or felting may occur. This method of scouring is also used for
all types of union goods containing wool. It is important to remember
that products such as sodium hypochlorite or bleaching powder are
unsuitable for bleaching wool. Where necessary, peroxides may be used,
or alternatively, acid 'Formosul' (see later). A chlorination treatment is
sometimes given to wool which minimises shrinkage and markedly
increases dyestuff uptake. Chlorination is a process requiring rigid
control and a high degree of skill, otherwise the material is spoiled. It is
not recommended that attempts are made to carry out the process on a
small scale. Optical bleaching is best applied to wool that has previously
been scoured and peroxide bleached. The dry weight of the fabric to be
treated should be known and used as the basis to calculate the following
dyebath additions: 2·0% formic acid (85%), 5·0% 'Formosul' and 10%
Glauber's salt. Previously dissolved 'Fluolite' *XNR* (0·5—1·5%) calculated
on the fabric weight is added and the temperature of the dyebath raised
slowly to 90°C (195°F), dyeing is continued at 90°C (195°F) for 30—45
min and the fabric is finally rinsed thoroughly and dried.

Natural Silk

When received in the grey state, silk contains both natural and
adventitious impurities which must be removed before printing to ensure

54

a smooth and even pattern. The main bulk of the natural gum present in raw silk is *sericin* which is a protein material which somewhat resembles gelatine in its general properties. Sericin is removed by a 'de-gumming' or 'boiling-off' operation. This consists of treating the fabric for 1–1·5 h at 95°C (205°F) in a solution of 10 parts olive oil soap per 1000 parts of water. This is followed by a thorough rinsing in warm and cold water and drying. If bleaching is required it is carried out after de-gumming, preferably using hydrogen peroxide with or without the addition of small amounts of sodium silicate. The colour of the fibre in wild silks is frequently a pale brown which cannot be completely removed even by bleaching. If an optical bleaching treatment is required for natural silk the process described for wool, using 'Fluolite' *XNR*, is recommended. Sodium hypochlorite should never be used in silk bleaching.

In former times natural silk was 'weighted' by a treatment with tin salts such as stannic chloride in order to deposit stannic hydroxide with the fibre. The process conferred a fuller and richer handle to the fabric but at the same time reduced the substantivity of certain types of dye, e.g. acid dyes. Owing to the high price level of tin and hence its derived salts, 'weighting' is uneconomic and is nowadays only very rarely encountered. Properly de-gummed natural silk has a very high substantivity for dyes and printing deep shades presents no problem. Should difficulties be encountered an insufficient scouring has been given to the fabric and it should be rescoured. No process analagous to wool chlorination is ever carried out on natural silk. This is because silk, lacking the surface scales present on a wool fibre, does not felt. In wool, the function of chlorination is to partially erode the surface scales and minimise felting due to them.

6

Printing Procedures

In its simplest terms a printing process involves the following stages:
(1) Preparation of print paste
(2) Printing of fabric
(3) Drying
(4) Fixing of dyestuff
(5) Washing-off.

PREPARATION OF THE PRINTING PASTE

The class of dyestuff and the fabric to be printed must first be chosen
to be compatible. The dyestuff may be water soluble and supplied as a
powder or water insoluble and supplied as a dispersion. On rare
occasions a print paste may be made using an insoluble dye marketed in
the form of redispersible grains.

Water soluble dyestuffs are often required in a concentrated solution
for addition to the thickening agent. Solvents or solution assistants are
sometimes necessary to ensure complete solution, e.g. glycerine, urea,
thiourea, 'Glydote' *BN*, Solution Salt *SV*. Any chemicals that may be
necessary to assist the fixation of the dyestuff are incorporated in the
dyestuff solution or added to the thickening later. The dyestuff solution
or dispersion must be thickened to form a print paste. A useful general
rule in the preparation of printing pastes is *add thin to thick*, i.e.
solutions or dispersions should be added to the thickening agent and
not vice versa. This is particularly important with large quantities
because it is difficult to disperse a thickening agent in a large volume of
dyestuff solution.

Thickening Agents

The choice of thickening agent is dependent on the class of dyestuff
used and the type of fabric to be printed. In the printing recipes
provided in this book a suitable thickening is recommended in each case.

The most suitable consistency of a printing paste varies for the particular method of application and the fabric being printed. It should be understood that the quantity of thickening in the detailed recipes is not rigid but may be increased or decreased as circumstances demand. This may prove necessary, for example, because thickening agents may become either thicker or thinner on standing. If an alteration of this kind is introduced then a compensating adjustment should be made to the water content of the print paste to ensure that the concentration of other chemicals in the print paste remains constant. Thickening agents are discussed in greater detail in Chapter 3.

PRINTING

The methods of printing by block and by screen are fully described in Chapter 4, where in addition some data on laboratory roller printing is given.

DRYING AFTER PRINTING

After printing, the fabric is dried to remove the moisture applied from the print paste. The drying operation is essential in order to retain a good printed mark and prevent the printed goods from marking-off during handling between printing and subsequent processing operations. The rate of drying may be important particularly if the fabric being printed has a low moisture regain. If, for example, in block or screen printing nylon or 'Terylene' the colours are seen to be bleeding slightly at the edges then the drying rate is too slow. Drying must be made more efficient by the provision of hot air blowers or by increasing the number or power of existing driers. Attempts to minimise colour bleeding by replacing the thickening by one of much higher colour content are apt to give rise to another problem. High solids thickenings often dry to give brittle films and small specks of print paste are apt to jump away during handling. Because nylon and 'Terylene' are very prone to acquire a static charge when hot the print paste specks become attached to other portions of the fabric. Here they become fixed during subsequent processing and greatly detract from the value and appearance of the print. The drying stage must not be confused with the baking process frequently given to fix 'Alcian', 'Procion' and pigment dyes. The baker is a separate piece of apparatus and baking invariably follows the drying operation. When printing vat dyestuffs by the alkali carbonate-sodium sulphoxylate formaldehyde ('all in') process, as well as all discharge styles and resist printed styles, it is very important to dry the printed goods quickly and thoroughly if optimum yields are to be obtained. Premature decomposition of the 'Formosul' (sodium sulphoxylate formaldehyde) occurs if improperly dried prints are stored. However if hard dried prints containing 'Formosul' are stored decomposition will also occur due to heating-up. Consequently the procedure should be thorough, and efficient drying followed by cooling if necessary.

DYESTUFF FIXATION

This may be achieved by a variety of methods depending on dyestuff class and substrate, e.g.:
(1) Baking (dry heat)
(2) Wet development
(3) Pad-batch development
(4) Flash ageing
(5) Pressure steaming
(6) High temperature steaming
(7) Normal steaming.
Of these, normal steaming is probably most suitable for use in colleges and schools of art and will be dealt with in most detail. Briefer descriptions of the other methods will now be given.

Baking (Dry Heat)

This method requires one of two different machines to be available, i.e. a gas-fired or an electric baker. This is a well ventilated chamber filled with air heated up to $160^{\circ}-180^{\circ}C$ ($320^{\circ}-355^{\circ}F$). Rollers at the top and bottom of the baker enable fabric to be run through the apparatus continuously over 2—5 min treatment time. There is no provision in a baker for control of weft shrinkage, so when higher treatment temperatures are required a high temperature stenter must be used. This latter apparatus represents a considerably larger capital outlay than a baker. Using a stenter a treatment of up to 1 min at $200^{\circ}C$ ($390^{\circ}F$) is possible with control of the fabric dimensions. On small patterns a baking treatment may be imitated by ironing on the reverse side of the print for 4—5 min with the iron set at a temperature appropriate to the fabric. For example, pigment printing compositions may be fixed on cotton using temperatures around $140^{\circ}C$ ($285^{\circ}F$). It has been suggested that somewhat larger pieces of fabric may be folded and baked in an electric oven. This requires times of $1 \cdot 5-2$ h because of the slow rate of heat penetration. Such a method is not without a certain element of risk if the pigment print has been prepared with a white spirit emulsion thickening. Ovens are far less well ventilated than an industrial baker and explosions resulting from pockets of solvent collecting in the oven cannot be ruled out. Gas-heated domestic ovens should never be used for this technique on safety grounds.

Wet Development

Industrially this is carried out in open width using a rectangular tank with guide-rollers at the top and bottom. The development tank may form the first tank of a multi-tank open soaper, or be a special addition to an existing soaper. Wet development is limited in its scope, being suitable for selected 'Procion' and other reactive dyes and some 'Soledon' dyes on cellulosic fabrics. The 'Soledon' dyes printed by the nitrite method, are wet developed through hot sulphuric acid. Reactive dyes are wet developed in a strongly alkaline bath to which large quantities of electrolyte have been added to suppress dyestuff bleeding.

Pad-Batch Development

This is essentially a process first developed for dyeing 'Procion' M and H dyes. For printed goods the process is best carried out by using a perforated beam type washing machine. Reactive dyestuffs are used and the printed fabric is padded on a mangle set to about 100% pick-up with sodium silicate at 48° Bé (100° Tw). Immediately after padding the cloth is run directly on to the perforated beam washing where it remains from 10 min–3 h depending on the 'Procion' dyes present. A thorough rinse in cold water follows. Both wet development and pad-batch development avoid the use of any form of steamer. This process is recommended only for cotton since sodium silicate has an adverse effect on the handle of viscose rayon.

Flash-Ageing

The basic essentials for this process are a pad mangle and a small relatively inexpensive ager. If very high running speeds are required then the ager length and cost increases considerably. The simplest ager is a vertical tower, but since the tower height cannot be increased beyond the limits imposed by the factory building containing it, alternative designs have been adopted for larger capacity agers. It is most undesirable that the printed side of the padded cloth comes into

59

contact with any rollers until the last possible moment during the process. For this reason the larger agers may be arc-shaped (the 'rainbow' ager), have a spiral cloth passage, or two vertical legs connected to a horizontal length (the 'Tower' ager). Flash ageing was originally developed for vat dyes but the process has now been adapted to allow a number of reactive dyes to be developed on this type of equipment.

Pressure Steaming

The use of steam under a pressure of $0.10-0.25$ MN/m^2 $(1-2.5$ atm)* accelerates the fixation of disperse dyes on fabrics composed of 'Terylene' and cellulose triacetate. Pressure steaming of prints is a discontinuous operation carried out in specially constructed Star steamers (e.g. the Dedeko steamer). The term *Star steamer* originates from the radiating arms used on the cloth carrying frame to wind the cloth in a spiral prior to inserting the frame in the steamer. The same system is of course used for non-pressurised steamers which are of much lighter construction and hence cheaper. Attempts have been made to produce continuous pressure steamers and while some success has been achieved with dyeing processes, difficulties arise with printed cloth. These are due to marking-off or smearing as the cloth passes between the pressure sealing devices at the entry and exit slots.

High Temperature Steaming

The use of high temperature steam to obtain rapid dye fixation has been pioneered by ICI and several firms now produce industrial models under licence. This system which is capable of operating, if required, up to $180°-200°$C $(355°-390°$F) combines the advantages of low treatment times with the avoidance of the need to use pressure seals. This extends the classes of dyes and fibres which may be processed by HT steaming when compared with pressure steaming. More recently, high temperature steamers working on a festoon system have been introduced by Arioli (Italy) and Stork (Holland).

Normal Steaming

This refers to steaming treatments carried out at, or only very slightly above atmospheric pressures with temperatures at $100°$C $(212°$ F) or a few degrees above this. The steam should be air-free and an abundant supply available. A variety of industrial steamers is available. It should

*$15-37$ lbf/in^2 gauge.

be noted that present day nomenclature includes agers in this general definition, hence the terms *ageing* and *steaming* are frequently synonymous. If any distinction is made then ageing refers to a somewhat shorter treatment carried out in a roller-ager (see also flash-ageing). Steaming being a somewhat longer treatment is carried out in a festoon steamer, a cottage steamer or a star steamer. The last two types are discontinuous devices and hence give much lower production rates than a festoon steamer which can process up to four layers of cloth simultaneously under favourable conditions.

Function of the Steaming Operation

The operation of steaming printed fabrics may be likened to a dyeing operation. Before steaming, the bulk of the dyestuff is held in a dried film of thickening agent; a small proportion may have penetrated into the fibre during drying but this is insufficient to be of much consequence. During the steaming operation the printed areas absorb moisture and form a very concentrated dyebath from which dyeing of the fibre takes place. The function of the thickening agent during this period is to prevent the dyestuff from spreading outside the area originally printed, that is, to prevent 'bleeding'. The concentrated 'dyebath' formed on the fibre exists more in the form of a gel than a solution and any tendency to bleed is restricted. If the steam is too moist or the printing paste contains too large a quantity of hygroscopic agent—for example, glycerine, urea, etc.—then the film of thickening agent becomes so diluted that bleeding occurs. Alternatively, if the steam is too dry the film of thickening cannot absorb sufficient moisture and the dyestuff does not fix satisfactorily. In addition to promoting the formation of a localised dyebath the steam may have other functions demanding more exact control on the steamer.

With acid and direct dyestuffs, the steaming period is usually lengthy, but since only a dyeing operation (or transfer of dyestuff) is taking place, the main practical problem is to ensure that the steam is not so moist as to cause bleeding. Slight air contamination is not deleterious although too large a volume of cold air being drawn into the steamer may lead to condensation of water on the fabric and thereby cause the print to bleed. Steaming times of up to 1 h are common with these dyestuffs. Much shorter steaming treatments are required to fix the 'Procion' dyestuffs where reaction with the fibre as opposed to a simple dyeing operation is involved. 'Procion' *M* brands will fix by steaming for as short a time as 15 s while the less reactive 'Procion' *H* brands require a minimum time of 10 min. Neither type is unduly sensitive to the quality of the steam and the presence of air in the steamer does not affect the fixation of dyes of this class.

61

More critical steaming conditions are necessary for the satisfactory steaming of 'Caledon' and 'Durindone' vat dyestuffs, and for white and illuminated printed discharges. The fixation of a vat dyestuff during steaming is a consequence of several reactions which require an abundant flow of air-free steam of reasonably high moisture content. Steaming times of 5–12 min are usually adequate, but in the special case of the flash-age process a steaming time of 20 s will suffice. The failure to fix vat dyestuffs or obtain white and illuminated discharges satisfactorily on a small scale can usually be traced to an insufficient supply of steam. When the printed patterns are introduced into a steamer, the air must be very rapidly displaced by an inrush of steam, or the fixation of the dyestuff will be seriously impaired. Air not displaced from the steamer rapidly attacks the sodium sulphoxylate formaldehyde in the printed areas at the high temperature reached during steaming, and decomposes it. Consequently the sodium sulphoxylate formaldehyde is not then available to fulfil its normal function of reducing the vat dye, and/or the dyed ground in discharge patterns, and thus fails to initiate the dyeing reaction which must take place during steaming. It will be appreciated that under such conditions the resulting prints will inevitably be unsatisfactory in appearance owing to inadequate and erratic fixation of the vat dyestuff or inadequate discharge of the dyed ground shade.

'Alcian' dyestuffs are converted by heat into insoluble products after they have dyed into the fibre. Steaming times of 5–20 min are adequate and the steam should be reasonably moist to allow maximum dye uptake but otherwise conditions are not critical. Steaming times longer than 20 min have no adverse effect on 'Alcian' dyes; hence, if required they may be printed and processed alongside dyes requiring a longer steaming treatment.

'Soledon' dyestuffs may be developed by a steaming treatment using the sulphocyanide printing process. In this case only a short steaming treatment is required but the temperature of the steamer must be at or near $100°C$ ($212°F$) to ensure that the acidic component necessary for development is liberated from one of the reagents added to the printing paste.

Disperse dyes on 'Terylene', acid dyes on nylon and basic dyes on acrylic fibres will all tend to bleed to varying extents if the steam is excessively moist because the fibres themselves are hydrophobic (i.e. they have low moisture regains). The most common cause of excessively moist steam is an inadequate supply and this is often coupled with an inadequately lagged steamer (see steam requirements described later).

Steaming Equipment
Steamers of the roller or festoon type are found in the majority of print works. These steamers, dependent upon an external source of steam,

62

are designed essentially for large-scale production and, as such, are considered to be outside the scope of this book. Few colleges and schools of art have a steam supply available. When access can be had to a steam supply, a Star steamer is frequently employed. Generally speaking, however, a simple steamer is used in which steam is generated by boiling water in the base, using a gas ring or electric immersion heaters.

'Dustbin'-type Steamer. The 'Dustbin'-type steamer illustrated in *Figure 6.1* suffices for most of the styles outlined in this book, but because of

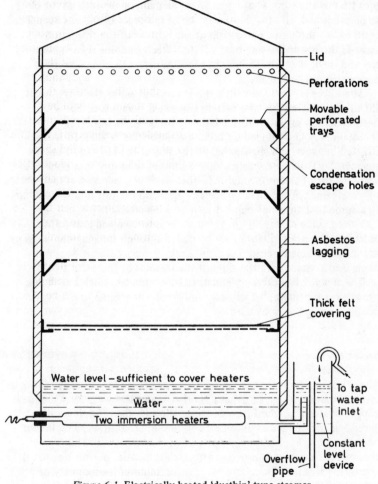

Figure 6.1. Electrically heated 'dustbin'-type steamer

63

the large volume of air that is admitted whenever the lid is removed for the purpose of loading or unloading, it is of very doubtful efficiency where vat dyes or discharge prints are concerned.

Tower Steamer. This type of steamer is comparatively simple to construct and, because of its design, is capable of providing suitable fixation conditions for vat dyestuffs or discharge prints. It is illustrated diagrammatically in *Figure 6.2*. As its name implies, it is a tower of variable height depending on the steaming capacity required. The breadth is made somewhat larger than the maximum width of the cloth to be processed, and the depth may be of the order of 0·3 m (1 ft). The cloth enters through a narrow slit at the bottom of the tower and ascends the tower, passing over a fluted, freely-running roller near the top and then, after descending the tower, it passes through a second narrow slit out to the air.

The tower is provided with a sloping roof in which there is a small slit to allow the escape of a certain amount of steam together with decomposition products formed during the steaming process.

Steam may be provided by boiling water in the 'V'-shaped troughs situated between and slightly below the slits at the bottom of the steamer. Sufficient steam should be admitted to ensure that there is a slight escape of steam through a further slit in the side and at the bottom of the steamer. When steam is seen escaping up the side it is reasonable to assume that air is not being drawn into the steamer.

Fluted guide rollers are provided at the entrance and exit to the machine. The printed cloth may be pulled through the machine by hand as long as sufficient tension is maintained to ensure that it does not come into contact with the sides of the steamer or the entry slits.

The steamer is preferably constructed of stainless steel, but if this proves too expensive, heavily galvanised mild steel plate or a suitable quality of wood may be used.

Steam Requirements

The primary reason for the failure of most 'home-made' steamers to give adequate fixation of dyestuffs other than vat dyes is an inadequate supply of steam. A good flow of steam through the printed goods should be maintained at all times, and in the 'Dustbin'-type sufficient heat should be applied to the water at the base to ensure that a reasonable flow of steam persists through the outlet perforations at the top of the steamer. The quantity of steam required varies with the volume of the steamer and a fair guide is to ensure that approximately

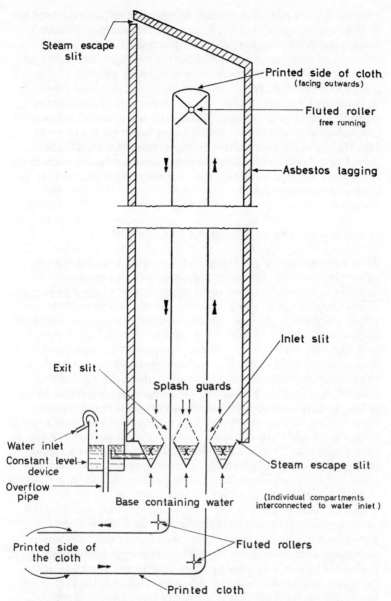

Steam escape slit

Printed side of cloth (facing outwards)

Fluted roller free running

Asbestos lagging

Inlet slit

Exit slit

Splash guards

Water inlet

Constant level device

Overflow pipe

Steam escape slit

Base containing water

(Individual compartments interconnected to water inlet)

Printed side of the cloth

Fluted rollers

Printed cloth

X – *Electric immersion heater* (*capacity dependent on the dimensions of the steamer*)

Figure 6.2. Tower steamer

65

1 litre (2 lb) of water is converted to steam per hour for every 30 litres (1 ft^3) capacity of the steamer. Thus with a conventional 'Dustbin' steamer which has a capacity of approximately 100 litres (3·5 ft^3) it is necessary to evaporate 3 litres (5·5 pints) of water per hour. A simple test can easily be made to ensure than an adequate quantity of water is in fact being evaporated.

If electric immersion heaters are employed for the production of steam it is useful to know that a 1 kW heater will convert 1·5 litres (3 lb) of water into steam per hour. Electric kettle-heaters of 1·5 kW capacity can be readily purchased, and, provided that the 'Dustbin' steamer is effectively lagged, two such heaters should suffice with this type on the assumption that the cubic capacity of the steamer is of the order of 100 litres (3·5 ft^3).

FINAL TREATMENT (WASHING-OFF)

After steaming, printed goods require rinsing well in a good supply of cold water to remove the thickening chemicals and surplus unfixed dyestuff. A soaping treatment in an appropriate detergent usually follows, the severity of this varying with the type of dyestuff and the fabric. Industrially, rinsing and soaping operations are carried out either in open width or in rope form. In an open soaper the fabric enters the first tank with guide rollers maintaining tension in the weft direction. This tension is maintained either by fluted conical rollers or by some other means as the cloth passes down the soaper, which is divided into from six to eight tanks with sprays and mangles between each tank. After emerging from the final mangle nip the fabric is either plaited down to await drying, or better still is passed immediately over a series of drying cylinders. Open soapers are capable of giving a very rapid wash if necessary under mild conditions. In former times they were used for treating such fugitive dyes as basic dyes printed on cotton or some of the pre-dyeing operations carried out on mordant-printed cloth.

In a rope soaper the cloth is processed in rope form, the term arising from the lack of weft tension causing the fabric to resemble a thick rope. This form is achieved by leading the fabric through a glazed ceramic ring (or 'pot-eye') into the machine and using similar pot-eyes at intervals to guide the cloth in its passage through the machine. The rope soaper may possess a single tank or several tanks running in tandem depending on the output required. The cloth progresses down the machine in a series of laps moved by a rotating, often elliptical, roller and prevented from entangling by guide rails. In another version the laps are held somewhat tighter and the elliptical roller is replaced by two mangle rollers and the cloth led between them.

66

There are several modern sophisticated models of rope soapers marketed in which attempts are made to combine the thorough washing of rope soaping with the high output of an open soaper.

For smaller scale operations in colleges and art schools the following possibilities should be considered. Small patterns may be rinsed in a rectangular laboratory sink. The rate of flow of water may be increased by fixing a tightly fitting wooden board in which several 12·5 mm (0·5 in) holes have been drilled about three quarters of the way along the sink's length, leaving the plug hole free. By connecting a rubber tube to the cold water tap and leading the tube through the board near the base a rapid flow of water is possible. This quickly fills up the greater portion of the sink in spite of the drainage holes and the top is then adjusted to maintain the level. By this means the excess water drains through the normal plug hole which has invariably a much greater capacity than the overflow. Furthermore, the board prevents the fabric undergoing washing from obstructing the drain or the overflow.

Soaping on this smaller scale is more difficult, admittedly large saucepans have been used heated by gas or electrically but these present a definite safety hazard. A washing machine is preferable particularly if rinsing and spin drying operations are possible on it. Where a piped steam supply is available very satisfactory washing and soaping tanks may be constructed in hard wood or preferably stainless steel. The minimum requirements for such tanks are a cold water inlet pipe, a low pressure steam inlet pipe, e.g. $0·10MN/m^2$ (1 atm), a drain valve and a perforated plate which prevents fabrics becoming entangled with the drain or the water and steam pipes. Experience has shown that these small tanks, of which two should be regarded as a minimum and up to six considered where circumstances permit, are best placed inside a larger tank. The larger tank is fitted with an adequate capacity drain which is normally left open. The smaller tanks when used for rinsing are allowed to overflow into the larger tank. Any accidental boiling over of the soaping tanks does not endanger the persons operating them.

For intermediate scale working, provided an adequate water and steam supply is available a winch beck should be installed. A winch beck normally processes fabric in rope form, either as a single endless loop, or, in the case of wider models, several loops. When the capacity of the winch allows several loops, the leading edge of the cloth is threaded back down the winch and joined to the last end. By this means as long a processing time as is necessary is possible irrespective of the running speed of the machine. These winches are virtually identical with the individual tanks of a rope soaper, but the term *winch* is often used to describe a dyeing machine. The fact that a stainless steel winch machine is suitable for scouring and dyeing fabrics as well as washing off prints should be borne in mind when considering this type of installation.

Similar machines in wood or with wooden fittings have considerable limitations both in regard to the cleaning down time required and the chemicals that may be used in them.

BIBLIOGRAPHY

There are three main sources of information relating to the processing machinery described in this Chapter:

(*a*)   Books showing diagrams or photographs of the machinery.

(*b*)   Journals and technical periodicals which may either have descriptive articles in them or may carry an illustrated advertisement.

(*c*)   Technical circulars and leaflets issued by the manufacturers of particular machines.

The following list, which is by no means fully comprehensive, does include a number of important sources of information.

1. HALL, A. J., *Standard Handbook of Textiles,* 7th edn., Butterworths, London, 1969 (Refer particularly to Chapt. 4, 164–304)
2. Textile Recorder Annual Machinery Review, Old Colony House, South King Street, Manchester 2, England (1966/67)
3. Teintex, Edition Teintex 60, Rue de Richelieu, Paris 2, France
4. Melliand Textilberichte KG, 69 Heidelberg, Rohrbacherstr. 76, W. Germany
5. Textil Praxis, 7000 Stuttgart 80, Hauptstr. 77, Postfach 800669, W. Germany
6. Textil Industrie, Mönchengladbach, Lüpertzender Str. 157–163, W. Germany
7. Textile Industries, W.R.C. Smith Publishing Co., 1760 Peachtree Road N.W., Atlanta, Georgia 30309, USA
8. Textile World, McGraw-Hill Inc., 330 West 42nd Street, New York, NY 10036, USA
9. Textile Chemist and Colourist, AATCC Technical Centre, PO Box 12215, Research Triangle Park, N. Carolina 27709, USA
10. American Dyestuffs Reporter, Howes Publishing Co. Inc., 44 East 23rd Street, New York, NY 10010, USA
11. Textile Manufacturer, 31 King Street West, Manchester M3 2PL, England
12. Textile Month, Textile Business Press Ltd., Statham House, Talbot Road, Stretford, Manchester M32 OEP, England
13. International Dyer, Textile Business Press Ltd., 30 Finsbury Sq., London, E.C.2., England

7

Colour Fastness Properties

The term *colour fastness* describes the resistance of dyed or printed textiles to various agencies to which they may be exposed during use or manufacture. Ideally the dyestuffs on a printed fabric or on a dyeing should last as long as the fabric itself. In addition the dyes used should not give rise to staining on the unprinted parts of a fabric or on other fabrics coming into close contact during wear or washing. In deciding what are the important fastness properties the fabric end-use should be borne in mind. Exposure to light and washing are often major factors but this may not enable a sufficiently good prediction of end-use performance to be made.

Furnishing fabrics clearly need to be fast to light but the fastness to washing or dry cleaning is also of importance. Dress fabrics, while not requiring such high light fastness, must have good washing and perspiration fastness. Dyes used on fabrics intended for bathing costumes must have good fastness to ordinary water and to the chlorinated water used in swimming baths, as well as to light. Cotton articles are usually required to stand up to much more severe washing than wool, so the washing fastness of dyes printed or dyed on cotton is usually more important than in the case of wool. Conversely, there are a number of processes used in the finishing of dyed wool for which the dyer expects from the dye maker an indication of the probable behaviour of the available dyestuffs when subjected to these finishing treatments.

Expression of Results of Fastness Tests

A 1–5 scale is used in all cases except light fastness. The principle used in assessment is to compare the loss of depth or change of shade (or both) of the treated pattern with an untreated control pattern. The difference between these two patterns is compared with the difference in a standard series of grey shades. The latter is termed a *grey scale* to distinguish it from a standard series of much paler greys and whites which form the 'staining scale'. The rating using the grey scale is quoted as 'effect on the print' (or dyeing) while the staining is quoted using the

1–5 Staining Scale as 'staining of adjacent material'. The material in question is named since frequently two adjacent materials are used, one being the same fabric as the test material but uncoloured, and the second material being an uncoloured pattern of a different fibre with which the test material might be expected to come into contact during use. In general, both 'effect' and 'staining' fastness gradings may be taken to have the following meanings:

5 excellent
4 good
3 fair
2 poor
1 very poor

If a figure is quoted without any qualification then the difference between the test pattern and the original is essentially one of weakness. Ratings such as '4–5 bluer' or '4 duller' indicate shade alterations. When two qualifications are added to the numerical rating, e.g. '3 redder, weaker' the first mentioned predominates but the overall effect still corresponds to 3 on the grey scale.

Standardisation of Fastness Testing

In the United Kingdom the Society of Dyers and Colourists appointed a committee to study fastness testing in 1927, and in 1947 when the International Organisation for Standardisation was formed it was appropriate that the Society appointed members to the appropriate I.S.O. Sub-Committee. Also on this Sub-Committee were members of the American Association of Textile Chemists and Colourists (AATCC) and the continental European organisation Europaisch-Continental Echtheits-Convention (ECE). During the years following 1948 the I.S.O. Sub-Committee has endeavoured, with a considerable amount of success, to replace all of the diverse systems of fastness testing employed in the United Kingdom, on the Continent and in the USA, by a single unified system employing the best features from each. When a particular fastness test has been agreed on a world wide basis the term *I.S.O. Recommendation* is applied to it. In practice most of the 44 national standardising bodies which form the I.S.O. take steps to establish the I.S.O. Recommendation as a national standard. Thus the Light Fastness: Daylight Test is BS 1006 in the UK, DIN 54003 in W. Germany, NF G07–012 in France, and so on.

In this publication the test results quoted are limited to those considered most important for each particular case. They include the fastness to light and the fastness to one washing test. Dyemakers are

70

able to quote fastness tests considerably wider in scope from their technical literature.

Light Fastness

The I.S.O. daylight fastness test which has been adopted by 21 countries uses eight blue-dyed wool standards. Standard 1 is very fugitive and the fastness increases stepwise to Standard 8 which is very fast. The test patterns are exposed alongside the standards. When a change of colour can just be perceived in the test pattern a note is made of the standard showing a similar change. A mask is used to cover part of the preliminary fade, and exposure is continued for as long as required to evaluate fully the light fastness. The final rating is given either as a single figure or where appropriate as a 'half' rating. Thus a rating of 5–6 means that the test pattern has better light fastness than Standard 5 but is not as good as Standard 6.

In the USA the I.S.O. method has not been adopted and methods based on a different set of blue wool standards numbered L2–L9 are used. The results are usually expressed in terms of the number of Standard Fading Hours necessary to produce a Grey Scale 4 contrast. Some attempts have been made to correlate findings by the two methods[1] but while reasonable correlation is possible where daylight fading is involved, difficulties arise when exposures on various fading lamps are involved.

Washing Fastness

There are five I.S.O. wash tests increasing in severity from 1–5 as follows:

Wash test	Treatment time	Treatment temperature	Composition of test solution
I.S.O. No. 1	30 min	40°C (105°F)	5 parts soap/1000 parts
I.S.O. No. 2	45 min	50°C (122°F)	5 parts soap/1000 parts
I.S.O. No. 3	30 min	60°C (140°F)	5 parts soap, 2 parts soda ash/1000 parts
I.S.O. No. 4	30 min	95°C (203°F)	5 parts soap, 2 parts soda ash/1000 parts
I.S.O. No. 5	4 h	95°C (203°F)	5 parts soap, 2 parts soda ash/1000 parts

Tests which differ very slightly from these are occasionally quoted in this publication, e.g. 'Once at 55°C (130°F)' differs from I.S.O. No. 2 in being carried out at 5°C (8°F) higher in temperature for 15 min less

71

time, and '5 times at 100°C (212°F)' differs from I.S.O. wash test No. 5 in being carried out for 5 h instead of 4 h and because a rinsing and drying operation is carried out after every hour's treatment in the earlier test.

Depth of Shade for Fastness Testing

As the fastness of a dye depends on the depth of colour it is necessary to specify standard depths at which fastness tests shall be carried out. A main range of standard depths referred to as 1/1 Standard Depth is available in 18 hues. Stronger 2/1 Standard Depth and weaker, referred to as 1/3, 1/6, 1/12 and 1/25 Standard Depth are also illustrated[2,3]. Dyemakers normally quote light fastness at three depths, e.g. 2/1, 1/1 and 1/25. Wet fastness tests should be assumed to have been carried out at 1/1 Standard Depth unless there is a statement to the contrary.

Abbreviations in Fastness Test Ratings

In the various tables of fastness properties the following standardised abbreviations are employed, where applicable, to indicate any change of shade:

B = bluer
Br = brighter
D = duller
G = greener
R = redder
W = weaker
Y = yellower

REFERENCES

1. *Light Fastness of Dyes: I.S.O. and A.A.T.C.C. Ratings,* Technical Information No. D1076, ICI Dyestuffs Division
2. 'Standard Methods for the Determination of the Colour Fastness of Textiles' (3rd Edition 1962) published by the Society of Dyers and Colourists, 19 Piccadilly, Bradford, England. Grey Scales, Staining Scales and Standard Depth illustrations may also be obtained from the same address
3. *The Determination of Colour Fastness,* Technical Information (Dyehouse) No. 647, ICI Dyestuffs Division

8

The Printing of Cotton and Viscose Rayon

Several classes of dyestuffs can be used for the printing of cotton and viscose rayon. The printer's choice of dyestuffs for any particular pattern is determined by the availability of the desired shade in any dyestuff range, by the fastness requirements of the final pattern, and, not least by the equipment and processing facilities available.

Linen. In general the recipes and processes referring to cotton and viscose rayon given in this chapter can also be used for the printing of linen. Typical recipes, processing details and fastness data to serve as a guide in the choice of dyestuffs are given below.

'PROCION' DYESTUFFS

General Information

The 'Procion' dyes are a range of reactive dyes whose fixation is achieved by chemical linkage of the dye with the fibre. By the use of 'Procion' dyes a wide range of shades possessing good fastness to light and washing can be obtained. Three distinct classes of 'Procion' reactive dyes are available:

'Procion' H Dyes. These are the less reactive type. Their lower reactivity is manifested by their excellent print paste stability and for this reason they are preferred for application by the steaming process.

'Procion' Supra Dyes. These dyes have reactivity and print paste stability comparable with 'Procion' *H* dyes. In addition they give very high yields and improved washing-off behaviour.

73

'Procion' M Dyes. These are the more reactive type and are therefore more versatile in application. They are suitable for use in various non-steaming print-on and resist styles, in addition to their use in the steaming process.

The Procion dyes, within each class, are miscible in all proportions with one another to produce a wide range of shades. The use of mixtures of 'Procion' *H* and *M* is not generally recommended but 'Procion' Supra and 'Procion' *H* dyes may be mixed if necessary.

Reaction Mechanism

The linkage of 'Procion' dyes with the fibre takes place in the presence of alkali and under the influence of heat. Development methods include:

Steaming process.
Baking (dry-heat) process.
Flash-ageing process.
Air-hanging process.
Wet development process.
Pad (alkali)-batch process.

These fixation methods call for slight variations of recipe, but all the 'Procion' recipes are based on the following simple system. 'Procion' dye is dissolved in water with the assistance of urea, and the solution obtained is mixed with a suitable thickening. Alkali is either incorporated in the print paste, supplied by a ground previously prepared in alkali, or applied by a subsequent padding operation. After fixation the prints are given a final washing-off treatment.

Choice of Thickening Agent

Because of the reactive nature of the 'Procion' dyes correct choice of thickening agent is essential. Thickenings of the sodium alginate type, either as aqueous solutions or in an emulsion, are the most satisfactory.

Preparation of the Fabric

When printing on cotton, the maximum yields are obtained from a mercerised fabric. As an alternative, causticisation of the fabric is recommended. On viscose rayon, improved yields are obtained when the fabric is causticised. It is essential that the final preparation treatments given to the cellulose substrate leave the fabric in a neutral or slightly alkaline condition. Any acidic reaction of the fabric, or the presence of residual starch on the fabric, will give rise to a lowering in the colour yield from 'Procion' dyes.

Use of Thickening Agents as Screen Table Adhesives

The practice of using a printing gum such as British Gum as a table adhesive in screen or block printing can result in a weak print or a harsh handle owing to reaction with dyestuff that has penetrated the fabric. Moreover, table adhesives should be neutral in reaction since acidity can adversely affect the fixation of the dyestuff. The use of a high-solids-content sodium alginate thickening such as 'Manutex' *F* or a methylated cellulose such as 'Celacol' *MM 10* is recommended.

Use of 'Procion' dyes in Admixture with other Classes of Dyes

'Procion' dyes are not normally suitable for use in admixture with other classes of dyes. They can be printed alongside certain conventional dyes but, with the wide range of shades obtainable from 'Procion' dyes, this mixed style is rarely operated.

Printing Recipes

The standard printing recipes for 'Procion' dyes quoted in *Table 8.1* are suitable for printing the majority of 'Procion' dyes by the steaming process on cotton and viscose rayon. Where modification for a particular 'Procion' dyestuff or 'Procion' printing process is required this is indicated under the appropriate development method. It has now become customary to designate 'Procion' printing methods as 'one-stage' or 'two-stage' processes. If alkali is present in the printing paste and steaming or baking follows this is a 'one-stage' process. Where the 'Procion' is printed without alkali on to fabric already containing alkali or to which alkali is subsequently applied this is a 'two-stage' process.

Table 8.1. GENERAL PRINTING RECIPE FOR 'PROCION' DYES

	Stock Paste	*Reduction*	
'Procion' dye	50	–	parts
Urea	50–200	50–200	,,
Water	490–240	540–290	,,
Thickening			
either sodium alginate	350	350	,,
or sodium alginate	150	150	,,
and			
emulsion thickening	300	300	,,
Resist Salt *L*	10	10	,,
Alkali			
either sodium bicarbonate	25	15	,,
or sodium carbonate (anhydrous)	15	15	,,
Bulk to	1 000	1 000	,,

75

Urea   Use on cotton   50—100 parts
         on viscose rayon   100—200 parts
Optimum urea concentration will depend on local steaming conditions.
'Procion' M dyes   Use as alkali 15 parts of sodium bicarbonate per 1 000 parts of
             print paste.

Preparation of the Print Paste

Either Prepare a stock thickening containing all the auxiliary products required for fixation of the 'Procion' dye. Then sprinkle the dye powder on to the stock thickening agitated by a high-speed stirrer (the sprinkle-in technique)

or Dissolve the urea in water, heat the solution and pour it on to the 'Procion' dye powder. Alternatively, mix the dye powder with urea and add hot water. Stir the mixture and, if necessary, heat until solution is effected. *Note:* Maximum temperature for 'Procion' *M* dyes is 70°C (160°F). Add the dye solution to the thickening containing previously dissolved Resist Salt *L*. Finally, add the alkali, preferably as a slurry.

Stability of Print Pastes and Printed Goods

'Procion' *H* and 'Procion' Supra dyes possess very good printing paste stability and, in general, can be stored for at least 28 days without any significant loss in printing strength. 'Procion' *M* dyes exhibit a lower level of print paste stability, the degree of stability varying with individual dyes. When using 'Procion' *M* dyes it is recommended that colleges and schools of art should prepare only sufficient print paste for immediate needs and the 'Procion' *M* print pastes should be freshly prepared each day.

    Prints produced with 'Procion' dyes may be stored without loss in colour yield until it is convenient to steam them. Prints so stored must be protected from contamination by acid or reducing fumes.

Mixture Shades

Calculate the total quantity of 'Procion' dye in the proposed mixture and make urea and alkali additions appropriate to this concentration of dye.

Antifrothing Agent

With sodium alginate thickening add 10—20 parts of 'Perminal' *KB* per 1 000 parts of print paste. With emulsion thickening add 0·5—1 part of 'Silcolapse' *5 000*.

Development

Steaming Process

The print pastes are prepared using the general recipe already given.
After printing and drying, the goods are steamed, the 'Procion' *H* and
'Procion' Supra dyes for 5–15 min and the 'Procion' *M* dyes for a
minimum of 15 s. The use of air-free steam is not essential, but the
presence of acidic or reducing fumes in the steamer must be avoided.
After steaming, the goods must be washed-off (see page 85). *Note:*
Avoid over-drying of the prints. Moist steaming conditions are
essential for viscose rayon. Suitable 'Procion' dyes include:

'Procion' Supra Dyes

Procion Supra Yellow H-8GP	*Procion Supra Blue H-3RP
Procion Supra Yellow H-4GP	Procion Supra Turquoise H-2GP
Procion Supra Yellow H-2RP	†Procion Supra Black H-LP
Procion Supra Red H-4BP	

'Procion' *H* Dyes

Procion Brilliant Yellow H-5G	Procion Rubine H-BN
Procion Brilliant Yellow H-4G	Procion Brilliant Purple H-3R
Procion Yellow H-G	*Procion Blue H-5R
Procion Golden Yellow H-R	Procion Navy Blue H-3R
Procion Brilliant Orange H-2R	Procion Brilliant Blue H-GR
Procion Orange H-4R	Procion Blue H-3G
Procion Printing Brown H-G	Procion Brilliant Blue H-5G
Procion Dark Brown H-B	Procion Turquoise H-A
Procion Red Brown H-4R	Procion Brilliant Blue H-3R
Procion Dark Brown H-6R	Procion Brilliant Blue H-4R
Procion Scarlet H-RN	Procion Olive Green H-7G
Procion Brilliant Red H-3BN	†Procion Black H-N.
Procion Brilliant Red H-8B	

Notes

(1) **'Procion' Blue H-5R and 'Procion' Supra Blue H-3RP*
Use as alkali 30 parts of sodium carbonate per 1 000 parts of
print paste (Blue *H-5R*) and 20 parts per 1 000 (Supra Blue *H-3RP*)

(2) † *'Procion' Black H-N and 'Procion' Supra Black H-LP*
Use as alkali 30 parts of sodium bicarbonate or 25 parts of
sodium carbonate and use 50 parts of urea per 1 000 parts of
print paste.

'Procion' *M* Dyes

Procion Brilliant Yellow M-6G   Procion Brilliant Red M-5B
Procion Yellow M-GR   Procion Brilliant Red M-8B
Procion Yellow M-4R   Procion Blue M-3G
Procion Brilliant Orange M-2R   Procion Brilliant Blue M-R
Procion Scarlet M-G   Procion Green M-2B
Procion Red M-G

Baking (Dry-Heat) Process

The print pastes are prepared using the general recipe already given *but* using at all depths of shade (1) a higher concentration of urea, i.e. 200 parts of urea per 1 000 parts of final print paste and (2) for 'Procion' *H* dyes 15 parts of anhydrous sodium carbonate and for 'Procion' *M* dyes 15 parts of sodium bicarbonate per 1 000 parts of final print paste.

After printing, the goods are dried, and then given a baking (dry-heat) treatment as shown in *Table 8.2.*

Table 8.2. BAKING TREATMENTS FOR 'PROCION' DYED FABRICS

Fabric	*Cotton*		*Viscose Rayon*	
Baking conditions	Temp.	Time	Temp.	Time
'Procion' Supra dyes	140°C (285°F)	5 min	150°C (300°F)	5 min
'Procion' *H* dyes	140°C (285°F)	5 min	150°C (300°F)	5 min
'Procion' *M* dyes	110°C (230°F)	3 min	140°C (285°F)	3 min

Note:

When an emulsion thickening is employed for printing 'Procion' dyes subsequently to be developed by the baking (dry-heat) process, attention is drawn to page 26 in respect of possible hazards.

In colleges and schools of art, where large scale baking equipment is not available, satisfactory fixation can be obtained by either baking for 5 min at 140°C (285°F) using, for example, an ordinary domestic electric oven fitted with temperature control, or, ironing for 5 min with a household hand iron, preferably of the thermostatically controlled type, or with a steam iron. After baking the goods must be washed off (see page 85). *Note:* Maximum yields are obtained on a mercerised cotton fabric, this process is only of minor interest on viscose rayon fabrics.

Suitable 'Procion' dyes include:

'Procion' Supra Dyes

Procion Supra Yellow H-8GP   Procion Supra Blue H-3RP
Procion Supra Yellow H-4GP   Procion Supra Turquoise H-2GP
Procion Supra Yellow H-2RP   Procion Supra Black H-LP
Procion Supra Red H-4BP

'Procion' *H* Dyes

Procion Brilliant Yellow H-5G   Procion Rubine H-BN
Procion Brilliant Yellow H-4G   Procion Brilliant Purple H-3R
Procion Yellow H-G   Procion Blue H-5R
Procion Golden Yellow H-R   Procion Navy Blue H-3R
Procion Brilliant Orange H-2R   Procion Brilliant Blue H-GR
Procion Orange H-4R   Procion Blue H-3G
Procion Printing Brown H-G   Procion Brilliant Blue H-5G
Procion Dark Brown H-B   Procion Turquoise H-A
Procion Red Brown H-4R   Procion Brilliant Blue H-3R
Procion Dark Brown H-6R   Procion Brilliant Blue H-4R
Procion Scarlet H-RN   Procion Olive Green H-7G
Procion Brilliant Red H-3BN   Procion Black H-N
Procion Brilliant Red H-8B

'Procion' *M* Dyes

Procion Brilliant Yellow M-6G   Procion Brilliant Red M-5B
Procion Yellow M-GR   Procion Brilliant Red M-8B
Procion Yellow M-4R   Procion Blue M-3G
Procion Brilliant Orange M-2R   Procion Brilliant Blue M-R
Procion Scarlet M-G   Procion Green M-2B
Procion Red M-G

Flash-ageing Process

Introduction. The fixation of prints on cotton or viscose rayon of selected 'Procion' dyestuffs by a high speed pad steam process or 'flash-ageing' is creating considerable interest and offers a means of obtaining better consistency of yield on viscose rayon fabrics. This 'two-stage' process consists essentially in printing a solution of the 'Procion' dyestuff in a suitable thickening, drying, and subsequently developing the print by padding in a cold solution containing alkali and common salt and passing immediately into the steamer. The thickening need not be capable of coagulation by alkali. The process

79

has three important features. First, the print pastes contain no alkali and this results in improved print paste stability. Second, fixation is achieved by a short steaming process normally of 40 s duration. The steamer is run in conjunction with a conventional two-bowl padding mangle and an open-width soaping range. Third, the printed fabrics can be stored for a considerable time before developing, provided that they are protected from contamination by acid or reducing fumes.

The following recipes are given as a guide:

Printing Recipe

50 parts	urea are dissolved in
580–510 ,,	water and the solution is heated. (Maximum temperature–'Procion' H dyes 90°C (195°F) 'Procion' M dyes 70°C (160°F). This solution is then added with stirring to
10–80 ,,	'Procion' dyestuff. When the dyestuff has dissolved the solution is stirred into
350 ,,	sodium alginate thickening containing
10 ,,	Resist Salt L
1 000 parts.	

Padding Solution (*cold*):

100 parts	sodium metasilicate
150 ,,	anhydrous sodium carbonate
50 ,,	anhydrous potassium carbonate
100 ,,	sodium chloride
500 ,,	water
100 ,,	Gum Tragacanth (7%)
1 000 parts.	

In order to obtain prints with sharp definition, high colour value and unstained whites, it is essential to choose the most suitable dyestuffs, and to ensure that the padding and steaming conditions are carefully controlled.

Dyestuff Selection. The following dyestuffs are considered to be of interest in respect of yield by the flash-ageing process.

80

'Procion' Supra Dyes

Procion Supra Yellow H-8GP
Procion Supra Yellow H-4GP   Procion Supra Red H-4BP
Procion Supra Yellow H-2RP   *Procion Supra Turquoise H-2GP

'Procion' *H* Dyes

Procion Brilliant Yellow H-5G   *Procion Brilliant Red H-3BN
Procion Brilliant Yellow H-4G   *Procion Brilliant Red H-8B
Procion Yellow H-G   *Procion Rubine H-BN
*Procion Golden Yellow H-R   *Procion Brilliant Purple H-3R
*Procion Brilliant Orange H-2R   Procion Blue H-5R
Procion Orange H-4R   Procion Brilliant Blue H-GR
*Procion Red Brown H-4R   *Procion Brilliant Blue H-5G
Procion Printing Brown H-G   *Procion Blue H-3G
Procion Dark Brown H-B   *Procion Turquoise H-A
Procion Dark Brown H-6R   *Procion Brilliant Blue H-4R
*Procion Red H-B   *Procion Olive Green H-7G
Procion Scarlet H-RN   Procion Black H-N

'Procion' *M* Dyes

*Procion Brilliant Yellow M-4G   Procion Brilliant Blue M-R
Procion Yellow M-GR   Procion Blue M-3G
*Procion Yellow M-4R   Procion Green M-2B

Notes:
(1)   'Procion' Brilliant Blue H-5G: increase urea to 150 parts per 1 000.
(2)   *Dyestuffs which are especially recommended.
(3)   The suggestions made to colleges and schools of art in connection
       with the flash-ageing of vat dyestuffs also apply to the flash-ageing
       of 'Procion' dyestuffs (see pages 101–105).

Air-Hanging Process

This process enables a reasonable degree of fixation of the more reactive
'Procion' brands to be obtained on cellulosic fibres. It is of interest when
only the simplest equipment is available. 'Procion' *H* dyestuffs are not
recommended for this process.
    The following sequence of operations is required:
(1)   Pad the unprinted cloth in a 2% solution of soda ash and dry. This
       operation is not critical and can be carried out either by hand
       squeezing or by padding on a mangle and drying.
(2)   Prepare the 'Procion' print pastes, using the recipes already given
       but omitting the addition of alkali.

(3)　　Print the 'Procions' on the alkali-prepared cloth and allow to dry by hanging in the air for several hours, preferably in a warm, humid atmosphere.

Notes
(1)　　The fullest yields by this process are obtained if the 'Procions' are printed on a mercerised cotton fabric or on viscose rayon, only relatively poor yields being obtained on an unmercerised cotton fabric.
(2)　　The duration of the air-hanging treatment depends on prevailing atmospheric conditions, and preliminary trials under local conditions would be advisable. As a guide, it has been found that hanging overnight in a warm, humid atmosphere is sufficient.
(3)　　If, for any reason, alkali preparation of the cloth is not convenient, the air-hanging technique can still be employed. The 'Procion' print pastes are prepared by the recipes already given but the normal quantity of sodium bicarbonate in the 'Procion' print paste is replaced by a mixture of 2 parts of soda ash per 1 000 parts of printing paste and 8 parts of sodium bicarbonate per 1 000 parts of printing paste. The 'Procions' are printed on unprepared cloth, then hung in air.
(4)　　The use of a mixture of sodium carbonate and sodium bicarbonate as the alkali component of the 'Procion' *M* print paste, instead of bicarbonate alone, lowers the stability of the printing paste. Pastes by this process must be prepared freshly each day and the alkali added immediately prior to printing.

Wet Development Process

This method enables selected 'Procion' dyes to be developed without the use of conventional steamers or flash-agers. It is mainly of interest for printing 'Procion' dyes on 'Brenthol' *AS* prepared cloth. The function of the 'Brenthol' *AS* is to form insoluble azoic dyes *in situ* when printed with 'Brentamine' Fast Bases or Salts. Because of the restricted range of shades available from these azoic combinations 'Procion' dyes are used to complete the range. While a steaming process would satisfactorily fix the 'Procion' dyes, it would simultaneously render the removal of the residual 'Brenthol' from the unprinted areas of the fabric more difficult. This two-stage wet development process is a compromise since in practice the treatment temperature and time range represent what is feasible using the first tank of an open soaper.

　　The print paste is prepared without alkali and after printing and drying the fabric is passed into a hot alkaline solution containing salt to minimise any bleeding of the dye, e.g.

Caustic soda 38°Bé (70°Tw) (by volume)	60 parts	
Sodium carbonate (anhydrous)	150 "	
Potassium carbonate (anhydrous)	50 "	
Sodium chloride (common salt)	100 "	
Bulk with water (by volume) to	1 000 parts.	

The bath is heated to 95°–98°C (205°–210°F) and the time of immersion is in the range 8–15 s. The prints are rinsed thoroughly, washed and dried.

The following dyes are recommended:

Procion Supra Yellow H-8GP

*Procion Brilliant Yellow H-4G	Procion Brilliant Red H-3BN
Procion Yellow H-G	Procion Brilliant Red H-8B
†Procion Brilliant Yellow M-4G	†Procion Brilliant Blue H-4R
†Procion Yellow M-4R	Procion Olive Green H-7G
*Procion Golden Yellow H-R	Procion Red Brown H-4R
Procion Brilliant Orange H-2R	Procion Dark Brown H-B
†Procion Red H-B	Procion Supra Turquoise H-2GP

The Pad(alkali)-Batch Printing Process

This process is of particular value where no steaming or baking facilities are available. It is suitable for the printing of mercerised cotton and of 'Brenthol' *AS* prepared cotton. The use of this process is not recommended for viscose rayon because the sodium silicate used at the padding stage makes the handle of the fabric harsh.

This two-stage process involves printing with 'Procion' pastes without added alkali, and drying in the normal way. The print is then padded in undiluted sodium silicate at 48°Bé (100°Tw) to get about 100% pick-up. The padding should, wherever possible, be a *nip-padding*, i.e. the printed cloth should be led face downwards directly into the mangle nip while the lower roller of the padding mangle revolves in the viscous sodium silicate. The preferred quality is Silicate of Soda *C 100* grade (ICI Mond Division) which has the following specification:

Weight ratio $SiO_2 : Na_2O$	=	2·0
Molecular ratio $SiO_2 : Na_2O$	=	2·05
Specific gravity at 20°C (70°F)	=	1·5
Approximate viscosity at 20°C (70°F)	=	200 cP

After padding and without intermediate drying the goods are batched cold. For 'Procion' *M* brands batching for a minimum of 10 min suffices, but if 'Procion' Supra or 'Procion' *H* dyes are used then batching for a

*Suitable only on 'Brenthol' *AS* prepared cloth.
†Suitable only on white cloth.

minimum of 3 h is required. To prevent any drying out, a sheet of 'Alkathene' should be wrapped around the batch and tied at each end. If more convenient, batching may be replaced by piling down for an equivalent length of time. Again the goods should be protected by a transparent impermeable sheet of 'Alkathene'.

A very thorough wash in cold running water preferably using spray pipes is needed to ensure the removal of sodium silicate, after which the fabric is washed-off in the normal way. The batching and washing off operations may be combined by using a perforated beam washer (e.g. as available from Sir James Farmer Norton & Co. Ltd., Salford 3, England). The goods are padded and batched directly on to the perforated beam. When the appropriate batching time has been completed the roll of fabric is washed on the beam first by pumping through cold water and then hot water at as high a temperature as practicable. After a final cold water rinse the goods are ready for removal from the beam for drying.

The following 'Procion' dyes are recommended for application to mercerised cotton and 'Brenthol' *AS* prepared cotton by the Pad (alkali)-Batch printing process.

'Procion' Supra Dyes

Procion Supra Yellow H-8GP
Procion Supra Yellow H-4GP   Procion Supra Red H-4BP
Procion Supra Yellow H-2RP   Procion Supra Turquoise H-2GP

'Procion' H Dyes

Procion Brilliant Yellow H-5G	Procion Brilliant Purple H-3R
Procion Brilliant Yellow H-4G	Procion Blue H-5R
Procion Yellow H-G	Procion Brilliant Blue H-GR
Procion Golden Yellow H-R	Procion Brilliant Blue H-3R
Procion Brilliant Orange H-2R	Procion Blue H-3G
Procion Orange H-4R	Procion Brilliant Blue H-5G
Procion Scarlet H-RN	Procion Olive Green H-7G
Procion Brilliant Red H-3BN	Procion Red Brown H-4R
Procion Brilliant Red H-8B	Procion Dark Brown H-6R
Procion Rubine H-BN	Procion Dark Brown H-B

'Procion' M Dyes

Procion Brilliant Yellow M-6G	Procion Brilliant Red M-2B
Procion Brilliant Yellow M-4G	Procion Brilliant Red M-8B
Procion Yellow M-GR	Procion Blue M-3G
Procion Yellow M-4R	Procion Brilliant Blue M-R
Procion Brilliant Orange M-2R	Procion Green M-2B
Procion Red M-G	Procion Olive Green M-3G

Washing-off 'Procion' Dyestuffs

Washing-off is an essential part of any 'Procion' printing process. The chemical reactivity of 'Procion' dyestuffs leads to the inactivation of a small proportion of the dye during the printing process. This dye does not combine with the cellulose, and must therefore be efficiently removed if the finished print is to have good washing fastness. As the inactive dye is still very soluble, normal washing processes are effective, but it is important that they be carried out thoroughly. A thorough water rinse and a treatment at or near the boil for 3–5 min in a solution of 'Lissapol' ND must be given to all 'Procion' dyes printed on cellulosic fabrics irrespective of the printing method used for the fixation of the 'Procion' dyes.

The following washing-off arrangements are suggested as a basis for trials:

(a) *In an eight-tank Open Soaper*

Tank 1	Cold running water
Tanks 2–6	2 parts of 'Lissapol' ND per 1 000 at as high a temperature as possible
Tanks 7–8	Cold water rinse

(b) *In a Washing Beck*

Beck 1	Cold running water
Beck 2	2 parts of 'Lissapol' ND per 1 000 at as high a temperature as possible
Beck 3	Cold water rinse

Smaller Scale Washing (for colleges and art schools). The fabric must be rinsed thoroughly for 5 min, preferably in open width in running water, until all the loose colour is removed. Finally, the fabric must be boiled for 5 min in 2 parts of 'Lissapol' ND per 1 000 of water and then rinsed in water. If either the rinsing water or the 'Lissapol' ND solution becomes highly coloured it should be thrown away and replaced by a fresh bath.

A Quick Test for the Efficiency of the Washing-off. A piece of the bulk washed and dried pattern is immersed for 1 min in a boiling solution of 'Lissapol' ND (2 parts per 1 000 parts), whereupon no more than a trace of 'Procion' dye should be evident in the test liquor.

Additional Printing Styles with 'Procion' Dyes

The 'Procion' dyes possess a high degree of versatility in textile printing. In addition to the direct printing styles mentioned earlier, the 'Procion' dyes are of considerable interest in a number of discharge and resist printing styles.

Discharge Printing

The use of 'Procion' dyes as dischargeable ground shades is discussed on pages 198—199.

Resist Printing

Procion-Illuminated Resists under Aniline Black. 'Procion' *H* dyestuffs are most useful in the production of multi-coloured resist effects of exceptional brightness under aniline black. This process is one which requires very careful control and it is not recommended for use in schools of art.

The 'Procion' *H* dye print paste is prepared by the recipe given on page 75, but using 40 parts sodium carbonate and making an addition of 100 parts zinc oxide (50% paste) per 1 000 parts of print paste. This is printed on cotton, dried, steamed for 5 min and then nip-padded in aniline black liquor. Aniline black liquor is made up from the following solutions:

Solution 1
- 50 parts — Gum Tragacanth thickening (7%)
- 47 " — aniline hydrochloride
- 3 " — aniline oil
- 125 " — hot water

Solution 2
- 12 " — sodium chlorate
- 125 " — hot water

Solution 3
- 25 " — potassium ferrocyanide
- 115 " — hot water

The solutions are cooled, then solution 2 is added to solution 1, and finally solution 3 added. After padding, dry, then steam again for 2 min, oxidise in acidified sodium dichromate (see page 98) and then wash off (see page 85). Avoid inhaling aniline fumes.

Fastness Properties of 'Procion' Dyes printed on Cotton

These can be seen by referring to *Table 8.3.*

Table 8.3. FASTNESS PROPERTIES OF
'PROCION' DYES PRINTED ON COTTON

	Light 1/1 Standard Depth	*Washing* I.S.O. Wash Test No. 5 4 h at 95°C (200°F) Effect on the print
'Procion' Supra Dyes		
Procion Supra Yellow H-8GP	7	5
Procion Supra Yellow H-4GP	6	5
Procion Supra Yellow H-2RP	4–5	4
Procion Supra Red H-4BP	4–5	4–5
Procion Supra Blue H-3RP	6	4–5
Procion Supra Turquoise H-2GP	6	3
Procion Supra Black H-LP	6–7	5
'Procion' H Dyes		
Procion Brilliant Yellow H-5G	6–7	4
Procion Brilliant Yellow H-4G	6	5
Procion Golden Yellow H-R	6	5
Procion Yellow H-G	5–6	3–4
Procion Brilliant Orange H-2R	4	4–5
Procion Orange H-4R	6	4–5
Procion Printing Brown H-G	5–6	4–5
Procion Dark Brown H-B	5–6	4
Procion Red Brown H-4R	4–5	4–5
Procion Dark Brown H-6R	4	4
Procion Red H-B	4–5	4–5
Procion Scarlet H-RN	4–5	4
Procion Brilliant Red H-3BN	4–5	4–5
Procion Brilliant Red H-8B	4–5	4
Procion Rubine H-BN	6	4–5
Procion Brilliant Purple H-3R	6–7	4–5
Procion Blue H-5R	6	4–5
Procion Navy Blue H-3R	6	4–5
Procion Brilliant Blue H-GR	5–6	4–5
Procion Blue H-3G	7	4
Procion Brilliant Blue H-5G	6	3–4
Procion Turquoise H-A	6	3–4
Procion Brilliant Blue H-3R	6	4–5
Procion Brilliant Blue H-4R	6	4
Procion Olive Green H-7G	6	4–5
Procion Black H-N	6–7	4–5
'Procion' M Dyes		
Procion Brilliant Yellow M-6G	6	3–4
Procion Yellow M-GR	5–6	4
Procion Yellow M-4R	4–5	3–4
Procion Brilliant Orange M-2R	4	4–5
Procion Scarlet M-G	4–5	3WY
Procion Red M-G	5	4
Procion Brilliant Red M-5B	4	4B
Procion Brilliant Red M-8B	4	4–5
Procion Blue M-3G	6–7	4–5
Procion Brilliant Blue M-R	6	4–5
Procion Green M-2B	4–5	5

DIRECT DYESTUFFS

The major defect of these dyestuffs is their lack of resistance to soaping. This has always been the barrier to their wider use in textile printing for there is an extensive range of shades available and a number of direct dyes possess very good light fastness. Some direct dyes that are tinctorially strong and economic to use are occasionally printed on cotton goods that are unlikely to be washed, e.g. mattress tickings. Hurst[1] drew attention to the use of a special type of direct dyestuff for furnishing printing some 15—20 years ago. These were marketed by the three Swiss dyemakers Sandoz, CIBA and Geigy who named them 'Cuprofix', 'Coprantine' and 'Cuprophenyl' dyes respectively. A careful selection of direct dyestuffs whose light fastness was improved by treatment with copper salts was made. Instead of using a conventional salt such as copper sulphate or acetate at the coppering stage a special copper compound of a synthetic resin 'Cuprofix' S (Sandoz) was employed. This resulted in both increased light fastness and washing fastness but as with all coppering treatments some shade dulling was introduced. In many countries direct dyestuffs along with a number of other classes have declined in importance in textile printing and have been overtaken by reactive or pigment dyestuffs. Large quantities of direct dyestuffs are still used in dyeing and some of this dyed material is used in discharge printing styles.

ACID DYESTUFFS

If acid dyestuffs are printed on cotton and steamed, virtually no dyestuff is fixed and the colour is almost completely removed by soaping. A variety of methods for improving the fixation of acid dyes on cotton were discovered but they never reached commercial importance. A number of patents have been granted that relate to dyeing or printing acid dyes in the presence of resin pre-condensates. These developments have been reviewed by Diserens[2]. On viscose rayon, studies by Meitner[3] using diffusion measurements led to conclusions which gave rise to a commercial process. It appeared that only acid dyes above a certain minimum particle size could be printed in the presence of urea. The dyes penetrated the fibre during steaming and aggregated so that when the urea was removed by washing off the acid dye was left behind. Although dyes printed by what became known as the *urea process* only possessed mediocre fastness to mild washing, the process was used fairly widely in the Middle East and India during the early 1950's particularly on lustrous filament viscose rayon fabrics, especially those with satin and sateen weaves. The

88

brilliance which characterised the acid dyes printed by the urea process, e.g. selected members of the 'Carbolan', 'Coomassie' and 'Lissamine' ranges was equalled by the reactive 'Procion' dyes. These new dyes which came into increasing use in the late 1950's possessed very much better wash fastness than acid dyestuffs. The result was a rapid decline in the urea process in favour of 'Procion' dyes which had the added advantage of reducing the steaming time required from 30—40 min to 5—10 min. Acid dyestuffs are still of importance for printing wool and natural silk and are used to an increasing extent for printing nylon. These outlets are discussed under the appropriate fibres.

BASIC DYESTUFFS

The usage of these dyestuffs on cellulosic fibres in printing has declined to very small proportions. Their lack of fastness is largely responsible for this in spite of their great brilliance and intensity as well as their relatively low price. Non-textile outlets account for much larger quantities of basic dyes, e.g. paper dyeing, lake making and spirit flexographic inks for paper printing. One textile application which has led to research for improved basic dyes is the printing and dyeing of acrylic fibres. The resulting dyes, e.g. 'Synacrils' are frequently referred to as *modified basic dyes*, and identified by a separate trade mark from ordinary basic dyes. The latter, having been marketed for many years by numerous firms seldom have a trade mark incorporated in their name, e.g. Rhodamine *6GBN*, Methylene Blue *ZF*, Malachite Green *AN*.

It is not proposed to give detailed recipes for printing basic dyestuffs on cotton and viscose rayon but the main features of the process are as follows.

The naturally occurring substance tannic acid is capable of forming a precipitate or 'lake' with a basic dyestuff. The formation of this lake may be temporarily delayed by the presence of acetic acid and a small amount of tartaric or citric acid in the print paste in addition to the tannic acid and dyestuff. During a somewhat lengthy steaming treatment of 30—45 min the volatile acetic acid is removed from the cloth and the tannic acid/basic dye lake formed. The lake is insufficiently fast to confer a measure of wash fastness so a 'fixing' treatment forms the first wet process. Fixing consists of a passage through warm tartar emetic, i.e. $KOOC(CH_2OH)_2 COOSbO.\frac{1}{2}H_2O$ and chalk. The tannic acid/dye lake abstracts the antimony (Sb) from the tartar emetic to form a more insoluble antimony/tannic acid/dye lake. The acid potassium tartrate left behind is neutralised by the chalk which forms a reservoir of alkalinity.

The preparation of basic dye print-pastes for cotton requires a considerable amount of skill, and so does the choice of thickening, so it is not difficult to appreciate why their use on cotton is so rarely encountered. As to fastness, their resistance to mild washing is much better than acid dyes on viscose but their light fastness is of a similarly low order. Direct dyestuffs on cotton are much faster to light than basic dyes but less fast to mild washing. Direct dyes are, of course, considerably duller.

MORDANT DYESTUFFS

Some of the earliest dyestuffs used for textile printing belonged to this class, e.g. Turkey red, Alizarin red, Madder purple, Logwood black, Quercitron bark and Persian Berry yellow, to name but a few. These dyes differ from other ancient dyes such as Tyrian purple, indigo and woad (which are vat dyes) in that they possess relatively little fastness and often not a great deal of colour unless applied in conjunction with a mordant. A mordant is the salt of a metal such as chromium, aluminium or iron and less frequently nickel, cobalt, zinc, tin or calcium. The metal salt used is one that easily hydrolyses, e.g. the acetate, thus releasing the metal to form an insoluble salt or lake with the mordant dye. In former times furnishing fabrics were printed with mordant dyes selected on the basis of good light fastness although some of the shades were relatively dull. Top quality furnishing fabrics at the present time are printed with vat dyes.

Some mordant dyes are polygenetic, i.e. they give a differently coloured lake with different metallic mordants. Alizarin (which was formerly extracted from the roots of the madder plant) gives a red with an aluminium mordant, purple with an iron mordant and claret with a chromium mordant. Fast Printing Green S, itself virtually colourless, gives a fast to light dull green with an iron mordant, a terra cotta shade with cobalt acetate and yellowish browns with nickel and chromium acetates.

The versatility of Alizarin in terms of shades produced had its drawbacks. When setting out to produce Alizarin Red or the more complex but brighter Turkey Red by printing, extreme precautions were necessary to prevent contamination by iron from the water supply or from any of the printing machinery, since marked shade dulling occurred due to the production of a mixed aluminium and iron lake.

The monogenetic mordant dyes give very similar shades when the mordant is changed and usually give the fastest results with chromium lakes. The Swiss firm of Durand and Huguemin specialised in chrome mordant dyes for many years and much research was directed towards reducing the long steaming times necessary to fix many mordant dyes. Several auxiliary products were introduced for this purpose, e.g. 'Fixer' *CDH* which accelerated lake formation and 'Chromate' *DH* which was used as a replacement for chromium acetate. An idea of the shade and fastness properties as well as application methods relating to the faster chrome dyestuffs may be obtained from a recent Durand and Huguenin publication[4].

AZOIC DYESTUFFS

'Brenthol' and 'Brentamine' Fast Salts*

Of the numerous methods recommended for the direct printing of insoluble azoic colours on cellulosic fibres, one of the most commonly used involves the following stages:

(*a*) impregnation of the cloth with an alkaline solution of the 'Brenthol', and drying

(*b*) printing with a thickened solution of the diazo component in the form of a 'Brentamine' Fast Salt, and finally

(*c*) the 'Brenthol' on the unprinted portion of the material is subsequently removed by a hot alkaline soaping treatment.

Consequently the 'Brenthols' that are of interest to printers are those which can be most easily removed in this manner. The 'Brentamine' Fast Salts available give an extensive range of shades when printed on cloth prepared with a single 'Brenthol'.

'Brenthols'

Only 'Brenthols' of low substantivity are of value in preparing grounds for the subsequent printing of 'Brentamine' Fast Salts. As a result, a considerable proportion of present-day printing is confined to 'Brenthols' *AS* and *AT*. 'Brenthol' *AS* is the standard 'Brenthol' for printing, yielding a wide range of shades—orange, scarlet, red, violet and blue—with various 'Brentamine' Fast Salts. A very fast red is obtainable with 'Brentamine' Fast Red *3GL* Salt. Blues with 'Brentamine' Fast Blue *VB* Salt, violets with Violet *B* Salt and navy blues with Blue *BB* Salt are all of importance. 'Brenthol' *AT* yields yellows with most 'Brentamine' Fast Salts. An exception is a bordeaux shade with 'Brentamine' Fast Black *K* Salt.

*No longer sold by ICI. See Appendix 2 for alternative suppliers.

Preparation of the 'Brenthol' Padding Solution.

15–20 parts	'Brenthol' are well pasted with
20 "	Turkey Red Oil *PO* and
100 "	boiling water until completely wet out. Then
16–26 "	caustic soda of 38° Bé (70° Tw) are added. When solution is complete the liquor is bulked with hot water to

1000 parts.

'Brenthols' padded at this strength are suitable for the production of all but very heavy shades, and may be diluted with water for weaker shades, but the concentration of caustic soda, i.e. 38° Bé (70° Tw) should not fall below 8 parts per 1 000.

Padding 'Brenthol' Solutions on Cotton Piece. Padding is usually carried out on a 2-bowl or 3-bowl mangle range set with a nip expression of, preferably, 70–80% but not more than 100%. The effect of · 'Brenthol' substantivity is minimised by padding at a high temperature– about 70°C (160°F)–as quickly as possible using a small trough (20–40 litre or 5–10 gal capacity) in which the liquor is kept at a constant level. The padded cloth is dried over heated cylinders or in a hot flue having uniform circulation of air. Cloth dried too slowly or at a very low temperature, and cloth that has been overheated, have a dull yellow appearance, instead of (in the case of 'Brenthol' *AS*) a bright, strong yellow appearance. This in turn will lead to inferior brightness and yield in the final print. If the apparatus described above is not available, padding may be accomplished by soaking the material well in the 'Brenthol' solution (about 30 s is sufficient) and then passing the material in open width, without creases, between the rubber rollers of an ordinary household wringing machine that have been screwed down as tightly as possible. The padded material is then ironed quickly with a hot iron or dried in a hot air stove at full width.

Storage of 'Brenthol'-Prepared Cloth. Whenever possible, cloth prepared with a 'Brenthol' should be printed and washed-off on the same day, as the longer the 'Brenthol'-prepared cloth is kept, the greater is the difficulty experienced in producing a good white ground. 'Brenthol'-prepared cloth should not be exposed to acid fumes or sunlight at any time during the processing and, if it is necessary to keep it for any length of time before printing, it should be wrapped in clean cloth and stored away from acid fumes. If these precautions are observed, it can be kept in a satisfactory condition for several days.

'Brentamine' Fast Salts

The 'Brentamine' Fast Salts are stabilised diazo compounds prepared from the corresponding 'Brentamine' Fast Bases. They are easy and convenient to use as they are readily soluble in cold water and, when thickened, the solution is ready for printing on the 'Brenthol'-prepared cloth.

General Recipe for Printing Pastes of 'Brentamine' Fast Salts

20–60 parts	'Brentamine' Fast Salt are dissolved in
360–320 "	water at a temperature below 30°C (85°F) and
600 "	'Indalca' *PA3* thickening (9%) and, as recommended,
20–0 "	acetic acid 40%; and the paste is bulked to
<u>1 000</u> parts.	

Addition of Acetic Acid to Printing Pastes. In many cases, the addition of 20 parts of 40% acetic acid per 1 000 parts to the printing paste improves the brightness of shade. An addition should be made in all cases when printing on 'Brenthol' *AT* or when printing weak shades of a 'Brentamine' Fast Salt on a strong 'Brenthol' prepare. It also improves the brightness of prints from the following:

Brentamine Fast Yellow GC Salt   Brentamine Fast Red TR Salt
Brentamine Fast Orange GR Salt   Brentamine Fast Violet B Salt
Brentamine Fast Red 3GL Salt

Special Recipe Applicable to Brentamine Fast Black K Salt:

40–80 parts	'Brentamine' Fast Black *K* Salt are pasted with
100 "	acetic acid (40%) and
260–220 "	water and stirred into
600 "	Indalca *PA3* thickening (9%). The paste is bulked to
<u>1 000</u> parts	and should be strained before use.

The stability of azoic print pastes can be improved by the addition of 'Azoguard' 35% solution. An addition of 20 parts per 1 000 parts of 'Azoguard' 35% solution is recommended especially with the following:

Brentamine Fast Scarlet GG Salt	Brentamine Fast Bordeaux GP Salt
Brentamine Fast Scarlet R Salt	
Brentamine Fast Red 3GL Salt	Brentamine Fast Black K Salt
Brentamine Fast Red B Salt	

Thickenings. 'Indalca' *PA3*, a Locust Bean ether, is a cold dissolving thickening and is thus more rapidly and conveniently prepared than Starch-Tragacanth thickening. The latter was frequently used in the past for machine printing while Gum Tragacanth alone or Gum Senegal was used for screen or stencil printing.

On no account must British Gum or any other type of dextrinised starch be used, because these greatly impair the stability of the 'Brentamine' Fast Salt. Sodium alginate thickenings should also be avoided with Brentamine Fast Salts.

Printing. The recipes given are primarily intended for machine printing but can equally well be applied to stencil, block or screen. It is advisable, when using hand-printing methods, to increase the concentration of caustic soda in the 'Brenthol' prepare, as the relatively long time the prepared cloth is exposed to the atmosphere during printing is liable to cause some deterioration (carbonation) of the caustic soda.

Finishing–Removal of Uncoupled 'Brenthol' from the Cloth

It is important to destroy any excess diazo compound that may remain on the printed and dried material before attempting to wash out the 'Brenthol', as otherwise it is liable to bleed on to the unprinted portion of the material and couple with the 'Brenthol', giving rise to bad whites. If the printed material is dried at a high temperature, as is usual in the case of machine printing, this is generally sufficient to decompose the excess diazo compound, but, if necessary, a short steam may be given. In screen or block printing, where the printed material is dried at a low temperature, the goods should be passed in open width through a bath containing 10 parts of sodium bisulphite liquor of 38° Bé (70° Tw) per 1 000 parts at 60°C (140°F) for about 30 s, and rinsed well in water before soaping.

94

Soaping is carried out for 5 min as near the boil as possible. To ensure complete removal of the uncoupled 'Brenthol', the following solution is recommended:

3 parts	'Lissapol' *ND*
2 "	soda ash dissolved in hot water. Then bulk to
1 000 parts.	

The material is then well rinsed with cold water and dried.

Notes
(1) All 'Brenthols' have a greater substantivity for viscose rayon than for cotton and this constitutes a disadvantage in that the removal of residual 'Brenthol' from the unprinted portions of the viscose rayon is rendered more difficult. Consequently on viscose rayon only the low-substantivity 'Brenthol' *AS* is used and care is necessary to ensure the minimum delay between padding and printing and between printing and clearing residual 'Brenthol'. Excessive delays make satisfactory removal of residual 'Brenthol' very difficult in practice.
(2) The use of mixtures of 'Brentamine' Fast Salts printed on a 'Brenthol' prepare is not recommended owing to the fact that not all 'Brentamine' Fast Salts are compatible, and difficulties may also arise owing to differing rates of coupling of the components of the mixture.
(3) The notable gaps in the range of shades obtainable on 'Brenthol' *AS* by the use of 'Brentamine' Fast Salts—namely yellow, green and greenish blue—can be filled by the use of the 'Alcian' dyestuffs (see page 113).

A representative range of shades, with details of certain of their fastness properties on cotton, obtainable by printing on 'Brenthol' *AS* and 'Brenthol' *AT*, is indicated in *Table 8.4*.

Stabilised Azoic Dyestuffs

Products of this type have been partly replaced by 'Procion' and other reactive dyes. There are however certain styles where stabilised azoics may be used alongside other classes of dyestuffs, combining both

Table 8.4. FASTNESS PROPERTIES ON COTTON

'Brenthol' *AS* printed with:	Shade Produced	*Light* (Full shade)	*Washing* I.S.O. Wash Test No. 5 Effect on the print
Brentamine Fast Orange GC Salt	Orange	5	3−4
Brentamine Fast Scarlet GG Salt	Scarlet	5	4B
Brentamine Fast Scarlet R Salt	Scarlet	5	4−5
Brentamine Fast Red 3GL Salt	Red	6	4−5B
Brentamine Fast Red TR Salt	Red	4−5	3
Brentamine Fast Red B Salt	Bluish-red	4−5	4
Brentamine Fast Bordeaux GP Salt	Bordeaux	4−5	3−4
Brentamine Fast Violet B Salt	Violet	5	4−5
Brentamine Fast Blue BB Salt	Blue	5	4−5WG
Brentamine Fast Black K Salt	Black	4−5	4−5
'Brenthol' *AT* printed with:			
Brentamine Fast Orange GC Salt	Greenish-yellow	4−5	4−5
Brentamine Fast Scarlet GG Salt	Greenish-yellow	5−6	4WR
Brentamine Fast Red 3GL Salt	Golden-yellow	5	4
Brentamine Fast Red B Salt	Golden-yellow	4−5	3−4
Brentamine Fast Black K Salt	Bordeaux	3	4

convenience and economy. Three distinct stages have taken place in the method and degree of stabilisation of the 'Brentamine' component. The first type were the Rapid Fast colours ('Brentamine' Rapid), these were followed by the 'Rapidogens' (Brentogens), both gave brighter shades when steamed in the presence of acetic and formic acid vapours. Such vapours rapidly corroded mild steel 'acid-agers' and while some factories (especially in the USA) invested in stainless steel agers there remained a target for an improved type of 'Rapidogen'. The introduction of the 'Neutrogens' by the French firm CFMC and the 'Rapidogen' *N* brands by the German dyemakers provided products which developed satisfactorily by neutral steaming. In the USA there are at least six firms offering stabilised azoics either in the form of powders or as concentrated solutions. Both neutral and acid steaming types are offered and a comprehensive list is available in Products/70 which shows both manufacturer and Colour Index number[5].

In the USA selected azoic dyestuffs are used alongside pigment printing compositions (especially in red shades), particularly on cotton to obtain improved dry cleaning fastness. While fast to dry cleaning pigment reds are available, they are more expensive than ordinary pigment reds.

VAT DYESTUFFS

Among the many qualities desirable in a textile fabric, one of the most important is durability, and where a fabric is to be produced in a coloured style the dyestuffs used for colouring it should possess fastness properties of a standard commensurate with the normal useful life of the fabric. On cellulosic fibres such as cotton and viscose rayon such a standard is only attained in general by the use of selected vat dyestuffs.

For textile printing 'Caledon' and 'Durindone' vat dyes are marketed as, *QF* Printing Pastes and as *FA* Pastes. The use of a particular brand depends upon availability and the proposed method of application.

Vat dyestuffs are insoluble in water, but when treated with alkaline reducing agents they are converted to a soluble reduced form. While in this reduced state they are capable of being absorbed by textile fibres. Subsequent oxidation converts this reduced form to the original insoluble vat dyestuff, which is firmly held within the fibre.

Vat dyestuffs may be applied in this way by several distinct processes which may be classified as single-stage or two-stage processes depending essentially on whether the reducing agent is present in the print paste or not. Where no reducing agent is present at the printing stage it is applied in a second stage, e.g.:

(1) *The Alkali Carbonate-Sodium Sulphoxylate Formaldehyde Method* (the All-in Method, a one-stage process)
(2) *The Flash-Age Method* (a two-stage process)
(3) *The Pad-Steam Method* (a two-stage process)

These processes will now be discussed.

The Alkali Carbonate-Sodium Sulphoxylate Formaldehyde Method

Printing Recipe

The method consists of printing the thickened dispersed vat dyestuff to which has been added an alkali, a reducing agent and a hygroscopic agent.

The following is the general recipe for vat printing pastes:

5–150 parts	'Caledon' or 'Durindone' *QF* paste are mixed with
195–50 "	cold water, then added to
800 "	stock thickening.
<u>1000</u> parts.	

A stock thickening is prepared as follows:

160 parts	potassium carbonate (anhydrous)
125 "	'Formosul' and
60 "	glycerine are dissolved in
600 "	thickening
<u>1000</u> parts.	

To obtain the best results it is advisable to mix the dyestuff paste with a small proportion of thickening that does not contain alkali or reducing agent, or to cold water, and then to add this mixture slowly with constant stirring to a specially prepared thickening in which the alkali and reducing agent have been incorporated. This procedure minimises any tendency for the vat dye paste to be aggregated or flocculated and give specky or uneven prints.

When printing reduced (pale) shades of vat dyestuffs it is often very important that the percentage of alkali and reducing agent does not fall below a certain minimum if optimum yields are to be obtained. In order to ensure good yields when printing reduced (pale) shades of vat dyestuffs, it is often the practice to prepare a full (strong) shade print paste on the lines of the last recipe and dilute it to the strength required by adding the appropriate quantity of the following reduction thickening:

50 parts	glycerine
60–80 "	potassium carbonate (anhydrous)
75–100 "	'Formosul'
815–770 "	thickening.

Bulk to <u>1000</u> parts.

Procedure after Printing

The goods are printed, dried, steamed for 5–10 min in air-free steam at 100°–102°C (212°–215°F), then, preferably in open width, washed in cold water, oxidised in a solution of sodium dichromate or sodium perborate made up at 0·75–1·5 per 1000 parts together with a little acetic acid. The time of treatment in this oxidising solution is of the order of 2—5 min. Finally, to obtain optimum brightness and fastness, the goods are treated at or near the boil for 5—10 min in either soap solution or a solution of 3 ml of 'Lissapol' *ND* and 0·5 parts of soda ash per 1 000 parts followed by rinsing and drying.

Notes

(1) Thickening agents used for printing vat dyestuffs must be capable of withstanding the relatively high concentration of alkali present in a vat printing paste. Mixtures based on British Gum are widely used as are thickenings based on starch mixed with either Gum Tragacanth or British Gum. Marketed under proprietary names are several modified starches, gums and other products that are suitable for printing vat dyestuffs. A thickening which has the advantage that it may be prepared cold using a high speed stirrer is based on 'Solvitose' *OFC 10* (1·6%) and 'Solvitose' *C5* (4·8%). Amounts of glycerine, alkali carbonate and 'Formosul' calculated as being adequate assuming the final thickening to be added at the rate of 80 parts per 100 parts of vat print paste, are first dissolved in water. The two 'Solvitose' thickenings are sprinkled in with stirring and then allowed to swell and dissolve for at least 1 h.

(2) Glycerine is present as a hygroscopic agent. Alternatives are 'Glydote' *BN* or urea. Under screen-printing conditions it is often found that urea is preferable to glycerine, especially if the drying conditions after printing are not good.

(3) The alkali carbonate most widely used is potassium carbonate. An alternative is sodium carbonate, which is often favoured by screen printers. The potassium carbonate in the above recipe may be replaced by 65 parts of anhydrous sodium carbonate (soda ash).

(4) Sodium sulphoxylate formaldehyde is the most important agent employed in the printing of vat dyestuffs. It is well known under several trade names, one of which is 'Formosul'. When using *QF* 'Caledon' Printing Blue *GCP* paste or *QF* 'Caledon' Printing Blue *3G* the amount of 'Formosul' in the stock paste should be reduced from 100 parts to 75 parts per 1 000 parts. This will avoid over-reduction and maintain the correct shade.

(5) After printing, the goods must be dried as quickly as possible and then steamed with the least possible delay. When this is impracticable, the dried goods should be stored in a dry atmosphere, free from draughts and acid fumes.

(6)   When printing with vat colours it is very important that the steam should be air-free if satisfactory results are to be obtained. The steam supply to the steamer should be such as to ensure that an adequate volume of moist steam is available to maintain the temperature as constant as possible within the range $100°-102°C$ ($212°-216°F$) and prevent air contamination. In a discontinuous steamer the flow of steam must be efficient and capable of sweeping out the air rapidly at the beginning of steaming.

(7)   In the case of *QF* 'Caledon' Printing Blue *GCP* paste the use of chemical oxidising agents should be avoided, if possible, as these tend to give greener and duller shades with this dyestuff. Oxidation in water alone yields the maximum brightness of shade from *QF* 'Caledon' Printing Blue *GCP* paste.

The vat dyes recommended for application by this process include those given in *Table 8.5*.

Table 8.5. FASTNESS PROPERTIES ON COTTON

'Caledon' and 'Durindone' Vat Dyestuffs	*Light* (Full shade)	*Washing* I.S.O. Wash Test No. 5 Effect on the print
QF Caledon Printing Yellow 5G Paste	4–5D	4–5R
QF Caledon Printing Yellow RK Paste	6–7	5
QF Caledon Printing Yellow GN Paste	5–6D	4–5
QF Caledon Printing Orange 6RS Paste	6–7	4–5R
QF Caledon Printing Red 3B Paste	6–7	4–5
QF Durindone Printing Orange R4F Paste	5	3–4
QF Durindone Printing Brown G Paste	6–7	4
QF Durindone Printing Pink FF Paste	6	4Y
QF Durindone Printing Red 3B Paste	6	4
QF Durindone Printing Scarlet 2B Paste	5	4
QF Durindone Printing Magenta B Paste	6	3–4
QF Caledon Printing Purple 4R Paste	7	5
QF Caledon Printing Blue GCP Paste	7–8	4–5
QF Caledon Printing Blue 3G Paste	7–8	4–5R
QF Caledon Navy Blue AR Paste	6–7	4 WR
QF Durindone Printing Blue 4BC Paste	5	3–4RW
QF Caledon Printing Jade Green 2G Paste	6–7	4–5D
QF Caledon Printing Jade Green XBN Paste	6–7	4
QF Caledon Printing Olive Green B Paste	7–8	3–4
QF Durindone Printing Black TL Paste	7–8	4B

The Flash-Ageing Method

The fixation of printed vat dyes by a high-speed pad-steam process (commonly referred to as *flash-ageing*) has recently grown in popularity owing to its suitability for producing, quickly and in simple equipment, high-quality prints of excellent fastness. The process consists essentially in printing a finely dispersed vat dye pigment in a suitable thickening (which must be capable of coagulation by alkali), drying, and subsequently developing the print by padding in an alkaline solution of sodium hydrosulphite and passing immediately into the steamer. The process has two essential features. First, the print pastes contain no reducing agent and the printed fabrics are, therefore, stable for an almost indefinite time on storage or on exposure to the atmosphere before steaming. Second, reduction and fixation are achieved by a very short steaming process, normally of 20–40 s duration. Since the steaming time is so short, considerable economies in the cost of steamer construction and in steam consumption can be achieved. The steamer is run in conjunction with a conventional two-bowl padding mangle and open-width soaping range.

In order to obtain prints with sharp definition, high colour value and unstained whites, it is essential when operating the flash-ageing process to choose the most suitable dyestuffs and thickening agent, and to ensure that the padding and steaming conditions are carefully controlled.

It will be appreciated that while the flash-age method is essentially simple in principle it does call for special equipment and technical control if its full value is to be realised. In the case of colleges and schools of art, where the necessary equipment is not available, it is suggested that attempts be made to approach experienced printers who would, on a commission basis, be prepared to pad, flash-age, oxidise and finish prints prepared by the flash-age method. Once printed and dried the goods have excellent storage stability, so padding and steaming may be delayed until convenient.

Printing Recipe

5–200 parts	'Caledon' or 'Durindone' *FA* Paste are mixed with
395–200 "	cold water and added to
600 "	stock thickening (see overleaf)
1 000 parts.	

Stock Thickenings

(*a*) cold dissolving

6 parts	of sodium hexametaphosphate ('Calgon' *PT*) are dissolved in
929 "	cold water. Then
40 "	'Solvitose' *C5* (Scholtens) and
25 "	'Manutex' *RS* (Alginate Industries) are added with high speed stirring. This is continued until a smooth paste is obtained.
1 000 parts.	

Alkali-coagulable thickening agents based on Locust Bean gum and sodium alginate are recommended. Additional suitable thickeners include 'Indalca' *S* (Cesalpinia) and 'Meyprogum' *CR New* (Meyhall Chemical). Occasionally wheat starch may be used in conjunction with Locust Bean gum and sodium alginate.

(*b*) hot dissolving

25 parts	wheat starch are mixed with
900 "	cold water. To this paste is added with stirring a mixture of
10 "	Gum Gatto and
10 "	ethanol. The mixture is boiled thoroughly for 20 min, cooled, and to the mixture is then added
2 "	sodium hexametaphosphate dissolved in
45 "	water and finally
8 "	'Manutex' *RS* are added slowly and with stirring

Bulk to 1 000 parts.

Allow to stand for 1–2 h to enable the sodium alginate to dissolve. If preferred, a 'Manutex' *RS* thickening (containing sodium hexameta-phosphate) may be prepared separately and mixed with the starch/Gum Gatto as required.

Padding Liquor

There are two types of reducing agent which may be used for flash ageing. They differ in stability which affects both the steaming time required and the exposure time possible after padding and before steaming.

102

Sodium hydrosulphite or 'hydros' (CI Reducing Agent 1) is the less stable product. Acetaldehyde sulphoxylate (CI Reducing Agent 13), e.g. 'Formosul' *FA* (ACC) and 'Rongal' *A* (BASF) is more stable than sodium hydrosulphite. This greater stability allows for an air passage of up to 2 min, but understandably requires a somewhat longer steaming time to effect dyestuff reduction.

Sodium hydrosulphite	*Acetaldehyde sulphoxylate*	
200	200 parts	Gum Tragacanth (8%) are diluted with
600	600 "	cold water. Then add
25	– "	sodium carbonate (anhydrous) and
75	90 "	(by volume) caustic soda of 38°Bé (70°Tw) plus
50	– "	sodium hydrosulphite or
–	100 "	(by volume) 'Formosul' *FA* and
Bulk to 1 000	1 000 parts	(by volume) with water.

To increase the coagulating effect of the padding liquors on the print paste thickening add 5 parts borax if locust bean gum is present, or 5 parts aluminium sulphate for sodium alginate based print pastes. Such additions minimise bleeding of the print at the padding stage or at the steaming stage.

The padding mangle should be a vertical type capable of a liquor pick up of about 70% or less, calculated on the dry fabric weight. The paddir trough should be small and padding liquor fed continuously across its full width to avoid accumulation of decomposed reducing agent. The method of padding will depend on the type of fabric being processed. To ensure complete wetting-out of the printed portions, especially with scree printed fabrics of heavy construction, 'slop-padding' is more satisfactory. In this method total immersion under the surface of the padding liquor precedes the mangling operation. For lighter fabrics 'nip-padding' is preferred and consists of applying the pad liquor directly by means of the lower pad mangle roller. Under these conditions the printed side of the fabric should touch the lower mangle roller which itself should be partially immersed in the padding liquor. This will ensure that the rolle surface is continuously washed with padding liquor and will minimise the risk of marking off.

The presence in the padding liquor of a small amount of thickening agent is very effective in ensuring that sufficient padding liquor is picked up by the cloth. Furthermore, such an addition is of value in preserving good definition during steaming and with sodium hydrosulphite exercises a marked stabilising effect by decreasing the permeability of the liquor to air. Naturally, the thickening used for this purpose must be one which is not coagulated by alkali.

Steaming

In the flash-ageing process steaming is carried out in an air-free atmosphere in a machine so constructed as to be capable of maintaining throughout a temperature of $110°-125°C(230°-260°F)$. The effect of raising the temperature from just over $100°-125°C(212°-260°F)$ is not to increase the rate of fixation appreciably, but rather to minimise any tendency of the print to flush because excess water is evaporated off. Excessive drying out is to be avoided, otherwise the degree of fixation may be impaired.

Compared with conventional roller agers or festoon steamers, flash-ageing equipment is of small volume and simple design, and should be constructed with the following purposes in mind:

(1) To provide a plentiful supply of saturated steam at $110°-125°C$ $(230°-260°F)$ to both sides of the printed fabric.

(2) To allow for a steaming time of 20—40 s at the required running speed; e.g. if it is desired to run at 30 m/min (33 yd/min) the steamer should be 10 m (11 yd) long to give a 20 s treatment.

(3) To preserve the printed mark and avoid contamination of the equipment by dyestuff. This depends to a great extent on the correct choice of dyestuffs and thickening agent, but, as far as the equipment is concerned, it is advisable to avoid contact of the printed side of the cloth with rollers, and to eliminate, as far as possible, too long vertical passages of the cloth since the pad liquor may flow down the fabric, giving loss of definition.

Oxidising and Washing

After leaving the ager the cloth must be passed immediately into the clearing and oxidising baths using a conventional open width soaping range. The first tank should preferably contain running cold water in order to eliminate caustic alkalinity from the cloth and to soften the thickening as quickly as possible. The rate of oxidation of the leuco vat dye may be increased in the following tanks by oxidising agents such as

104

sodium dichromate, sodium perborate, sodium percarbonate or hydrogen peroxide. The brightest shades are usually obtained when oxidation is carried out by water alone. This is particularly important where 'Caledon' Blue *GCP* and 'Caledon' Blue *XRC* are used, since the shades of these dyestuffs become duller and greener by the action of the oxidising agents previously mentioned.

To develop full brightness and optimum fastness properties the goods are treated at or near the boil for 5–10 min in soap or a solution containing 3 parts of 'Lissapol' *ND* per 1 000 parts and 0·5 parts soda ash per 1 000 parts, followed by rinsing and drying.

The *FA* Paste brands of the 'Caledon' and 'Durindone' dyes are specifically designed for application by the two-stage (flash age) vat printing process for cellulosic fabrics. The *FA* paste range includes:

Caledon Yellow 5G-FA Paste	Caledon Navy AR-FA Paste
Caledon Yellow 4GL-FA Paste	Durindone Blue 4BC-FA Paste
Caledon Yellow GN-FA Paste	Caledon Blue XRC-FA Paste
Caledon Golden Yellow	Caledon Blue GCP-FA Paste
RK-FA Paste	Caledon Jade Green 2G-FA Paste
Caledon Gold Orange 3G-FA	Caledon Jade Green XBN-FA Paste
Paste	Caledon Olive Green B-FA Paste
Caledon Brilliant Orange	Caledon Olive OMW-FA Paste
6R-FA Paste	Caledon Olive R-FA Paste
Caledon Red 2GN-FA Paste	Caledon Dark Brown 2G-FA Paste
Durindone Pink FF-FA Paste	Caledon Brown R-FA Paste
Caledon Brilliant Red 3B-FA	Caledon Brown 2R-FA Paste
Paste	Caledon Dark Brown 6R-FA Paste
Caledon Brilliant Red 5B-FA	Caledon Grey M-FA Paste
Paste	Caledon Black P-FA Paste
Durindone Magenta B-FA	Caledon Black 2R-FA Paste
Paste	Alcian Blue 7GX 300
Caledon Brilliant Purple	Alcian Blue 8GX 300
4R-FA Paste	

The Pad-Steam Method

The pad-steam method differs in two important details from the flash-ageing process. Firstly, the reducing agent used is sodium formaldehyde sulphoxylate CI Reducing Agent 2 (trade names 'Formosul', 'Rongalit' *C*, 'Hydrosulphite' *C*, etc.) and secondly as a consequence of the use of this more stable reducing agent the steaming time is much longer than in flash-ageing and is of the order of 15–25 min. The thickening used for printing must be one that is coagulated by alkali assisted if necessary by borax, both being present at the padding stage. The process is sometimes described as the *Collorescine process* after the trademark of a cellulose derived thickening which formed the original recommendation. A number of thickenings were evolved based on Locust Bean gum (e.g. Gum Gatto) mixed with starch. The latter gave higher yields of dye but the Locust Bean gum which was coagulated by alkali had to be present up to a certain minimum level, otherwise the printed dyes bled during steaming.

Printing Paste

A typical recipe for the pad-steam process is:

65 parts	wheat starch are mixed with
900 ”	cold water and to the mixture is added with stirring, a mixture of
10 ”	Gum Gatto
10 ”	ethanol. The mixture is thoroughly boiled for 20 min, cooled, and finally
1 ”	acetic acid (40%) and
10 ”	mineral oil are added. The whole is bulked to
1000 parts.	

An addition of 0·3 parts of borax to each 1 000 parts of the thickening may be made if desired. The addition of the borax renders the thickening more sensitive to alkali and, by increasing the rate at which coagulation occurs as the cloth enters the padding liquor, reduces the risk of dyestuff entering the padding trough.

The final print paste is prepared as follows:

100–200 parts	dyestuff paste are mixed with
300–200 ”	water and then adding with constant stirring to
600 ”	pad-steam thickening as described before. The paste is finally bulked to
1000 parts.	

If the dyestuff is in powder form, it must be thoroughly dispersed in water before adding to the thickening. The addition of a small amount of acetic acid to the thickening prevents coagulation when slightly alkaline vat pastes are added.

106

Padding Liquor

The padding liquor contains an alkali and a reducing agent. Examples
of typical padding liquors are:

	Alkali Carbonate Recipe	Caustic Alkali Recipe
Sodium sulphoxylate formaldehyde	100 parts	150 parts
Sodium carbonate (anhydrous)	50 ”	50 ”
Caustic soda at 38°Bé (70° Tw)	–	75 ”
Common salt (or calcined Glauber's salt)	100 ”	100 ”
and bulked with water to	1 000 parts.	1 000 parts.

The goods are usually 'nip-padded' and the mangle is adjusted to give
an expression of approximately 100%.

Steaming

Prints by the pad-steam process are steamed immediately after padding,
without intermediate drying. Steaming times of 15−25 min are normally
employed. A festoon steamer is frequently employed by roller printers.
Where production is not sufficient to justify the use of a festoon steamer,
e.g. in the case of screen printing, a star or tower steamer will provide an
economic output.

Oxidising and Washing

After steaming, the prints are oxidised and finally treated at or near the
boil for 5−10 min in soap solution or a solution containing 3 parts of
'Lissapol' *ND* per 1 000 parts of liquor and 0·5 parts of soda ash per
1 000 parts of liquor, followed by rinsing and drying.

Vat dyestuffs suitable for application by the pad steam printing
processes include the majority of those members of the *FA* range
listed earlier. An exception is 'Caledon' Blue *XRC−FA* paste which
gives inferior fixation with the alkali carbonate pad liquor and is apt to
be erratic even with the caustic alkali recipe. For this reason 'Caledon'
Blue *GCP−FA* paste is the preferred product.

'Alcian' Blue 8GX (or 7GX) in the two-stage (flash-age) process
The unique turquoise shade of 'Alcian' Blue *8GX* (or *7GX*) is of great

107

value in augmenting the range of shades obtainable from vat dyes printed on cotton. The following printing recipe is recommended:

5–20 parts	'Alcian' Blue *8GX 300* (or *7GX 300*)
50 "	glacial acetic acid and
40 "	cold water are mixed. Then
205–190 "	water at 60°C (140°F) are added.
	The solution is added to
550 "	thickening (Note 1) containing
50 "	sodium acetate dissolved in
50 "	cold water. Finally
50 "	glucose syrup (80%) are added
	(Note 2)

1000 parts.

Notes
(1) Suitable thickenings include 'Indalca' *U* (Cesalpinia) and 'Meyprogum' *CRX* (Meyhall Chemical). With 'Alcian' dyestuffs sodium alginate thickenings must not be used.
(2) Glucose syrup maintains the correct shade of the 'Alcian' dye during the padding and steaming operations. After printing the goods are dried very thoroughly. They are then steamed and washed-off as for vat dyes.

'SOLEDON' DYESTUFFS

All 'Durindone' or 'Caledon' dyestuffs contain two or more carbonyl ($>C=O$) groups. In the presence of alkali and a suitable reducing agent the alkaline leuco compound, e.g. ($\geqslant C - O^-$ Na^+) forms and the insoluble vat dye becomes water soluble. A more stable soluble vat derivative which can be isolated and marketed in powder form is obtained by forming a sulphuric acid ester group from each leuco group in the dye. This gives ($\geqslant C - O . SO_3^- Na^+$) groupings and because the dye is in the leuco form its colour bears no relation to the parent vat dye. Such dyes are marketed as 'Soledons', 'Indigosols', etc., and are often referred to in N. America simply as *soluble vats*. The printing processes evolved for 'Soledons' and their equivalents have two aims:

(1) To maintain the dye in its 'Soledon' form long enough to enable fibre penetration to take place.
(2) To regenerate the parent vat dye inside the fibre using acid oxidising conditions.

'Soledon' dyestuffs were often used in the paste alongside stabilised azoic dyestuffs since the two ranges gave shades which were complementary to each other. They were also used in the years immediately following their introduction to replace some vat printing styles. The appearance of more sophisticated forms of vat printing pastes specifically designed for printing reduced the extent to which printers used 'Soledon' dyes. Furthermore, the increasing replacement of 'Soledon'/stabilised azoic mixed styles by 'Procion' and other reactive dyes decreased the offtake of solubilised vats even further. Nevertheless they are ideal for obtaining vat fastness prints with the minimum amount of equipment. 'Soledon' dyestuffs are inevitably more expensive than vat dyestuffs but some allowance must be made for the fact that as powders they are more concentrated than 'Caledon' and 'Durindone' pastes.

Printing Methods

The two methods most commonly employed for printing cellulosic fibres are:

(1) The *Nitrite* process
(2) The *Sulphocyanide* process.

The Nitrite Process

In this process sodium nitrite, the potential oxidising agent, is added to the print paste and the dyestuff developed by treatment with sulphuric acid.

A typical printing recipe is the following:

50 parts	'Soledon' dyestuff are dissolved in a mixture of
50 "	'Glydote' *BN*
50 "	urea and
250 "	hot water. The solution, which may be heated up to 80°C (175°F) to ensure complete solution, is added to
600 "	*thickening.

Bulk to $\overline{1000}$ parts.

Thickenings:

968 parts	Gum Tragacanth (7%) thickening
30 "	sodium nitrite crystals
2 "	sodium carbonate (soda ash)

Bulk to $\overline{1000}$ parts, or if a cold dissolving thickening is preferred:

40 parts	'Manutex' *RS* powder are added with high speed stirring to
920 "	water containing
10 "	sodium hexametaphosphate and
30 "	sodium nitrite crystals.
1000 parts.	

After printing, the goods are dried, steamed for 5–10 min (optional; see Note 1) and then developed in a bath containing 20 parts of sulphuric acid at 66° Bé (168°Tw) by volume, per 1000 parts of water held at 70°C (160°F). The immersion in the acid bath, which should be of 2–4 s duration, is followed by a nip and an air passage of 10–20 s, then a thorough rinse in water and finally a soap at or as near the boil as practicable, as detailed for vat dyestuffs (see Note 3 later). This recipe is a general one designed for obtaining medium-depth prints on cotton (for printing on viscose rayon see Note 1 and 4). If heavy-depth shades of 'Soledons' are required some adjustment in the type and quantity of the solution assistant and/or modification of the quantity of sodium nitrite in the print paste may be required.

Attention is drawn to the following notes on certain individual 'Soledons'.

Notes

(1)   Steaming prior to passage through the sulphuric acid bath:

On cotton the nitrite process is generally regarded as a non-steam style, but a short steaming treatment of 5–10 min is very beneficial in the case of 'Soledon' Pink *FFS* and 'Soledon' Olive *DS.*

On viscose rayon a short steaming treatment is beneficial in the case of these two 'Soledons' and with:

Soledon Yellow 3RS	Soledon Blue 2RCX
Soledon Dark Brown 3RS	Soledon Jade Green XS
Soledon Red 2BS	Soledon Green GS
Soledon Blue 4BC 125	

(2)   In the case of 'Soledon' Pink *FFS* the temperature of the sulphuric acid bath should be held at 70°–80°C (160°–175°F). An addition of 5 parts of 'Dispersol' *VL* per 1000 parts and 25 parts of Glauber's salt per 1000 parts minimises any tendency of these dyes to stain the unprinted portions of the fabric. In the case of 'Soledon' Indigo *LLS*, development is carried out at room temperature. For all other 'Soledons' development is satisfactory when the acid bath is maintained at 55°–70°C (130°–160°F).

110

(3) 'Soledon' Indigo *LLS* and 'Soledon' Golden Yellow *GKS* are soaped at 60°C (140°F), other 'Soledons' at the boil.

(4) When printing with 'Soledon' dyes on viscose rayon, improved results are often obtained if the 'Glydote' *BN* in the recipe is increased from 50 to 100 parts per 1 000 parts of print paste.

(5) Avoid inhaling fumes and provide good ventilation.

The Sulphocyanide Process

The 'Soledon' print paste in this process contains an oxidising agent, an oxidising catalyst and a chemical substance which during steaming develops acidity. A typical recipe is the following:

50 parts		'Soledon' dyestuff are dissolved in a mixture of
50	"	'Glydote' *BN*
50	"	urea and
150	"	hot water. The mixture, which may be heated up to 80°C (175°F) to ensure complete solution, is added to
550	"	*Gum Tragacanth 7% thickening containing
50	"	ammonium sulphocyanide (50% solution),
80	"	sodium chlorate (10% solution) and
20	"	ammonium vanadate (1% w/v solution).

Bulk to 1 000 parts.

After printing, the goods are dried, then steamed for 5–10 min, rinsed well in water and soaped at or as near to the boil as practicable, as described for vat dyestuffs. This recipe is a general one designed to obtain medium-depth prints on cotton. (When printing on viscose rayon, see Note 2 later.) If heavy-depth shades of the 'Soledons' are required, some adjustment in the type and quantity of the solution assistant and/ or modification of the quantity of ammonium sulphocyanide (50% solution) and sodium chlorate (10% solution) in the print paste may be required.

*This thickening should be made slightly alkaline with ammonia before adding tl 'Soledon' dyestuff solution. As with the sodium nitrite process a 4% 'Manutex' *RS* thickening may be used as an alternative.

111

Notes

(1) The sulphocyanide process for 'Soledons' is sometimes used where development by acid steaming is required, for example when printing 'Soledons' alongside 'Brentogens'. A 5—10 min acid steam will develop both classes of dyestuff.

(2) When printing on viscose rayon, improved levelness and yields are often obtained if the steaming time for the 'Soledons' is increased to 10—15 min.

(3) 'Soledon' Indigo *LLS* and 'Soledon' Golden Yellow *GKS* are soaped at 60°C (140°F), other 'Soledons' at the boil.

(4) When printing on viscose rayon, improved results are often obtained if 'Glydote' *BN* in the above recipe is increased from 50 parts to 100 parts per 1 000 parts of print paste.

The following 'Soledons' are not recommended for the printing of viscose rayon by the sulphocyanide process:

Soledon Jade Green *XS*   Soledon Olive *DS*
Soledon Green *GS*

The fastness properties of 'Soledon' dyestuffs on cotton are listed in *Table 8.6*.

Table 8.6. FASTNESS PROPERTIES OF 'SOLEDON' DYESTUFFS ON COTTON

'Soledon' Dye	*Light* (Full shade)	*Washing* I.S.O. Wash Test No. 5.* Effect on the print
Yellow 3RS	6—7D	4—5
Golden Yellow GKS	5—6D	3
Golden Yellow RKS	6—7D	5
Dark Brown 3RS	7	4—5
Red 2BS	6—7YD	4
Pink FFS	6	4Y
Blue 4BC 125	5	3—4WR
Blue 2RCX	7	4—5R
Indigo LLS	4	3
Jade Green XS	7	4
Green GS	7—8	3—4
Grey BS	6	4
Olive DS	7	3

*4 h at 95°C (200°F).

112

An example of an oxidation black has already been given in connection with the production of 'Procion' illuminating colours under aniline black. The aniline used in the padding liquor is mainly in the form of its hydrochloride, which is a small molecule and virtually colourless. However, when steamed in the presence of acid oxidising agents, a much larger molecule is formed to which the term *aniline black* is given. The fastness properties of the aniline black depend upon the degree of the oxidation. The process always involves the risk of fabric degradation by the liberated acid. One advantage of aniline blacks was that they were cheap to produce and even when it was found that *p*-amino diphenylamine (Diphenyl Black Base) would produce oxidation blacks without fabric damage, the extra cost of the base prevented its wide adoption. Although aniline black print pastes possessed low print paste stability those based on Diphenyl Black Base were lower still. Chemical modifications to Diphenyl Black Base resulted in products such as 'Soloxan' Black (ICI) and 'Solanile' Black (CFMC) which were equivalents, as well as the chemically different 'Aminosol' Black *M* (F. Bayer) and 'Nigranilina' *MR* (ACNA).

The printing recipes used for these stabilised Diphenyl Black Base derivatives resemble those of 'Soledon' dyestuffs. Ammonium chlorate was used in these recipes, functioning both as an acid liberating component and an oxidising agent. For this purpose a solution was prepared by the admixture of ammonium sulphate and barium chlorate. Ammonium chlorate itself is not usually available as a solid because of its unstable nature.

At the present time the usage of these oxidation blacks seems to be declining.

'ALCIAN' DYESTUFFS

With the discovery of 'Alcian' Blue it was found possible to produce prints of unique bright turquoise shade possessing excellent fastness. With the subsequent introduction of further members of the 'Alcian' range, a wide variety of fast shades, outstanding in their ease of application, can be produced on cotton. The 'Alcian' dyestuffs are not recommended for the printing of fibres other than cotton.

Several 'Alcian' printing recipes are available, but each consists essentially of an aqueous solution of the 'Alcian' dyestuff with an acidic and/or solubilising component together with thickening agent.

Printing Recipes

The following are two typical recipes which will now be described.

Recipe A (The 'Alcian' Developer X recipe):

5–30 parts	'Alcian' dyestuff are mixed with
40 "	'Alcian' Developer X, then
255–230 "	warm water at 60°C (140°F) are added and the resulting solution is added to
650 "	thickening agent in which has been dissolved
50 "	'Alcian' Developer X.
Bulk to 1000 parts.	

Recipe B (The acetic acid–urea recipe):

5–30 parts	'Alcian' dyestuff are mixed with
125 "	acetic acid (40%),
75 "	urea and
145–120 "	warm water at 60°C (140°F). The solution obtained is added to
650 "	thickening agent.
Bulk to 1000 parts.	

Procedure after Printing

After printing, using either Recipe A or Recipe B, the goods are dried and then developed by:

either steaming the goods for 5–10 min,
or hard-drying the goods, preferably over steam-heated cylinders.

Both these treatments are followed by treatment of the fabric in open width in an 'Alcian' fixing bath using:

either a solution of

1—4 parts	sodium dichromate crystals and
2·5—5 ,,	acetic acid (40%) dissolved in water and bulked to 1 000 parts.

or

7·5—15 parts	'Azoguard' 35% solution diluted with water and bulked to 1 000 parts.

Both solutions are used cold, and a treatment of 15—30 s duration is sufficient. After passage through either of these two solutions the goods are rinsed in cold water and treated at or near the boil (as facilities permit) for 5 min in soap solution or a solution containing 3 parts of 'Lissapol' *ND* and 2 parts of soda ash per 1 000 parts followed by rinsing and drying.

Notes
(1)   If the goods have been printed using Recipe B (acetic acid—urea recipe) the sodium dichromate or 'Azoguard' aftertreatment may be omitted at the expense of a slight loss in yield, provided the prints have either been steamed for 5—10 min or printed on a 'Brenthol'-prepared cloth and dried hard after printing.
(2)   Provided an addition of 50 parts sodium acetate crystals per 1 000 parts of print paste is made to the 'Alcian' print paste prepared by Recipe B, quite good fixation of 'Alcian' Blue *8GX 300* and 'Alcian' Blue *7GX 300* at all depths of shade, and of 'Alcian' Yellow *GXS*, 'Alcian' Green *2GX* and 'Alcian' Green *3BX* at strengths up to 1%, can be obtained with a steaming treatment or a fixing bath aftertreatment, by either
   (*a*) Baking at $105°—110°C$ $(220°—230°F)$ for 5—10 min
   or
   (*b*) Hanging the goods in the air for a period of not less than 24 h.
   The prints are finished off with a boiling soap or 'Lissapol' *ND/* soda ash treatment as described above.
(3)   Thickenings based on starch-tragacanth are generally recommended for use with the 'Alcian' dyestuffs. In certain circumstances Locust Bean gums or modified Locust Bean gums give very smooth and attractive prints with the 'Alcian' dyestuffs. British Gums, sodium alginate thickenings, Gum Senegal and many modified starch and cellulose preparations are not, however, suitable for use with this class of dyestuff.

The fastness properties of 'Alcian' dyestuffs on cotton are shown in *Table 8.7.*

115

Table 8.7. FASTNESS PROPERTIES OF 'ALCIAN' DYESTUFFS ON COTTON

'Alcian' Dye	*Light* (Full shade)	*Washing* I.S.O. Wash Test No. 5.* Effect on the print
Yellow GXS	4–5	4–5
Green 2GX	5	4
Green 3BX	6–7	4–5
Blue 8GX 300	6–7	4–5
Blue 7GX 300	6–7	4G
Blue 5GX	6–7GD	4–5
Blue 2GX	6–7D	4

*4 h at 95°C (200°F).

PIGMENT PRINTING COMPOSITIONS

The idea of fixing insoluble dyes by means of gums on to fibres is not new. Various gums, albumens and resins were used for this purpose for a long time together with organic and inorganic pigments. More significant progress took place in 1938 when the American Inter-chemical Corporation (now *Inmont Corp.*) produced their 'Aridye' compositions with a synthetic resin binder. These were of the water-in-oil (w/o) type of emulsion. This nomenclature is used to describe the nature of the emulsion into which the pigment and resin are incorporated. In a w/o emulsion the 'oil' forms the continuous phase and the viscosity results from the emulsification of water droplets into the oil. The 'oil' used is that described earlier in the preparation of emulsion thickenings for 'Procion' dyes. It is sold under various names including 'White Spirit', 'Distillate' and 'Safety Solvent'. These solvents should meet the following specifications:—

(1) Non toxic.
(2) Flash point of 30°C (85°F) or above (determined by the Pensky-Martens closed-cup flash tester).
(3) Boiling range of 127°–205°C (260°–400°F).
(4) KB value of approx. 45. (The Kauri-butanol number is a measure of the aromatic hydrocarbons present, and these should not exceed 15%).
(5) Specific gravity of 0·780–0·80.

The final choice of a solvent which meets these specifications will depend on availability, price and odour. By changing the type of emulsifying agent used to disperse the pigments and the resins an oil-in-water (o/w) emulsion system may be prepared. Because they contain a

116

greater proportion of solvent the o/w thickening system is somewhat more expensive than the w/o type, however, since water forms the continuous phase (o/w) it may be used for cleaning down purposes. Interchem introduced an o/w system in 1953 and named it the 'Aquaprint' system. European dyemakers have invariably favoured o/w systems. *Table 8.8* lists the brand names of a number of well known companies making textile pigment printing compositions:

Table 8.8. MANUFACTURERS AND BRAND NAMES OF
SOME TEXTILE PIGMENT COMPOSITIONS

Country	Manufacturer	Brand Name
W. Germany	BASF	Helizarin
	F. Bayer	Acramin
	FH	Imperon
France	CFMC	Neopralac
Italy	Minerva*	Minerprint
	Lamberti†	Lifebond
	ACNA	Velesta
UK	Tennants*	Hifast
USA	Verona	Acramin
	Hilton-Davis Chemical Division	{ Lifebond Seabond
	Inmont	Hifast (type *O*)
	Inmont	Hifast (type *W*)
	Roma	Questrol

*Manufactures under licence from Inmont
†Manufactures under licence from Hilton-Davis

In pigment printing there is no penetration of the pigment into the fibre and the fastness of the final print depends upon the extent to which the resin binder is surrounding the pigment particles and binding them to the fibre surface.

There are some differences in terminology in pigment printing between N. America and Europe. The Americans' use of the phrases *concentrated clear* (*conc clear*) and *cut clear* refers to the practice of supplying a binding resin in concentrated form which has to be diluted or reduced, i.e. 'cut' before use. The term *binder* is more often used in Europe. The concentrated binder is reduced to make a 'stock thickening' which includes all the necessary ingredients except the pigment. A 'reduction thickening' is also prepared containing a lower amount of binder.

The additives invariably necessary include some form of cross-linking agent, e.g. a low-crock auxiliary, a fixer, etc., as well as an acid

117

liberating catalyst (ammonium nitrate, diammonium phosphate). Sometimes special softening agents are included. To obtain the necessary viscosity and flow properties in the emulsion paste a small quantity of a conventional thickening agent is often incorporated. The fixation of pigment prints is normally achieved by baking (curing) for 3—4 min at 140°C (285°F) in specially constructed gas or electrically heated chambers. Ample ventilation is essential at this stage to avoid the build-up of explosive solvent/air mixtures.

The term *crock-fastness* which is synonymous with rubbing fastness, is important in pigment printing since some of the earlier products fell down in this respect. The handle ('hand') of the fabric, i.e. the relative stiffness or softness of the printed areas compared with the unprinted areas, is equally important. It is often found that a good fastness to rubbing is associated with a stiff fabric handle. The addition of a softening agent usually lowers the rubbing fastness if present in excess. Clearly a balance must be found between the various print paste additives within a given pigment printing system.

One of the major claims made for pigment printing compositions is that they may be printed on all fibres. Certainly they are more versatile in this respect than any other dye class used for textile printing. It is usually necessary to use different binders for synthetic fibres and glass fibre fabrics than for cellulosic fabrics in order to obtain optimum results. When the printing of fibre mixtures is required pigment printing compositions are in a very strong position and it is invariably possible to use a mixed binder system.

PRINTING WITH 'ACRAMIN' PIGMENTS

A typical print paste for the 'Acramin' pigment system of Bayer using 'Acramin' *LC* binder is prepared as follows:

1—100 parts	'Acramin' dyestuff
9—900 ”	Stock Emulsion *LC* (i.e. 9 times the dyestuff amount)
990— 0 ”	Reduction Emulsion *LC*
1 000 parts.	

For 'Acramin' dye strengths of up to four parts per 1 000 parts it is possible to use only Reduction Emulsion *LC*. It is recommended that on synthetic fibres, linen, cellulose acetate and viscose filament satin fabrics an addition of 10—25 parts 'Acramin' *M* (or *CN*) per 1 000 parts is made depending on the depth of shade. The recipes for Reduction Emulsion *LC* and Stock Emulsion *LC* are as follows:

	Reduction Emulsion LC	Stock Emulsion LC
Prepare a mixture consisting of:		
'Acramin' *LC*	60—80 parts	300 parts
Emulsifier *3240*	20 ,,	20 ,,
Thickening Agent 3—4% (See note 1)	40 ,,	40 ,,
Water	x ,,	x ,,
Diammonium phosphate 1:2	20—30 ,,	20— 30 ,,
Urea	0—10 ,,	0— 25 ,,
and		
'Acrafix' *M* (or *CN*).	10 ,,	10 ,,
Emulsify using a high speed stirrer, then add slowly		
White Spirit	600—650 ,,	500—500 ,,
	1 000 parts.	1 000 parts

Note

1. For example, sodium alginate or 'Tylose' *DKL* (FH). Prints made on the basis of these recipes would be fixed by baking (curing) for 10 min at 140°C (285°F). For further details see Reference 6.

PIGMENT PRINTING BY THE 'BEDAFIN' *2101* (or *2001*) PROCESS

The 'Bedafin' *2101* (*2001*) process was one of the earliest pigment printing systems to be available for textiles. It utilises selected 'Monastral' and 'Monolite' pigments in either their aqueous '*V*' paste or '*HD*' paste forms. (Where both brands are available the '*HD*' paste is the more concentrated.) The process provides a range of bright fast shades for printing on cotton and viscose rayon but is not recommended for other types of textile fabrics.

'Bedafin' *2101* (*2001*) is a non-drying oil urea/formaldehyde modified alkyd resin dissolved in 'Cellosolve'. The addition of a weak alkali such as triethanolamine or ammonia renders it soluble in water. After application to textile materials and heating at a temperature of 100°C (212°F) or higher, 'Bedafin' *2101* (*2001*) is insolubilised, and it is this property that is utilised for the fixation of pigments on textiles. Provided that fixation is carried out under the best conditions, the 'Bedafin' process for pigment printing yields prints of good fastness to washing. A selected range of pigments is listed in *Table 8.9*.

119

The Printing Paste

In making up the print paste it is important that the triethanolamine or ammonia be thoroughly mixed with the pigment before adding the 'Bedafin' *2101* or *2001*. The 'Bedafin' resin should be added slowly in one portion with vigorous stirring; otherwise there may be a tendency to curdle the paste and spoil it. Although the printing pastes possess good keeping properties, triethanolamine is to be preferred to ammonia on account of the superior stability it confers. Addition of electrolytes should be avoided as they precipitate 'Bedafin' *2101* or *2001*.

By using 30% or more of 'Bedafin' resin in the paste, thickening can be dispensed with, but if a thicker printing paste is desired, a little Gum Tragacanth or starch thickening, neutralised with triethanolamine or ammonia, may be added. The viscosity of the print paste may be reduced where necessary by replacing some of the water stipulated in the recipe by 'Cellosolve'. Frothing, if experienced, may be controlled by an addition of butyl alcohol.

A typical printing recipe is the following:

50–200 parts	pigment paste are thoroughly mixed with
20 "	triethanolamine;
350 "	'Bedafin' *2101* or *2001* are then added gradually with continuous stirring. The print paste is then made up to 1 000 parts with
580–430 "	water.

It is emphasised that this printing paste recipe and baking treatment are recommended for obtaining the highest wash fastness. In styles where this factor is not so important, however, it will be found that by using a smaller quantity of 'Bedafin' resin together with a thickening—for example, gum tragacanth or starch—washing fastness adequate for many purposes is obtained. Moreover, the use of a smaller quantity of 'Bedafin' *2101* or *2001* will effect a saving in cost and will give the printed material a softer handle.

Fixation Treatments

After printing, the fabric should be dried prior to being given the heat treatment necessary to effect fixation. This heat treatment may be carried out at temperatures from 100°C (212°F) upwards.

The best fixation is obtained by baking the printed goods at 120°–150°C (250°–300°F). Steaming is unsuitable. Baking is carried out for

3–5 min. The higher the temperature, the shorter is the time required for fixation. Temperatures higher than the range specified are not recommended, however, since certain azoic pigments are liable to sublime or mark-off under such conditions. The necessary baking treatment may readily be accomplished in continuous baking chambers of the type used in the processing of fabrics with urea/formaldehyde condensates for crease-resist finishes; or, alternatively, discontinuous hot air baking is very satisfactory for the fixation of 'Bedafin' *2101* or *2001* provided that good air circulation is maintained. Since the 'Bedafin' *2101* (*2001*) system does not employ a white spirit emulsion system there is no potential solvent hazard at the baking stage.

In the case of colleges and schools of art where bulk-scale equipment of this nature is not available, small quantities of printed cloth may be baked in an ordinary domestic oven fitted with a temperature control. Alternatively, constant ironing for 3–5 min with a household hand iron, preferably of the thermostatically-controlled type, is effective.

After the heat fixation treatment, the printed material is soaped for 5 min at 60°C (140°F). The soaping treatment (after baking) may be omitted, although soaping improves the handle of the printed fabric. An improvement of finish may be achieved by working the material with the hands after the baking and soaping treatments.

The pigment pastes listed in *Table 8.9* are suitable for printing by the 'Bedafin' *2101* (*2001*) process. The above pigment pastes may be mixed with one another, as required, to produce compound shades. White effects can be obtained by using zinc oxide or titanium dioxide as the pigment in the 'Bedafin' *2101* (*2001*) print paste.

Table 8.9. FASTNESS PROPERTIES OF PIGMENT PASTES USED FOR PRINTING ON COTTON BY THE 'BEDAFIN' *2101* (*2001*) PROCESS

Pigment Paste	*Light* (Medium depth)	*Washing* I.S.O. Wash Test No. 5.* Effect on the print
Monolite Fast Yellow GNVS Paste	6–7	3–4
Monolite Fast Yellow 10GVS Paste	7	4
Monolite Fast Paper Orange 3GS Paste	6	2–3
Monolite Fast Red 2RVS Paste	6	4–5
Monolite Red 4RHVS Paste	7	4
Monastral Fast Blue BVS Paste	8	3–4
Monolite Fast Green BNS Paste	7–8	3–4
Carbon Black VS Paste	8	4

*4 h at 95°C (200°F).

The printing paste prepared as described for the 'Bedafin' *2101* (*2001*) process has been found to have a solvent action on the usual type of flocking mordant, causing a deleterious action on flocked blocks used for printing. To overcome this defect it is recommended that the printing blocks be prepared by using 'Bedafin' *2101* or 'Bedafin' *2001* as a flocking mordant. After flocking the treated linoleum surface the block is stoved for 5 min at 135°C (275°F), this process rendering the flocked surface immune to the solvent action of the printing paste.

PHTHALOGEN DYESTUFFS

These are a range of novel products made by the Bayer Company which are suitable for printing on cotton and viscose rayon. Their novelty lies in the fact that they are phthalocyanine precursors, i.e. they are compounds which when treated with the appropriate auxiliaries and under the correct conditions will form metal phthalocyanines inside the fibre. There are two Phthalogen ranges, the '*M*' brands which are low molecular weight precursors and the '*K*' brands which are higher molecular weight products which closely resemble the final phthalocyanine. Different solvents are required for the two brands to obtain optimum results in terms of fibre penetration and brightness. The combined range includes bright-royal blues, turquoises and greens as well as a blue-black. All possess a high level of light fastness and wet fastness. Application details including the use of Phthalogens alongside other dyestuff classes together with shade illustrations are given in *Phthalogen dyestuffs in Textile Printing*[7].

REFERENCES

1. KNECHT, FOTHERGILL and HURST, *Principles and Practice of Textile Printing*, 2nd edn., Griffin and Co., London, 1952
2. DISERENS, L., Chemical Technology of Dyeing and Printing, **2**, 333, 1951, Rheinhold Publishing Corp., New York
3. MEITNER, *JSDC*, **61**, 33—36 (1945)
4. *Selection of Faster Chrome Dyestuffs, Ref. D71, 2nd edn.*, Emulsion Printing Method in Roller and Screen Printing, Durand and Huguenin A. G., Basle, Switzerland, 1962
5. 'Products 70', *Textile Chemist and Colourist*, Sept., 1969, American Association of Textile Chemists and Colourists
6. *Acramin Dyestuffs in Textile Printing*, Le 1185 d—e—f Bayer Verkauf Farben 509 Leverkusen — Bayerwerk, W. Germany
7. *Phthalogen Dyestuffs in Textile Printing*, Sp 367C/Fa Bayer Verkauf Farben 509 Leverkusen — Bayerwerk, W. Germany

9

The Printing of Wool and Natural Silk

As with other natural fibres success in the printing of both wool and natural silk cannot be achieved without adequate fabric preparation. Wherever possible the thoroughly scoured wool should be given a chlorination treatment preferably by a specialist firm (see Chapter 5). Unless otherwise stated, all the data in this chapter refers to chlorinated wool fabric. Natural silk is not chlorinated, but the natural and adventitious impurities must be removed by 'boiling-off' or 'degumming'. Details for the application of optical brightening agents for both fibres have been given in Chapter 5.

Dye classes suitable for printing wool and natural silk include 'Procion', 'Procilan', acid, direct and basic, although the usage of the last two classes is declining.

'PROCION' DYES

'Procion' dyes enable a wide range of self and mixture shades to be obtained on chlorinated wool and natural silk. The general application methods are similar to those used on cellulosic fibres and only relatively short steaming times are required. With 'Procion' dyes a higher degree of all-round fastness is produced than is normally associated with chlorinated wool and natural silk, particularly where acid or direct dyestuffs have been used. This is due to the reactive 'Procion' dyes forming strong covalent links with the fibre instead of the weaker 'salt-linkages', i.e. ionic bonds formed by acid and direct dyes. Printing pastes used for chlorinated wool and natural silk should be stored only for the length of time recommended for cellulosic fibres. Storage for longer periods produces little visual effect on the final print, but the fastness to subsequent wet processing is markedly reduced. This appears due to the loss of reactive chlorine atoms from the 'Procion' dye precluding the formation of covalent bonds. Fixation then depends only on the formation of weaker salt-linkages through the 'Procion' dye solubilising groups as with acid and direct dyes. Where a particular 'Procion' *M* or *H* dye is not recommended for printing on chlorinated wool this is because the fibre is capable of causing the removal of metal from the dye molecule. This results in alteration of shade and loss of fastness. The effect does not occur with all metals present in metallised 'Procion' dyes, and natural silk does not appear to possess de-metallising properties.

Printing on Chlorinated Wool with 'Procion' Dyestuffs

'Procion' dyestuffs are recommended for printing chlorinated wool; in the absence of a chlorination treatment, low yields result and the prints have an uneven appearance. Some improvement is obtained on unchlorinated wool by adding 40 parts of benzyl alcohol and 20 parts of 'Lissapol' *NX* per 1 000 parts of printing paste. This procedure should only be resorted to when it is impossible or impracticable to have the wool chlorinated.

The printing recipe recommended for chlorinated wool is similar to that recommended for printing the 'Procions' on cotton or viscose rayon but *without* an addition of sodium bicarbonate or carbonate. The addition of sodium bicarbonate to a paste used for printing chlorinated wool generally gives a slight reduction in yield, which varies from dye to dye but is normally of the order of 10–15%.

High-viscosity sodium alginate thickenings, such as 'Manutex' *RS* (Alginate Industries), on account of their low solids content, may tend to give prints of poor definition on chlorinated wool in certain designs. Prints of better definitions are obtained by the use of a high-solids content sodium alginate such as 'Manutex' *F* (Alginate Industries). 'Manutex' *F* thickens at 150 parts per 1 000 and should be used in amounts ranging from 500–600 parts per 1 000 parts of 'Procion' printing paste. Prints from gum tragacanth have only a slightly harsh handle, which may be acceptable in many cases. After printing, the goods are steamed for a minimum of 10 min under the conditions normally used for wool fabrics. While 'Procion' dyestuffs are not unduly sensitive to steaming conditions, it is recommended that the chlorinated wool fabrics be conditioned before steaming if optimum yields are to be obtained, particularly if steaming is to be conducted on a continuous basis. After steaming wash-off (preferably in open width) using the following sequence:

1. Rinse thoroughly in cold water.
2. Rinse for 10 min in water at 60°C (140°F).
3. Treat for 5 min at 50°C (120°F) in a solution containing 2 parts ammonia (sp. gr. 0·880) and 2 parts of 'Lissapol' *ND* per 1 000 parts of water.

124

4. Finally, rinse cold in a solution containing 1 part of formic acid (85%) and 2 parts of 'Fixanol' *PN* per 1 000 parts of water.

Printing on Natural Silk with 'Procion' Dyestuffs

The behaviour of 'Procion' dyestuffs on natural silk differs slightly from their behaviour on chlorinated wool, since the recommended recipe contains sodium bicarbonate. *Tables 9.1* and *9.2* show the fastness

Table 9.1. 'PROCION' *H* DYES: FASTNESS PROPERTIES ON WOOL AND ON SILK

'Procion' *H* Dye	Wool		Silk	
	Light 1/1 Standard depth	*Washing* I.S.O. Wash Test No. 2 45 min at 50°C(120°F) Effect on the print	*Light* 1/1 Standard depth	*Washing* I.S.O. Wash Test No. 2 45 min at 50°C(120°F) Effect on the print
Supra Yellow H-8GP	6	5	6R	5
Supra Yellow H-4GP	6−7	5	6	5
Supra Yellow H-2RP	6−7	5	5	5
Supra Red H-4BP	4−5	4−5	4−5	5
Supra Blue H-3RP	Not recommended		5−6	4−5
Supra Black H-LP	7	3−4WB	7	5
Brilliant Yellow H-5G	6−7	4R	6	3−4
Brilliant Yellow H-4G	7	3	6	5
Golden Yellow H-R	6−7	3	6	5
Yellow H-G	5−6	4D	5−6	4−5
Brilliant Orange H-2R	4−5	3−4	5−6	5
Orange H-4R	6	4−5	6	5
Printing Brown H-G	Not recommended		6	4Y
Dark Brown H-B	6−7	5	6−7	5
Red Brown H-4R	6−7	5	6	5
Red H-B	4−5	4	Not recommended	
Scarlet H-RN	6	4−5	5	4−5
Brilliant Red H-3BN	6	3WB	6	3
Brilliant Red H-8B	5	4−5	4	5
Rubine H-BN	Not recommended		5−6	4−5B
Brilliant Purple H-3R	Not recommended		6	4−5
Brilliant Blue H-3R	6	4	5	5
Brilliant Blue H-4R	6	4−5	5	5
Brilliant Blue H-GR	6	3−4	5−6	5
Blue H-3G	6	2	5−6	4
Brilliant Blue H-5G	5−6G	3−4	6	4−5R
Navy Blue H-3R	Not recommended		5R	5
Blue H-5R	5−6	3	6	4
Turquoise H-A	6	4−5	5−6	4−5
Black H-N	7	3−4WB	7	5

Table 9.2. 'PROCION' *M* DYES: FASTNESS PROPERTIES ON
WOOL AND ON SILK

'Procion' *M* Dye	Wool		Silk	
	Light 1/1 Standard depth	*Washing* I.S.O. Wash Test No. 2 45 min at 50°C(120°F) Effect on the print	*Light* 1/1 Standard depth	*Washing* I.S.O. Wash Test No. 2 45 min at 50°C(120°F) Effect on the print
Brilliant Yellow M-6G	6–7	4–5	6	5
Yellow M-GR	6–7	5	6–7	4–5R
Yellow M-R	6–7	4	6	4WR
Yellow M-4R	4–5	3–4R	4–5	5
Brilliant Orange M-G	6	5	5	3–4
Brilliant Orange M-2R	5	4–5	4–5	5
Scarlet M-G	5	5	4–5	3–4
Red M-G	6	5	5–6	5
Brilliant Red M-2B	6	4–5	5–6	4–5
Brilliant Red M-5B	5	4B	4	3–4
Brilliant Red M-8B	4–5	4–5	4–5	5
Rubine M-B	Not recommended		6–7	4–5
Brilliant Blue M-R	6	4	6	3–4
Blue M-3G	6	3–4	6	3–4
Green M-2B	4–5WB	4	5WB	5

properties of 'Procion' *H* and *M* dyes respectively on wool and silk. The recommended recipe is that given for printing the 'Procions' using sodium bicarbonate as alkali on cotton or viscose rayon. In the absence of sodium bicarbonate slightly lower yields are produced on natural silk with most members of the 'Procion' range.

The choice of thickening agent is of particular importance in silk printing, and the best results have been obtained using 'Manutex' *F* thickenings already described for chlorinated wool. Gum Tragacanth gives prints with a slightly harsh handle, while sodium alginate thickenings of the 'Manutex' *RS* type tend to lack definition. As with other dyestuffs printed on natural silk the volume of 'Procion' printing paste applied should be kept to the minimum consistent with adequate furnishing and covering of the printed design.

Steaming conditions should be dry, and a steaming time of 10 min gives excellent fixation of all members of the range. If the steaming time is prolonged or the steam is too moist, the urea concentration in the printing paste may lead to slight bleeding or a loss of print definition. In cases where insufficient control of steaming conditions is possible, some improvement may be achieved by decreasing the quantities of urea in the printing paste. Any decrease so made should have regard to the quantity of urea necessary to ensure that a satisfactory solution of the dyestuff is produced. After steaming, the processing should be finished (preferably in open width) using the following sequence:

1. Rinse thoroughly in cold water.
2. Rinse for 5 min in water at 60°C (140°F).
3. Treat for 10 min at 85°C (185°F) in a solution containing 1 part of sodium carbonate and 2 parts of 'Lissapol' *ND* per 1 000 parts of water.
4. Finally, rinse in a solution containing 1 part of formic acid (85%) and 2 parts of 'Fixanol' *PN* per 1 000 parts of water.

'PROCILAN' DYES

The 'Procilan' dyes contain a reactive group that forms a stable chemical linkage with the wool fibre. As a result they possess wet fastness properties that are superior to those of conventional (i.e. non-reactive) 1:2 metal complex dyes. At the same time, 'Procilan' dyes have the high light fastness normally associated with 1:2 metal complex dyes. When 'Procilan' dyes are printed on wool their superiority is particularly apparent in regard to severe wet treatments such as repeated washing. 'Procilan' dyes are for this reason of special interest for the melange (vigoureux) printing of wool slubbing. For further information on this outlet see Reference 1.

Printing of 'Procilan' Dyes on Chlorinated Wool and Natural Silk

The printing paste is prepared as follows:

30 parts	'Procilan' dye (Note 1) and
50 "	Urea are dissolved in
395 "	Boiling water.

The solution is added to:

500 parts	Thickening (Note 2). Finally
10 "	'Perminal' *KB* and
15 "	Sodium bicarbonate (Note 3) are added.

1 000 parts.

Notes
  (1) 'Procilan' Black *RS* is not recommended for natural silk.
  (2) Suitable thickenings include:

127

'Nafka' Crystal Gum Supra (Scholtens), 'Meyprogum' *AC* (Meyhall), 'Indalca' *V* (Cesalpina) and 'Thickening *301*' (Grünau).

(3)   Omit sodium bicarbonate when printing on chlorinated (or unchlorinated) wool.

After printing and drying the chlorinated wool or silk patterns are steamed for 30 min. This is followed by rinsing in cold water, preferably in open width, and a treatment for 3 min at 50°C (120°F) in a solution containing 2 parts 'Lissapol' *ND* per 1 000 parts. A final rinse in cold water is then given followed by drying.

The fastness properties of 'Procilan' dyes on chlorinated wool and natural silk are shown in *Table 9.3*.

Table 9.3. 'PROCILAN' DYES: FASTNESS PROPERTIES ON CHLORINATED WOOL AND NATURAL SILK

'Procilan' Dye	Chlorinated Wool		Silk	
	Light 1/1 Standard depth	*Washing* I.S.O. Wash Test No. 3 30 min at 60°C(140°F) Effect on the print	*Light* 1/1 Standard depth	*Washing* I.S.O. Wash Test No. 3 30 min at 60°C(140°F) Effect on the print
Yellow 2G	7	5	6–7	5
Orange R	6–7	4–5	5–6	5
Red G	5	4–5	4–5	4
Dark Brown B	6	4–5	6	4
Grey BR	6	4–5	5–6	4
Black R	6–7	4–5	Not recommended	

ACID DYES

The following is a typical printing recipe:

5–30 parts		dyestuff are pasted with
20 "		Solution Salt *SV* (when required)
50–75 "		glycerine and
235–185 "		hot water. The mixture, which may be boiled if necessary to ensure complete solution, is added to
600 "		thickening in which
20 "		'Perminal' *KB* and a solution of
20 "		ammonium oxalate in
50 "		hot water have been incorporated.

Bulk to 1 000 parts.

128

Table 9.4 indicates the acid dyestuffs suitable for application to chlorinated wool and natural silk by printing methods, and details the more important fastness properties.

Table 9.4. FASTNESS PROPERTIES ON CHLORINATED WOOL AND SILK

| Acid Dyestuff | Chlorinated Wool | | Silk | |
	Light (Full shade)	Washing Once at 55°C(130°F) Effect on the print	Light (Full shade)	Washing Once at 55°C(130°F) Effect on the print
*Carbolan Yellow 3GS	3–4	3	4	4–5
Carbolan Yellow 4GS	6	3–4	3–4	4
Carbolan Yellow RS	6	3WG	4–5	4
Lissamine Fast Yellow 2G 125	6–7	1	6	1
Coomassie Yellow R200	4	3WD	5	3–4
Naphthalene Fast Orange 2GS	5	1	Not recommended	
Coomassie Fast Orange G 150	5	3	4	3
Coomassie Fast Brown RS	5–6	4Y	5	4–5
Coomassie Milling Scarlet G 150	3	3WB	3–4	4
Napthalene Scarlet BS	4	1	3–4	1
Azo Geranine 2G 200	4–5	1	4–5	1
*Coomassie Red PG 150	4–5	3–4B	4	5
*Carbolan Crimson BS	3	3–4	3–4	5
*Carbolan Crimson 3BS	4	3–4	4–5	3–4
*Carbolan Violet 2RS	4	3–4	4–5	4–5
Coomassie Violet R 150	2	3–4	2	3
*Carbolan Blue BS	5	3–4	4	4–5
*Carbolan Brilliant Blue 2R 140	5–6	4–5	5	4
Coomassie Brilliant Blue FF 200	2	4	2	4
Coomassie Brilliant Blue R 250	3	4–5	3	4
Coomassie Brilliant Blue G 250	3	4	3	4–5
*Carbolan Green G 125	5–6	4	4–5	4
Lissamine Green V 200	3	2	3	1
*Carbolan Brilliant Green 5GS	6	4–5	4–5	4
Coomassie Fast Grey 3GS	6–7	3	6–7	3–4
Ultralan Black RN 150	6–7	5	6–7	3–4

*Addition of Solution Salt *SV* recommended when using these dyestuffs; see previous recipe.

After printing, the goods are dried and then steamed for 45–60 min at 100°–102°C (212°–215°F). When steaming prints on wool, optimum yields will only be obtained under moist steaming conditions. If

129

unsaturated steam is used or the steam 'dries out' during steaming, unlevel prints and poor yields may result. To guard against this undesirable feature the printed fabric is often conditioned prior to steaming by hanging in a cool damp room for several hours. Another technique is to steam the fabric for 30 min, then remove it from the steamer, allow it to condition in a cool damp room and finally continue the steaming for the final 30 min. When processing natural silk these precautions are not usually necessary.

After steaming, prints on both wool and silk should be rinsed thoroughly in cold water. The faster dyestuffs of the 'Coomassie' and 'Carbolan' ranges may be given a short treatment in a solution of 2–3 parts of 'Lissapol' ND per 1000 parts of water at 40°C (105°F), whereby brighter shades are often obtained.

Notes
(1) The thickening agents used for printing both wool and natural silk must be readily removable from the fabric. 'Nafka' Crystal Gum, sodium alginate thickenings and natural gums of the senegal and tragacanth types are widely used.

(2) An addition of sodium chlorate at the rate of 2–5 parts per 1000 parts is often made to the print paste, when printing blacks or other deep shades, to prevent dyestuff loss by reduction.

(3) When printing on silk, with moist steaming conditions, the glycerine should be reduced or omitted.

(4) In all cases, the brand of the highest concentration available should be used.

DIRECT DYES

The following is a typical printing recipe:

5–30 parts	dyestuff are pasted with
50–75 "	glycerine and
255–205 "	hot water. The mixture, which may be boiled if necessary to effect solution, is added to
600 "	thickening containing
20 "	'Perminal' KB. Finally, a solution of
20 "	disodium hydrogen phosphate dissolved in
50 "	hot water is stirred in.

Bulk to 1000 parts.

130

Notes (1), (2), (3) and (4) given on page 130 are also applicable here. Steaming and washing are carried out exactly as for acid dyestuffs, details of which are given on pages 129–130.

The fastness properties of direct dyestuffs on chlorinated wool and silk are listed in *Table 9.5*. The dyes listed in the table are all suitable for application to chlorinated wool and natural silk by printing methods.

Table 9.5. FASTNESS PROPERTIES ON CHLORINATED WOOL AND ON SILK

Direct Dyestuff	Chlorinated Wool		Silk	
	Light (Full shade)	*Washing* Once at 55°C(130°F) Effect on the print	*Light* (Full shade)	*Washing* Once at 55°C(130°F) Effect on the print
Chrysophenine G 200	6	3	6	3
C.R. Durazol Flavine RS	6–7	3	6	2
C.R. Durazol Yellow GR 200	6–7	3	6–7	4
Durazol Yellow 4GS	6–7	3	6	4
Durazol Yellow 6G 150	4–5	3	4–5	4
C.R. Durazol Orange 2G 125	6–7	4	6–7	3–4
Durazol Orange 4R 150	5	3–4	5	4
Chlorazol Orange PO 150	4–5	3WR	4–5	4
Durazol Brown BR 150	3	3WR	5	3–4D
C.R. Chlorazol Fast Scarlet 4B 150	3–4	3WB	3–4	3–4
C.R. Chlorazol Fast Pink BK 200	5	3	4–5	2WD
C.R. Durazol Red 2B 150	5	3WB	6	3–4
C.R. Durazol Brilliant Red BS	4–5	2B	4–5	4
Chlorazol Bordeaux BS	5	4	5–6	3–4
Chlorazol Fast Helio 2RK 200	4–5	3	3	3
Durazol Helio B 200	5	3	4	2
C.R. Durazol Blue 2GN 200	5	1	4	1
Durazol Blue 8G 150	6	3–4WR	6	3–4R
C.R. Durazol Blue 2R 150	5	3–4	5	3
C.R. Durazol Blue 4R 200	5–6	3W	5	3R
C.R. Chlorazol Sky Blue FF 200	2	3–4	1	3WG
Chlorazol Dark Green PL 125	4	3	3–4	4
Chlorazol Green BN 125	3	3	3	4–5
Durazol Grey RGS	3	3	3	3

BASIC DYES

The usage of basic dyes on chlorinated wool and natural silk is declining because although they enable brilliant shades to be obtained, such shades possess only very moderate fastness properties. The following is a typical printing recipe:

10 parts	basic dyestuff are dissolved in a mixture of
50 "	'Glydote' *BN*
100 "	acetic acid 40% and
170 "	water. Then
20 "	tartaric acid are added and the solution is stirred into
650 "	thickening (Note 1)

Bulk to 1 000 parts.

The printed goods are dried then steamed for 30—45 min and afterwards rinsed well in cold water and dried. The following basic dyestuffs are suitable for application by printing methods:

Acronol Yellow TC 180	Rhodamine 6GBN 500
Auramine ON 150	Magenta Large Crystals
Safranine TN 125	Methyl Violet 2BN 200
Victoria Pure Blue BON 110	Acronol Brilliant Lake Blue A 220
Methylene Blue ZFS	Malachite Green ANS Crystals
Rhodamine 6GDN 500	Brilliant Green YNS Crystals

Note

(1) It must be borne in mind that basic dyes are cationic, i.e. they are positively charged and hence will precipitate negatively charged thickenings such as sodium alginate. Alginate thickenings cannot, therefore, be used with basic dyes. Suitable thickenings for both chlorinated wool and natural silk include 'Nafka' Crystal Gum and natural gums of the senegal and tragacanth type. In addition, 'Polyprint' *S-145* ('Polygal' *A-G*), 'Thickening *301*' (Grünau) and 'Meyprogums' *NP* and *NP16* (Meyhall) are recommended. None of these thickenings should be mixed with Gum Senegal or crystal gums without preliminary trials, since abnormal viscosity losses are apt to occur.

REFERENCE

1. *'Procilan' Dyes for the Mélange (Vigoureux) Printing of Wool,* ICI Technical Information (Dyehouse) No. 829

10

The Printing of Nylon

For the printing of nylon fabrics, 'Nylomine' Acid P dyes and 'Procinyl' dyes are widely used. 'Procion' dyestuffs are used to a lesser extent because although they give prints of excellent wet fastness and light fastness, difficulties are encountered in obtaining deep shades. A few acid dyes are employed occasionally to get novelty shades where brightness of shade is the principal requirement. Disperse dyes of the 'Dispersol' and 'Duranol' type are seldom used on nylon because they show poor wet fastness properties. Pigment printing compositions are also used in pale to medium depths, but difficulties can arise with full shades and also on nylon stretch fabrics. The two types of nylon, i.e. nylon 66 and 6 have some points of difference. Nylon 6 needs less swelling agent in the print paste than nylon 66 and generally takes up more dyestuff. On the other hand, prints on nylon 66 usually show slightly better light and wet fastness properties than nylon 6.

In special cases in which a particular fastness property is of prime importance, printers are recommended to carry out fastness tests on their own material under their own specific conditions.

'NYLOMINE' ACID P DYES

There are three ranges of 'Nylomine' Acid dyes for dyeing which have the letter A, B or C in the brand name and this classifies the products according to their dyeing behaviour. The 'Nylomine' Acid P range has been compiled with printing requirements in mind including good solubility and printing behaviour coupled with a wide range of shades of good all round fastness.

Printing Recipe

30– 60 parts		'Nylomine' Acid *P* dye are dissolved in
50 ,,		'Glydote' *BN* and
360–330 ,,		hot water containing
10 ,,		'Dispersol' *VP* (Note 1). The solution is added to
450 ,,		thickening (Note 2) containing previously dissolved
50 ,,		thiourea (Note 3) and
20 ,,		'Perminal' *KB*. Finally
30 ,,		ammonium sulphate (Note 4) are added.
1 000 parts.		

Notes
(1)   'Dispersol' *VP*. A coacervating agent to improve colour yield and levelness, especially on fabrics composed of bulked yarns. A coacervate process involves the formation of an aqueous two-phase system in a dye impregnating liquor[1].
(2)   Suitable thickenings include:
      'Nafka'Crystal Gum Supra (Scholtens), 'Meyprogum' *AC* (Meyhall), 'Indalca' *U* and 'Indalca' *PA/3* (Cesalpinia) and Thickening *301* (Grünau).
(3)   Thiourea. On nylon 6 fabrics reduce to 20 parts.
(4)   Ammonium sulphate. Can be replaced by 50 parts of ammonium tartrate at 20° Bé (32° Tw). With 'Nylomine' Acid Navy *P–2RS* and mixtures containing it, omit ammonium salts.

Printing

From a printing point of view nylon differs from the textile fabrics discussed previously in this book in that the amount of water taken up by nylon is very limited. For example, at 100% r.h. the moisture regain of viscose rayon, wool and silk is 33%, while nylon is only 7%. Consequently, to obtain prints which maintain a satisfactory definition during drying and steaming it is advisable to use
(1)   in machine printing, rollers having a fine, i.e. shallow engraving
(2)   in screen printing, a fine mesh screen
(3)   a thickening agent of high solids content and
(4)   a wetting-out agent in the print paste, e.g. 'Perminal' *KB*.

Processing after Printing

The printed and dried fabric is steamed for 30 min. at atmospheric pressure. After steaming the fabric is washed-off (preferably in open width) using the following sequence:

A cold rinse for 5–10 min in a solution containing 1 part of sodium carbonate (anhydrous) per 1 000 parts of water. This process removes a large proportion of the unfixed dye and the sodium carbonate suppresses any tendency for this dye to stain the unprinted areas of the fabric. Next, the fabric is treated for 5–10 min in a solution containing 2 parts 'Lissapol' *ND* and 1 part of sodium carbonate per 1 000 parts of water heated to 60°C (140°F). This is followed by a rinse in cold water and a further rinse in a solution containing 1 part of acetic acid (80%) per 1 000 parts of cold water. A final cold water rinse is given followed by drying. This washing sequence is essential if optimum wet fastness is to be achieved and the handle of the fabric maintained. Complexing agents of the synthetic tanning agent type are sometimes employed in washing-off prints, but there is always the possibility that there will be some effect on the fabric handle and also on the unprinted whites. This procedure is more commonly used in nylon dyeing than in printing and it is often referred to as a *back-tanning* process.

Fastness Properties

The fastness data given in *Table 10.1* refers to patterns that have not been aftertreated with a complexing agent. The data on nylon 66 refers to a fabric made from ICI bulked yarn and the nylon 6 data to a 'Celon' (Courtaulds) 40-denier fully delustred fabric.

Dye Selection for End Use

For furnishing fabrics, upholstery, loose covers, etc.:

Nylomine Acid Yellow P-4GS   Nylomine Acid Navy P-RS
Nylomine Acid Yellow P-3R 200   Nylomine Acid Green P-3G 150
Nylomine Acid Orange P-RS   Nylomine Acid Brown P-3RS
Nylomine Acid Blue P-3R 140   Nylomine Acid Brown P-2BS
Nylomine Acid Blue P-BS   Nylomine Acid Black P-RS
Nylomine Acid Blue P-2GS

For swimwear, etc.:

Nylomine Acid Yellow P-4GS   Nylomine Acid Blue P-2GS
Nylomine Acid Yellow P-3R 200   Nylomine Acid Navy P-RS
Nylomine Acid Orange P-RS   Nylomine Acid Green P-3G 150
Nylomine Acid Orange P-2RS   Nylomine Acid Brown P-3RS
Nylomine Acid Scarlet P-RS   Nylomine Acid Brown P-2BS
Nylomine Acid Blue P-3R 140   Nylomine Acid Black P-RS
Nylomine Acid Blue P-BS

For dress goods, etc.:

All 'Nylomine' Acid *P* dyes are suitable. For maximum productivity and brightness, attention is especially drawn to the following:

Nylomine Acid Yellow P-4GS   Nylomine Acid Blue P-RS
Nylomine Acid Yellow P-5RS   Nylomine Acid Blue P-2GS
Nylomine Acid Orange P-2RS   Nylomine Acid Navy P-2RS
Nylomine Acid Scarlet P-RS   Nylomine Acid Green P-3G 150
Nylomine Acid Scarlet P-2RS   Nylomine Acid Green P-2BS
Nylomine Acid Red P-4BS   Nylomine Acid Brown P-3BS
Nylomine Acid Violet P-4RS   Nylomine Acid Black P-RS
Nylomine Acid Blue P-2RS

Table 10.1. FASTNESS PROPERTIES OF 'NYLOMINE' ACID *P* DYES ON NYLON 66 AND NYLON 6

'Nylomine' Acid *P* Dye	Nylon 66		Nylon 6	
	Light 1/1 Standard Depth	*Washing* I.S.O. Wash Test No. 3 30 min at 60°C (140°F) Effect on the Print	*Light* 1/1 Standard Depth	*Washing* I.S.O. Wash Test No. 3 30 min at 60°C (140°F) Effect on the Print
Yellow P-4G	6−7	4−5	6−7	3
Yellow P-3R	7	5	5−6	4
Yellow P-5R	4−5	4−5R	4−5	4R
Orange P-R	6−7	5	6	5
Orange P-2R	5	4−5	5	4
Scarlet P-R	5	5	4	5
Scarlet P-2R	5	4−5	4−5	4
Red P-4B	4	3−4B	4	2B
Violet P-4R	3−4	4−5	3	4−5
Blue P-B	6−7	5	5	4
Blue P-3R	7	5	4−5	4−5
Blue P-2R	7	4−5	4−5	3
Blue P-R	7	4−5	5	3
Blue P-2G	7	5	5	4−5
Navy P-2R	4	4	3	3
Navy P-R	7	5	5	4
Green P-3G	6−7	5	5−6	5
Green P-2B	4	4	4	4
Brown P-3R	7	4−5	5	4−5
Brown P-2B	7	5	5	5
Brown P-3B	3−4	4−5	3−4	4
Black P-R	7	5	4−5	4R
Acid Dyes				
Lissamine Flavine FF	2	4−5	2	2
Lissamine Rhodamine B	2	4B	2	3−4B
Disulphine Blue VN	2	3−4	2	3−4
Lissamine Green V	2	3	2	2

In addition, for the production of novelty effects where brightness of shade is the principal requirement, the following four acid dyes, selected for their outstanding brilliance of shade, are also recommended:

'Lissamine' Flavine *FFS*, 'Lissamine' Rhodamine *B 200*, 'Disulphine' Blue *VN 150*, 'Lissamine' Green *V 200*.

'PROCION' DYES

Selected 'Procion' dyes may be used for printing nylon to give shades of good fastness to light and washing. The 'Procion' dyes are of particular value for the production of full bright golden-yellow, orange, red and turquoise shades. In this respect they are of interest in supplementing the shade range obtainable with 'Nylomine' Acid *P* dyes. Not all 'Procion' dyes are suitable for nylon printing and this appears to be due either to molecular size, shape or a combination of the two. Support for this view is seen in the fact that a few dyes will print nylon 6, but not nylon 66. Further details of the suitability of the complete 'Procion' *H* and 'Procion' Supra ranges together with some members of the 'Procion' *M* range may be obtained from Reference 2.

Printing Recipe

The general recipe is as follows:

10–30 parts	'Procion' dye are dissolved in
50 „	'Glydote' *BN* and
330–310 „	water at 70°C (160°F) containing
10 „	'Dispersol' *VP* (Note 1). The solution is added to
500 „	thickening (Note 2) containing previously dissolved
50 „	thiourea (Note 3)
30 „	ammonium sulphate (Note 4) and
20 „	'Perminal' *KB*
1 000 parts.	

Notes
(1) See corresponding note under 'Nylomine' Acid *P* recipe.
(2) See corresponding note under 'Nylomine' Acid *P* recipe. In this application the 'Procion' dye is not restricted to sodium alginate thickenings, and those given in the footnote are to be preferred.
(3) Thiourea. Reduce amount to 20 parts on nylon 6 fabrics.

Table 10.2. FASTNESS PROPERTIES OF PROCION DYESTUFFS PRINTED ON NYLON 66

'Procion' Dyestuff	*Light* 1/1 Standard depth	*Washing* I.S.O. Wash Test No. 2 45 min at 50°C (120°F) Effect on the print
Procion Brilliant Yellow M-6G	6	4−5
Procion Brilliant Yellow M-4G	6	4−5
Procion Yellow M-GR	6	4−5
Procion Golden Yellow H-R	5−6	4−5
Procion Yellow M-R	5−6	4R
Procion Yellow M-4R	3	4R
Procion Brilliant Orange M-G	5R	4R
Procion Brilliant Orange H-GR	5	4−5
Procion Brilliant Orange M-2R	5	4−5
Procion Brilliant Orange H-2R	5	4−5
Procion Brilliant Red H-3B	5	4Y
Procion Brilliant Red M-5B	4	4−5
Procion Brilliant Red M-8B	5	5
Procion Red M-G	5	5
Procion Scarlet M-G	4−5	4−5
Procion Scarlet H-RN	5	4−5
Procion Brilliant Blue M-R	6	4
Procion Brilliant Blue H-GR	5	4
Procion Blue H-B	6	4−5
Procion Brilliant Blue H-5G	3−4Y	4−5
Procion Brilliant Blue H-7G	3−4Y	4−5
Procion Olive Green M-3G	5	3−4WY

(4) See corresponding note under 'Nylomine' acid *P* recipe for alternative.

(5) Additions of up to 40 parts of phenol have been recommended in the past. Care must be taken to protect the hands and eyes when using this substance. Some attack on the screen lacquer may also take place.

Printing Process

Print dry and steam for 30 min. at atmospheric pressure and then follow with the washing-off sequence already given for 'Nylomine' Acid *P* dyes.

Compound Shades

'Procion' dyes can be mixed with one another to give a range of compound shades. 'Procion' and acid dyes when applied by the above recipe can be used in admixture or to obtain 'fall-on' effects. Disperse dyes are compatible with 'Procion' dyes, but the general level of fastness of disperse dyes is lower than that obtained from selected 'Procion' dyes. Mixtures of 'Procion' and 'Procinyl' dyes are not recommended.

Dyestuff Selection

A list of suitable 'Procion' dyes, selected on the basis of build-up, together with details of the fastness properties when printed on nylon 66 is given in *Table 10.2.*[3]

'PROCINYL' DYES

The 'Procinyl' dye molecules contain reactive groupings, but no solubilising sulphonic acid groupings. They are, therefore, reactive disperse dyes in which the reactive groups are able to react with the amide (−NH−) groups along the nylon molecular chains as well as with those amino (NH_2) groups present at some of the chain ends. The effect of such reactions is to produce prints of high wet fastness. The wet fastness of 'Procinyl' dyes printed on nylon is considerably higher than that achieved with conventional disperse dyes and is generally superior to that obtained from many 'Nylomine' and other acid dyes. The 'Procinyl' dyes show good compatibility in admixture with one another and have the advantage of retaining the printed mark under moist steaming conditions and in 'fall-on' effects.

After steaming, surplus colour and thickening are readily removed by a cold water rinse followed by a treatment in warm 'Lissapol' *ND*. During the wet processing treatments, 'Procinyl' printed goods may be piled wet without danger of staining on to the adjacent unprinted portions of the pattern.

Printing Recipe

The general printing recipe is:

139

10–60 parts	'Procinyl' dye are dispersed in
300–250 ,,	water and
10 ,,	glacial acetic acid.
	The suspension is stirred into
600 ,,	thickening (Note 1) containing
50 ,,	sodium acetate,
10 ,,	sodium chlorate (Note 2) and
20 ,,	'Perminal' *KB*
1 000 parts.	

When prepared by this recipe, print pastes of 'Procinyl' dyes may be stored for 28 days at 15°C (60°F) without significant loss in printing strength.

Notes
(1)   Suitable thickenings include:
       'Nafka' Crystal Gum Supra (Scholtens)
       'Meyprogum' *AC* (Meyhall)
       'Indalca' *U*, 'Indalca' *PA/3* (Cesalpinia)
       Thickening *301* (Grünau)
(2)   Sodium chlorate prevents reduction of dye in the print paste and during steaming. On nylon it is not advisable to use Resist Salt *L* which is used for this purpose on cellulosic fibres.

Experience has shown that when a print paste containing Resist Salt *L* (but no dye) is applied to nylon and processed normally, some of the Resist Salt *L* is absorbed by the nylon and cannot be removed during the usual washing after-treatment. When such a print is exposed to light, the residual Resist Salt *L* causes the pattern (originally colour-less) to go appreciably yellower.

When a dyestuff is present in addition to Resist Salt *L*, this yellowing may result in an apparent decrease in the light fastness of the dye. For this reason it is now recommended that Resist Salt *L* should not be used for prints on nylon. However, when printing heavy shades, the addition of Resist Salt *L* may be permissible, and the printer should decide, on the basis of experiments under his own conditions, whether the protection offered by Resist Salt *L* against dye reduction is out-weighed by any possible change in the print on exposure to light.

Where protection against reduction is desirable without incurring the risk of this yellowing on exposure, an addition of sodium chlorate (5–10 parts per 1 000 parts) may be made instead of Resist Salt *L*. Although laboratory tests have failed to show any tendency for residual sodium chlorate in the nylon to become yellower when the print is exposed to light, the printer is strongly advised to check the suitability of any particular dye combination under his own conditions. No tendering has been observed in nylon fabrics printed with the quantities of sodium chlorate recommended above and then processed in the normal manner.

Process

After printing, the goods are dried, steamed at atmospheric pressure for 30 min, rinsed in water and then treated for 5—10 min at 50°C (120°F) in a solution containing 2 parts of 'Lissapol' *ND* per 1 000 parts of water, then finally rinsed in water and dried.

Dyestuff Selection

Fastness properties of 'Procinyl' dyes printed on nylon are listed in *Table 10.3*.

Table 10.3. FASTNESS PROPERTIES ON NYLON

'Procinyl' Dye	*Light* 1/1 Standard depth	*Washing* I.S.O. Wash Test No. 2 45 min at 50°C (120°F) Effect on the print
PQ Procinyl Yellow G Paste	6—7	5
PQ Procinyl Orange G Paste	5	5
PQ Procinyl Scarlet G Paste	6	5
PQ Procinyl Red G Paste	5	5
PQ Procinyl Rubine B Paste	4	5
PQ Procinyl Blue R Paste	4—5R	5

Compound Shades with 'Procinyl' Dyes

For compound shades, 'Procinyl' dyes can be recommended with confidence. Their behaviour in admixture with one another follows their behaviour when printed individually. The 'Procinyl' dyes are compatible with disperse dyes, but not with 'Nylomine' or acid dyes. The predictable behaviour in compound shades is due to the lack of sulphonic acid (SO_3H) groups in the molecule.

141

'NYLOMINE' ACID AND OTHER ACID DYES

Due largely to the presence of differing numbers of sulphonic acid groups present in their dye molecules, the compatibility of 'Nylomine' Acid and other acid dyestuffs is not easy to forecast from their behaviour when they are printed individually. The observed effects are the displacement of one dye from the fibre by another when mixture shades are printed, so that the build up of one component does not increase in proportion to the presence of increased amounts in the print paste. This is especially true with deep shades such as dark greens, dark browns and navies. If it is desired to use mixtures of 'Nylomine' Acid dyes from the various available ranges, viz. *A, B, C* or of the 'Nylomine' Acid *P* dyes with other acid dyes for heavy compound shades, then preliminary trials should be carried out. These trials should be aimed at determining the most suitable combinations under the particular conditions employed. Nylon which has been heat set at too high a temperature may have incurred a loss of amine end groups. If this nylon has subsequently or previously been given an optical bleaching treatment with a product containing sulphonic acid groups, then the total number of sites on the nylon where dye fixation can take place is reduced. Such fabrics will exaggerate difficulties due to dye incompatibilities. Another reason for the failure to build up heavy printed shades on nylon arises from the incorporation at the fibre-extrusion stage of a white pigment for delustring purposes. This is usually titanium dioxide, and one of its functions is to render less transparent, fabrics woven or knitted from these delustred yarns. It is practically impossible to build up blacks and other deep shades on heavily delustred nylon with soluble dyes. Recourse to pigment printing compositions may be necessary provided those chosen will meet the end use fastness requirements. An exception to the general rule of avoiding admixture of different 'Nylomine' Acid ranges is the use of 'Nylomine' Yellow *A-GS* and 'Nylomine' Acid Green *P-3G 150*. Mixtures of these two dyes are of value for the production of bright yellowish green shades that do not exhibit catalytic fading (i.e. the behaviour on light exposure which results in the preferential fading of one component due to the presence of the other).

DISPERSE DYES

Compatibility

These dyes may be recommended for the production of compound shades. They are free from solubilising sulphonic acid groups and their behaviour in admixture with one another follows their behaviour when printed individually.

Printing Recipe

The general printing recipe is as follows:

30–100 parts	'Duranol' or 'Dispersol' dyestuff paste are diluted with
340–270 „	water and the suspension is stirred into
600 „	thickening (Note 1) containing
20 „	'Perminal' *KB* and
10 „	sodium chlorate (Note 2)
1 000 parts.	

Notes
(1) The same thickenings recommended for 'Nylomine' Acid *P* dyestuffs will be found satisfactory for disperse dyes.
(2) Sodium chlorate. Refer to the corresponding note under the 'Procinyl' recipe.

Table 10.4. FASTNESS PROPERTIES: DISPERSE DYES PRINTED ON NYLON 66

'Dispersol' or 'Duranol' Dye	*Light* 1/1 Standard depth	*Washing* I.S.O. Wash Test No. 2 45 min at 50°C (120°F) Effect on the print
Dispersol Fast Yellow G Liquid	6	3
Dispersol Printing Yellow 3GS Paste	3	3
Dispersol Fast Orange B Liquid	6	3–4
Duranol Printing Brown G Paste	4	4R
Dispersol Fast Red R Liquid	3	4
Dispersol Fast Scarlet B Liquid	4	4R
Duranol Red X3B Liquid	5	3
Duranol Printing Blue B 200 Paste	4R	3
Duranol Blue G Liquid	4–5	3
Duranol Dark Blue T Liquid	4	3
Duranol Blue Green B Liquid	4	3–4
Duranol Printing Black R Paste	5	4–5B

Note
The 'Duranol' and 'Dispersol' colours when printed on nylon do not necessarily give the same shade as on cellulose acetate, and this is more or less pronounced with the scarlets, reds and violets, which tend to become bluer and/or duller.

Process

After printing, the goods are dried, steamed for 30—45 min at atmospheric pressure, and then well rinsed in cold water and dried.

Dyestuff Selection

A list of suitable disperse dyes for printing on nylon, together with fastness properties will be found in *Table 10.4.*

REFERENCES

1. CASTY, R., *Melliand Textilber,* **41,** 1365–1376 (1960). See also Swiss Patent No. 386 387 and British Patent No. 930 429
2. *Pattern Card Procion Dyes Printing* (14570), ICI Dyestuffs Divn. and subsequent insert sheets
3. *Use of Nylomine Acid P dyes for the printing of polyamide fabrics,* Technical Information Note No. D 1178, ICI Dyestuffs Division

The Printing of 'Terylene' Polyester Fibre

Some details have already been given in Chapter 5 relating to the scouring of 'Terylene' and the application of 'Fluolite' *XMF* as an optical brightening agent. More detailed information on fabric preparation and also on finishing operations subsequent to printing is available in the ICI Fibres Ltd. publication entitled *"Terylene" Manual*. When considering the printing of polyester fabrics it is necessary first to survey the equipment available for fixing the 'Dispersol' and 'Duranol' disperse dyes that will be used in their coloration. These development methods are:

(*a*) Atmospheric Steaming
       This method does not require a pressure vessel, but in order to obtain moderate-good yields of dye a 'carrier' must be added to the print paste. The former ICI product, 'Tumescal' *PH* (parahydroxydiphenyl), was selected from a large number of products and worked efficiently. Chemical equivalents to 'Tumescal' *PH* are available in some countries. Not all disperse dyes respond to carriers of this type, and dyes which do invariably give prints whose light fastness is lower than if such products had not been used.

(*b*) Pressure Steaming
       A discontinuous pressure steaming treatment of 30 min at 1.4×10^5 N/m^2 (20 lbf/in^2) gives a good yield with the majority of disperse dyes. No carriers are necessary, but the steamer must be capable of operating safely at such pressures. In the U.K., pressure vessels of this type are required to pass at intervals a hydraulic test in which water is pumped in up to twice the safe working pressure to check for the absence of flaws. Printers operating this process usually have a pressurised star-steamer, a good example of which is the 'Dedeko' steamer (Dupuis, München Gladbach). Laboratory models of this steamer are made.

(c) High Temperature Steaming

The ICI High Temperature Steamer uses superheated steam to obtain accelerated dye fixation. The print paste contains an addition of urea which aids dye transfer to the polyester fibre. High temperature steaming is a continuous process and no pressure seals are necessary. For 'Terylene', temperatures up to 180°C (360°F) are usually employed with a treatment time of 1 min., or alternatively, a treatment of 5 min at 150°C (300°F) may be given.

(d) Dry Heat (Baking) Fixation

This method operates at the highest temperature range of the four, viz. 180°–200°C and at times of 120–30 s respectively. At these temperatures polyester fabrics will begin to shrink unless restrained. For this reason a high temperature stenter

Table 11.1. SUITABILITY OF 'DISPERSOL' AND 'DURANOL' DYESTUFFS FOR VARIOUS DEVELOPMENT METHODS

'Dispersol' and 'Duranol' Dyestuff	Development Method			
	a	b	c	d
	Atmospheric steaming with carrier	Pressure steaming	High temperature steaming	Dry heat baking
Dispersol Fast Yellow T	N	S	S	S
Procinyl Yellow G	N	S	S	S
Dispersol Fast Yellow G	S	S	S	N
Dispersol Fast Yellow A	S	S	S	S
Dispersol Fast Yellow T3R	N	S	S	S
Dispersol Fast Yellow T4R	S	S	S	S
Dispersol Fast Orange B	S	S	S	S
Dispersol Fast Scarlet B	S	S	S	N
Dispersol Fast Red TB	N	S	S	S
Dispersol Fast Red T3B	N	S	S	S
Duranol Red X3B	S	S	S	S
Dispersol Fast Rubine BT	N	S	S	N
Duranol Turquoise TG	S	S	S	S
Dispersol Navy P-R	N	S	S	N
Dispersol Fast Navy TG	N	S	S	N
Duranol Dark Blue T	S	S	S	S
Duranol Fast Blue T2R	N	S	S	N
Durnaol Blue G	S	S	S	S
Dispersol Fast Brown T3R	N	S	S	N
Dispersol Black P-MF	N	S	S	N
Duranol Direct Black T	S	S	S	S
Dispersol Fast Black T2B	N	S	S	N

S = Suitable   N = Not Suitable

('tenter') is frequently used in industry, since the fabric dimensions are maintained to pre-set levels by the stenter chains to which the fabric is attached by clips or pins, and the process is continuous. Laboratory baking stoves are available which will operate within this temperature range. They may be fitted with a frame to hold the fabric to its original dimensions. This is a discontinuous process intended only for small scale operation, the maximum pattern size which may be processed being limited by the size of the frame that slides in and out of the baker. Dry heat fixation is best avoided when processing 'Crimplene' and other fabrics constructed from stabilised bulked yarns, since loss of bulk may occur.

Table 11.1 lists the suitability of 'Dispersol' and 'Duranol' dyestuffs for these four development methods.

General Printing Recipe for Disperse Dyes

This requires modification according to the development method used. Details of the recommended recipe changes are given in the paragraphs on 'Processing After Printing'.

10–100 parts	'Dispersol' or 'Duranol' dye are dispersed in
360–270 „	water. The dispersion is then stirred into
600 „	thickening (Note 1) containing previously dissolved
10 „	Resist Salt *L* and
20 „	'Perminal' *KB*
1 000 parts.	

Note

(1) Suitable thickenings include 'Manutex' *F* (Alginate Industries), 'Meyprogum' *AC* (Meyhall), 'Indalca' *U* and 'Indalca' *PA/3* (Cesalpinia) for the pressure steaming method), Thickening *301* (Grünau) and an emulsion thickening based on 'Dispersol' *PR* and white spirit with 'Manutex' *F* or 'Indalca' *PA/3* as film former. The latter mentioned thickening is recommended especially when fixation is by dry heat (baking) or by high temperature steaming.

Thickenings should be made slightly acid with acetic acid to avoid any possibility of aggregating the disperse dye pastes.

When using an emulsion thickening replace the anti-frothing agent, 'Perminal' *KB*, by 0·5—1·0 part of 'Silcolapse' *5 000* (ICI).

Recipe Changes and Dye Fixation Processes after Printing

(*a*) Atmospheric Steaming with 'Carrier'
The addition of a suitable carrier is made to the print paste, e.g. 20 parts *p*-hydroxydiphenyl which have previously been dispersed in 100 parts water, per 1 000 parts. Steaming for up to 1 h is carried out at atmospheric pressure. If only pale to medium shades are involved it may be possible to avoid using a carrier and still get an acceptable result in terms of yield of dye.

(*b*) Pressure Steaming
No recipe modifications are required. A steaming treatment of from 20 — 30 min at a pressure of $2·0 \times 10^5 - 1·4 \times 10^5$ N/m² (30—20 lbf/in²) is given.

(*c*) High Temperature Steaming
An addition of 200 parts of urea per 1 000 parts of print paste is made. The use of an emulsion thickening in place of a conventional thickening may prove beneficial in obtaining more rapid dye-to-fibre transfer. Steaming for 1 min at 180°C (355°F) is recommended using the ICI High Temperature Steaming Process[1].

(*d*) Dry Heat (Baking) Fixation
An addition of 100 parts of urea per 1 000 parts of print paste and the use of an emulsion thickening is recommended. A treatment of from 30—120s at 200°—180°C (390°—355°F) is given and the fabric held so as to prevent shrinkage.

Washing-Off

After fixing the dyestuff by one of the four methods just described, the fabric is rinsed in cold water and then treated for 5—10 min at 65°—70°C (150°—160°F) in a solution containing 2 parts of 'Lissapol' *ND* per 1 000 parts of water. This treatment is followed by a further rinse in cold water and then drying. With patterns containing deep shades and/or a considerable proportion of 'fall-ons', a 'reduction

clearing' treatment should be inserted between the water rinse and the
warm 'Lissapol' *ND* treatment. This enables the maximum brilliance and
fastness to be obtained. 'Reduction clearing' consists of treating the
fabric for 10 – 20 min at 50°C (120°F) in a solution of:

2 parts		caustic soda flakes
2	,,	'Lissolamine' *RC*
2	,,	sodium hydrosulphite, adding
water to	1000 parts.	

In addition to choosing dyestuffs for 'Terylene' according to their
suitability for fixation by an available method, it may be important to
meet specified end use suitability requirements. *Table 11.2* gives those
'Dispersol' and 'Duranol' dyestuffs classified according to their end use
suitability for the ICI Fibres Ltd. labelling scheme.

Table 11.2. END USE SUITABILITY OF 'DISPERSOL' AND 'DURANOL' DYES
ON 'TERYLENE' POLYESTER FIBRE

'Dispersol' and 'Duranol' Dyestuff	End Use Suitability			
	Furnishings	*Furnishings (supplementary)*	*Rainwear, swimwear*	*Dress goods*
Dispersol Fast Yellow T	S	S	S	S
Procinyl Yellow G	N	N	S	S
Dispersol Fast Yellow G	N	N	S	S
Dispersol Fast Yellow A	S	S	S	S
Dispersol Fast Yellow T3R	N	S	S	S
Dispersol Fast Yellow T4R	S	S	S	S
Dispersol Fast Orange B	S	S	S	S
Dispersol Fast Scarlet B	N	N	N	S
Dispersol Fast Red TB	N	N	S	S
Dispersol Fast Red T3B	S	S	S	S
Duranol Red X3B	N	N	S	S
Dispersol Fast Rubine BT	S	S	S	S
Duranol Turquoise TG	S	S	S	S
Dispersol Navy P-R	N	N	N	S
Dispersol Fast Navy T2G	S	S	S	S
Duranol Dark Blue T	N	N	S	S
Duranol Fast Blue T2R	S	S	S	S
Duranol Blue G	N	S	S	S
Dispersol Fast Brown T3R	N	N	S	S
Dispersol Black P-MF	N	N	N	S
Duranol Direct Black T	N	S	S	S
Dispersol Fast Black T2B	N	N	S	S

S = Suitable for this outlet   N = Not suitable

Detailed fastness properties of selected 'Duranol' and 'Dispersol' dyes
are given in *Table 11.3*. A wider selection of fastness tests, mainly in
relation to pleating fastness is to be found in Reference 2.

Table 11.3. FASTNESS PROPERTIES OF DISPERSE DYES PRINTED ON 'TERYLENE'

Disperse Dye	Light (Daylight) 1/1 Standard depth	Washing I.S.O. Wash Test No. 4 30 min at 95°C (200°F)		Pleating (dry heat) 30s at 180°C (355°F)		Pleating (dry heat) 30s at 210°C (410°F)	
		Effect on print	Stain on polyester	Effect on print	Stain on polyester	Effect on print	Stain on polyester
Dispersol Fast Yellow T	7R	4–5	5	5	4–5	5	3–4
Procinyl Yellow G	6	5	5	5	5	5	5
Dispersol Fast Yellow G	7	4–5	5	4	3	4	2
Dispersol Fast Yellow A	7	4–5	5	4–5	4–5	4–5	3
Dispersol Fast Yellow T3R	6	5	5	4–5S	5	4S	4–5
Dispersol Fast Yellow T4R	6–7	4–5R	5	4–5S	4–5	4–5S	4
Dispersol Fast Orange B	7	4–5	5	5	4	4	3–4
Dispersol Fast Scarlet B	4	4–5	5	5	3	4	2
Dispersol Fast Red TB	5	5	5	5	4–5	5	4–5
Dispersol Fast Red T3B	6–7	4–5	5	5	4	4–5	3
Duranol Red X3B	5–6	4–5	4–5	4–5	3–4	4	2
Dispersol Fast Rubine BT	6–7	4–5	4–5	5	4	5	4
Duranol Turquoise TG	7	4–5R	5	4–5	4	4–5	2–3
Dispersol Navy P-R	5	4–5	5	5	4	4–5	3
Dispersol Fast Navy T2G	6	4–5	5	4–5S	5	4S	3–4
Duranol Dark Blue T	6R	4–5	4–5	5	3–4	4–5	2
Duranol Fast Blue T2R	6–7	4–5	4–5	4–5S	5	4S	4–5
Duranol Blue G	6	4–5	4–5	4–5	3–4	4	2
Dispersol Fast Brown T3R	5–6	5	5	5	4	4–5	4
Dispersol Black P-MF	5	4–5	5	5	4	4–5	2
Duranol Direct Black T	6	4–5	3–4	5	3–4	4	2
Dispersol Fast Black T2B	5–6	4–5	5	4–5	4–5	4–5	4

R = redder   S = stronger

A union fabric is one that is composed of more than one fibre and this effect may be achieved by weaving:

(a) A warp composed of a spun blend of two or more fibres with a weft yarn composed of a spun blend of two or more fibres *or* a weft yarn composed of a single fibre.

(b) A warp composed of yarns containing only one fibre and weft yarns composed of a different fibre.

A fabric of type (b) may be designed to exploit the presence of two different fibres, e.g. by dyeing the two fibres in contrasting shades. In textile printing, fabrics of type (a) are more frequently encountered. The object of fibre blending is generally to obtain an improvement in the physical properties of the resulting fabric. Alternatively, a more expensive fibre may be blended with a less expensive one in proportions which represent a compromise between optimum properties and price. In either event, since the desired end product of blending is fabric properties, it is far more usual for the dyer or printer to be expected to produce solid shades (i.e. those in which the two fibres appear coloured to equal depths) on blended fabrics. The printing of polyester/cellulosic blends provides an interesting example of how this problem is approached. Three polyester/cotton blends are normally available containing respectively 80/20, 67/33 and 50/50 polyester/cotton. Depending on the fabric construction and the depth of shade required it is often possible to print polyester/cotton 80/20 blends solely with disperse dyes. The fact that the cotton fibres have not been penetrated by the disperse dye is not obvious because surface staining of these fibres by disperse dye particles has occurred.

Printing of a 67/33 or a 50/50 'Terylene'/cotton blend involves coloration of both fibres. Since 'Terylene' is not coloured by water soluble dyes, 'Procion' and other reactive dyes are fixed only on the cotton fraction. Conversely, cotton is not usefully coloured by insoluble dyes unless they are formed *in situ* or made to undergo a solubilisation stage.

Vat Dyestuffs

An interesting development took place in 1957[3] when Müller *et al.* of Cassella introduced the 'Polyestren' ranges for dyeing and printing. These were vat dyestuffs carefully chosen for their ability to colour polyester fibres under dry heat conditions. This property was assisted by the extremely fine state of division of the vat dyes compared with pastes intended for cellulosic fibre printing. When printing vat dyes on cotton, too fine a particle size leads to low printing efficiency, and too coarse a particle size to the production of specks. The process adopted with the 'Polyestren' dyes on polyester/cotton blends involved two stages:

1. Dry heat fixation for 45–60 s at 200°C (390°F) to enable the 'Polyestren' dye to penetrate the polyester fibre.
2. Padding the fabric in a reducing solution and then steaming, i.e. using a flash ageing process. At this stage the reduced vat dye was able to colour the cellulosic fibre.

Another factor limiting the choice of vat dyes available for 'Polyestren' dyes used on polyester-cellulosic blends is the possibility that there may be appreciable differences in shade and fastness properties between the same dye on the two fibres. Such dyes would be excluded from the 'Polyestren' range.

'Dispersol' and 'Duranol' Dyes Combined with 'Procion' Dyes

This method aims to colour the two components of a polyester-cellulosic blend with two dyestuff ranges, one for each fibre. It has the advantage that a low cost single stage fixation process is used to fix both dye classes. A wide range of attractive shades of good all-round fastness can be obtained.

For information on the preparation of polyester/cellulosic fibre blends prior to printing reference should be made to the fibre manufacturers. In the case of regenerated cellulosic fibres, e.g. 'Vincel' (Courtaulds) a polynosic viscose rayon fibre, the pre-treatment may well differ from when cotton is present in the blend. Information on the preparation of blends containing 'Terylene' polyester fibre is available from ICI Fibres Limited, Harrogate, Yorkshire, England, or their publications. Maximum colour value is obtained on polyester/cellulosic blends if the fabric preparation includes mercerisation or causticisation.

To enhance the overall appearance of the print, 'Fluolite' *XMF* Paste (a fluorescent brightening agent for synthetic fibres) is applied. Prior to printing, pad the fabric in a solution containing two parts of 'Fluolite' *XMF* Paste per 1 000 parts of water, then dry. The optical brightening agent will become fixed on the 'Terylene' in the blend at the dye fixation stage. To achieve maximum brightness and solidity of shade on a particular polyester/cellulose blend, match the shade required with 'Duranol' or 'Dispersol' dyes on the polyester in pre-liminary tests. Next, rematch the shade on mercerised or causticised cotton using 'Procion' reactive dyes. These two matchings combined together will form the basis for obtaining the required match on the fibre blend. Attention is drawn to a useful technique for separating the fibre components of such blends in order to check the shades and depths achieved[4].

Printing Recipe (Conventional Thickening)

20–100 parts	'Dispersol' or 'Duranol' dye are dispersed in
345–225 „	water. The dispersion is then stirred into
500 „	thickening (see Note 1) containing (previously dissolved)
100 „	urea
10 „	Resist Salt L and
15 „	sodium bicarbonate. Finally, sprinkle in while stirring with a high speed stirrer
10–50 „	'Procion' dye
<u>1 000</u> parts.	

Note
(1) Since 'Procion' dyes are present the thickening must be a sodium alginate type. 'Manutex' F (Alginate Inds.) has been found satisfactory. Alternatively, a semi-emulsion thickening in which 'Manutex' F acts as a film former, may be used.

Preparation of an Emulsion Thickening

Two techniques are available, but both require a high speed stirrer (1 000 rev/min or faster), e.g. a 'Greaves' Mixer[5].

Method 1. An emulsion thickening (o/w) is prepared without film former using 'Dispersol' PR as emulsifying agent. A sodium alginate thickening is prepared separately. The two thickenings are mixed together to form a semi-emulsion thickening (*half-emulsion* thickening is an analogous term). Depending on the operating method preferred, this mixed sodium alginate/emulsion thickening is incorporated

153

either directly in a print paste or used for the preparation of a stock thickening containing the remaining print paste ingredients.

Method 2. A solution of 'Dispersol' *PR* is prepared containing the auxiliary products required for the fixation of the dye. To this solution either a previously prepared solution of sodium alginate or dry sodium alginate powder, is stirred in. Next, using high speed stirring the white spirit or other hydro-carbon oil is slowly added to form a semi-emulsion.

Method 2 is more readily adapted to give final print paste viscosities higher than those obtainable by Method 1, and so it is the recommended technique where very viscous pastes are required, e.g. on flat-bed or rotary screen printing machines.

Printing Recipe (Emulsion Thickening – Method 2)

100	parts	urea
10	,,	Resist Salt *L*
15	,,	sodium bicarbonate
1·5	,,	'Calgon' *PT* (sodium hexameta-phosphate) and
4·5	,,	'Dispersol' *PR* are dissolved in
330	,,	Water at 60°–70°C (140°–160°F). To this solution (after cooling) is added, with high speed stirring,
16	,,	'Manutex' *F* powder followed by
320	,,	white spirit or distillate, etc. Stirring is continued until the mixture is thoroughly emulsified. Then
20–100	,,	'Dispersol' or 'Duranol' dye are dispersed in
173–53	,,	water and mixed and stirred into the thickening. Finally,
10–50	,,	'Procion' dye are sprinkled in with high speed stirring.
1 000	parts.	

Process after Printing

The printed and dried goods are developed by one of the following methods:

either   Dry Heat (Baking). Treat for 60 s at 200°C (390°F)

or   High Temperature Steaming. Steam for 60 s at 180°–190°C
            (355°–375°F) using the ICI High Temperature Steaming
            Process

or   Pressure Steaming. Steam for 20–30 min at a pressure of
            $1 \cdot 4 \times 10^5$ N/m² (20 lbf/in²).

Washing-Off

This is one of the most important stages since there are two classes of
dyestuff present, and all possible precautions must be taken to prevent
the unprinted areas of the fabric becoming soiled by unfixed dye. The
'Procion' dye will have been chosen for printing on the grounds of its
lack of staining of cotton during washing-off; being sulphonated, it will
not stain the polyester fibre, and the surplus disperse dye will not be
subjected to sufficiently high temperatures to dye back heavily on to
the polyester component. The potential staining arises from the disperse dyes originally printed on to both polyester and cotton, but not
fixed on the latter. On washing-off the disperse dye is readily removed
from the printed cotton, but a proportion of it is redeposited on the
surface of cotton and 'Terylene' fibres in the unprinted areas. To
minimise this difficulty, additions of activated charcoal are made to
the washing-off bath to absorb the disperse dye preferentially and
reduce the amount available to be deposited on the cotton. The
recommended washing-off sequence for polyester/cotton fabrics is as
follows:

1. Rinse thoroughly in an ample supply of cold water.
2. Treat for 5 min at or near the boil in a liquor containing 2 parts of
   'Lissapol' *N* and 2–4 parts of activated charcoal per 1 000 parts of
   water, e.g. 'Actibon' *S* or activated charcoal Grade 338. [6] A liquor
   to goods ratio of approximately 30:1 is recommended and this is
   achieved conveniently using a winch which should preferably be
   constructed of metal rather than wood. To reduce the possibility
   of dusting and consequent contamination of white goods, etc., by
   the dry activated charcoal powder, it is recommended that, prior
   to use in the washing-off sequence, the activated charcoal be pasted
   with an equal weight of 'Lissapol' *N*.
3. Rinse thoroughly in cold water preferably using a spray rinse to
   facilitate the removal of adhering particles of activated charcoal.
4. Treat for 5 min at 60°C (140°F) in a solution containing 2 parts
   'Lissapol' *N* per 1 000 parts of water.
5. Rinse thoroughly in cold water and dry.

SELECTION OF DISPERSE AND REACTIVE DYES FOR PRINTING POLYESTER/CELLULOSIC BLENDS

'Dispersol' and 'Duranol' Dyes

Table 11.4 gives the suitability of certain disperse dyes for various development methods when used in printing 'Terylene'/cotton 67/33 blends.

Table 11.4. SUITABILITY OF DISPERSE DYES FOR VARIOUS DEVELOPMENT METHODS WHEN USED IN PRINTING 'TERYLENE'/COTTON 67/33 BLENDS

Disperse Dye	Development Method		
	Dry heat	*High temperature steaming*	*Pressure steaming*
Dispersol Fast Yellow T Liquid	R	R	R
Dispersol Fast Yellow T3R Liquid	R	R	R
Dispersol Fast Yellow T4R Liquid	R	R	R
Dispersol Fast Orange B Liquid	R	R	R
Dispersol Fast Scarlet TR Liquid	N	R	R
Dispersol Fast Scarlet B Liquid	N	R	R
Dispersol Fast Red TR Liquid	R	R	R
Duranol Red X3B Liquid	N	R	R
Dispersol Fast Rubine BT Liquid	R	R	R
Duranol Blue G Liquid	N	R	R
Duranol Fast Blue T2R Liquid	R	R	R
Dispersol Fast Navy T2G Liquid	R	R	R
Duranol Turquoise TG Liquid	R, PM	R	R
Dispersol Fast Brown T3R Liquid	R	R	R
Duranol Direct Black T Liquid	N	R	R
Dispersol Fast Black T2B Liquid	R	R	R

R = Recommended for this dye
N = Method not recommended for this dye
PM = Pale to medium shades only

'Procion' Dyes

All 'Procion' H and 'Procion' Supra dyes recommended for printing cellulosic fibres are suitable[7]. A few 'Procion' H dyes and 'Procion' M dyes which have been developed specifically for dyeing purposes are not recommended, primarily because they stain the cellulosic portion of the fibre during washing-off. In *Table 11.5* the main fastness properties of selected 'Duranol', 'Dispersol' and 'Procion' mixtures are given. The members of the disperse and reactive dyes used have been chosen to give similar shades on the polyester and cotton portions of the fabric.

PRINTING WITH PIGMENT PRINTING COMPOSITIONS

Many modern pigment printing systems are printed on polyester/cellulosic unions occasionally using the water-in-oil system, but more frequently the oil-in-water types. When the emulsion containing the pigment and binding resin is printed on a polyester/cellulosic blend, the emulsion breaks. The distribution of pigment and binder between the two fibres is uneven, and microscopically it may be seen that more is attached to the cellulosic fibres than to the polyester fibres. Visually, however, the fabric appears to be printed in a solid shade. To obtain optimum fastness to rubbing and maintain the fabric handle it is necessary to balance out the various print paste additives, resin binders, cross-linking agents, etc. according to the recommendations of the makers of the particular system in use. A typical system is the 'Hifast' *W* system* of Inmont, USA (formerly Interchemical Corp.)[8]. The example given in the next paragraph relates to a roller printing recipe. To modify such a recipe for screen printing it would be necessary to reduce proportionally the pigment content, the resin binder (carrier) and fixative (cross-linking agent). A reduction of around 40% should be made as a first step and further smaller adjustments made as required.

'Hifast' carrier stock paste (oil-in-water system) is prepared as follows:

35 parts (by volume)	'Hifast' Carrier *59124* are diluted with
35 „ (by volume)	water using a high speed stirrer (Note 1). When mixed,
165 „ (by volume)	water are stirred in followed by
800 „ (by volume)	white spirit, distillate or other 'safety solvent'. The solvent is added more slowly as the full amount is reached, as the viscosity rises rapidly.

1 000 parts (by volume).

* Supplied in the UK by Tennants Textile Colours, Belfast.

Table 11.5. EXAMPLES OF MIXTURES OF 'DISPERSOL' AND 'DURANOL' DYES WITH 'PROCION' DYES: FASTNESS ON A CAUSTICISED 'TERYLENE'/COTTON (67/33) BLEND

Dye Mixture	Parts of dye per 1 000 parts of print paste	Light (daylight) 1/1 standard depth	Washing I.S.O. Wash Test No. 4 30 min at 95°C (200°F) Effect on Print	Washing Stain	Pleating (dry heat) 30 s at 180°C (355°F) Effect on Print	Pleating Stain	Pleating (dry heat) 30 s at 210°C (410°F) Effect on Print	Pleating Stain
Dispersol Fast Yellow T Liquid Procion Supra Yellow H-4GP	75 35	7	4–5	5 (T) 5 (C)	5	4–5 (T) 4–5 (C)	5	3–4 (T) 4 (C)
Dispersol Fast Yellow T3R Liquid Procion Supra Yellow H-4GP Procion Supra Yellow H-2RP	100 20 3	5–6	4–5	5 (T) 3–4 (C)	5	5 (T) 5 (C)	5	5 (T) 5 (C)
Dispersol Fast Yellow T4R Liquid Procion Supra Yellow H-2RP	50 25	5	4–5	5 (T) 5 (C)	5	5 (T) 5 (C)	5	4 (T) 4–5 (C)
Dispersol Fast Orange B Liquid Procion Golden Yellow H-R Procion Orange H-4R	50 15 10	6	4–5	5 (T) 5 (C)	4–5	4–5 (T) 4–5 (C)	4–5	4 (T) 4–5 (C)
Dispersol Fast Scarlet TR Liquid Procion Scarlet H-RN	75 25	5	5	5 (T) 4–5 (C)	4–5	4 (T) 4 (C)	4	3 (T) 3 (C)
Dispersol Fast Scarlet B Liquid Procion Scarlet H-RN	50 25	4	4–5	5 (T) 5 (C)	4–5	3–4 (T) 4 (C)	4	2 (T) 2 (C)
Dispersol Fast Red TB Liquid Procion Brilliant Red H-3BN Procion Supra Yellow H-2RP	40 15 1	5	5	5 (T) 5 (C)	5	5 (T) 5 (C)	5	4–5 (T) 4–5 (C)
Duranol Red X3B Liquid Procion Brilliant Red H-8B Procion Brilliant Purple H-3R	75 14 3	4–5	4–5	4–5 (T) 4–5 (C)	4–5	3–4 (T) 3–4 (C)	4	2 (T) 3 (C)

Dye	Amount							
Dispersol Fast Rubine BT Liquid	50	5–6	4–5	4–5 (T)	5	4–5 (T)	5	4 (T)
Procion Brilliant Red H-8B	15			4–5 (C)		5 (C)		4 (C)
Procion Brilliant Purple H-3R	6							
Duranol Turquoise TG Liquid	150	6–7	4	5 (T)	5	4–5 (T)	4–5	3 (T)
Procion Turquoise H-A	30			4 (C)		5 (C)		4 (C)
Procion Brilliant Blue H-3R	15							
Dispersol Fast Navy T2G Liquid	150	5–6	5	5 (T)	5	5 (T)	4 (S)	4–5 (T)
Procion Blue H-5R	50			5 (C)		5 (C)		5 (C)
Procion Supra Black H-LP	7·5							
Duranol Fast Blue T2R Liquid	100	6	5	5 (T)	5	5 (T)	4–5	4–5 (T)
Procion Brilliant Blue H-3R	60			5 (C)		5 (C)		4–5 (C)
Duranol Blue G Liquid	100	5–6	4–5	4–5 (T)	4–5	4 (T)	4	3 (T)
Procion Brilliant Blue H-3R	30			4–5 (C)		4–5 (C)		4 (C)
Procion Supra Turquoise H-2GP	15							
Dispersol Fast Brown T3R Liquid	100	5	5	5 (T)	5	5 (T)	4–5	4 (T)
Procion Orange H-4R	50			4 (C)		5 (C)		4–5 (C)
Duranol Direct Black T Liquid	150	6	4–5	4 (T)	5	4 (T)	4	2–3 (T)
Procion Supra Black H-LP	60			4–5 (C)		4 (C)		3 (C)
Dispersol Fast Black T2B Liquid	200	6	4–5	5 (T)	5	4–5 (T)	5	4–5 (T)
Procion Supra Black H-LP	60			5 (C)		4–5 (C)		4–5 (C)

S = stronger   C = cotton   T = 'Terylene'

Note

(1)   The dilution of a carrier (resin binder) with a small amount of water in this manner is termed *pre-cutting* in N. America. The pre-cut carrier is then *cut* (i.e. reduced or diluted) further to form a stable emulsion of high viscosity.

The print paste is prepared according to the strength of the pigment required, as follows:

Colour strength	Amount of 'Hifast' fixative	Amount of 'Hifast' carrier stock paste
30%–10%	15%	55%–75%
10%–2%	10%	80%–88%
2% or less	5%	93% or more

The pattern card from which this data was abstracted illustrates a range of nearly thirty 'Hifast' *W* colours printed on a 67/33 polyester/cotton blend and fixed by curing (baking) for 2 min at 175°C (350°F).[8] Readers wishing for further information of the printing of 'Terylene' and 'Terylene' blends should refer to the following Technical Information Notes "D" Series, published by ICI Dyestuffs Division:

No. D 568   "Printing of 'Terylene'/Wool Fibre Unions"
No. D 979   "Printing of Polyester Fibres"
No. D 980   "Dispersol, Duranol and Procinyl Dyes: Textile Printing Review"
No. D 1088   "The use of Activated Charcoal as a Washing-off Agent"
No. D 1099   "Printing of Polyester/Cellulosic Blended Fabrics"

REFERENCES

1. The brochure entitled *The ICI High Temperature Steaming Process,* ICI Dyestuffs Division (Ref. 15351), lists the names of manufacturers of commercial high temperature steamers
2. Technical Information Note D. 979, *Printing of Polyester Fibres,* issued by ICI Dyestuffs Divison, 13 Dec. 67
3. MULLER, J., WALKER, R. and ILG, H., *Melliand Textilberichte, 38,* 1032–1043 (1957)
4. Technical Information Note D. 1051, *A simple method of separating the fibre components in dyed polyester/cellulose blends*
5. The Greaves High-Speed Mixers are supplied in a variety of sizes by Joshua Greaves & Sons Ltd., Ramsbottom, Nr. Manchester, England
6. 'Actibon' *S* is supplied by the Clydesdale Chemical Co. Ltd., 142, Queen Street, Glasgow C1, Scotland. Recommended usage is 2 parts/1 000 parts of wash liquor. Activated Charcoal Grade 338 is supplied by Sutcliffe Speakman and Co. Ltd, Leigh, Lancashire, England. Recommended usage is 4 parts/1 000 parts of wash liquor
7. *Pattern Card Procion Dyes – Printing* (Ref. 14570), ICI Dyestuffs Division
8. *Pattern Card Hifast System for Roller Printing.* Interchemical Corporation, Hawthorne, New Jersey, USA (1966). *Note:* Interchemical Corporation is now renamed *Inmont*

12

The Printing of Cellulose Acetate and Cellulose Triacetate

The chemical differences between cellulose acetate and cellulose triacetate have been outlined in Chapter 1. There are also physical differences, cellulose triacetate takes up less moisture than cellulose acetate and is less easily penetrated by dyestuffs. The use of swelling agents or more rigorous fixation conditions is necessary with cellulose triacetate, but once a dyestuff is fixed on this fibre it invariably shows better wet fastness than on cellulose acetate itself. Because of these differences in behaviour it is most important to determine which cellulose derivative is present before printing. This is best done by testing the fibre for solubility in an acetone/water mixture (see Chapter 1). Cellulose triacetate is not soluble in this solvent mixture. The term *acetate rayon* invariably refers to the secondary acetate but confusion does sometimes occur. Trademarks are of more assistance, e.g. 'Dicel' and 'Tricel' (Courtaulds) easily distinguish cellulose diacetate from cellulose triacetate while 'Arnel' (Celanese Corp. of America) refers only to cellulose triacetate in filament or staple form. Occasionally, a blend of cellulose triacetate with another fibre is given a separate trademark, e.g. 'Tricelon' (Courtaulds) is a blend of 65:35 'Tricel'/'Celon', i.e. cellulose triacetate and nylon 6, marketed by Courtaulds. Such blends are dealt with separately later in this chapter.

The dyestuffs used for printing cellulosic and protein fibres usually give little or no colour value on acetate rayon fabrics, and when this fibre was introduced it was necessary to devise special ranges of dyes capable of dyeing and printing it satisfactorily. The 'Dispersol' and 'Duranol' dyes were developed for this purpose, and in recent years 'Procinyl' dyes have also been used. 'Procinyl' dyes do not react with these fibres but function as disperse dyes giving very good wet fastness properties. All three ranges are suitable for printing both cellulose acetate and cellulose triacetate fabrics. The makers of 'Tricel' recommend that it should be given an *S* finish before printing. This is a controlled surface saponification of the fibre using caustic soda. If the

161

treatment is overdone the dye uptake will be depressed, so in industry the treatment is carried out until the bulk matches up to a control pattern. The result of the treatment is to produce a thin layer of cellulose around the cellulose triacetate fibres. This increases the moisture uptake at the surface and minimises the formation of static charges on the fabric.

'Procinyl', 'Dispersol' and 'Duranol' dyestuffs are insoluble in water and for printing are usually applied in the form of finely divided pastes. These are termed either *PQ* pastes or *liquid* brands. In the occasional case where these brands are not available then the 'Grain' or 'Powder Fine' brands normally used only for dyeing may be considered. In preparing the initial concentration needed to form a print paste, care must be taken with the powder brands to ensure that sufficient time is allowed for dispersion to ensure that specks are not apparent on the final print.

THE PRINTING OF CELLULOSE ACETATE

Printing Recipe

A typical printing recipe for the printing of cellulose acetate with 'Dispersol', 'Duranol' and 'Procinyl' dyes is as follows:

10–100 parts	'Dispersol', 'Duranol' or 'Procinyl' dye are dispersed in
360–270 ,,	water
	The dispersion is then stirred into
600 ,,	thickening (Note 1) containing previously dissolved
10 ,,	Resist Salt *L*
20 ,,	'Perminal' *KB*
1 000 parts.	

Notes
(1) Suitable thickenings, which should be made slightly acid with acetic acid, include 'Manutex' *F* (Alginate Industries), 'Nafka' Crystal Gum (Scholtens) — not recommended for high temperature steaming, 'Meyprogum' *AC* (Meyhall), 'Indalca' *U* and 'Indalca' *PA/3* (Cesalpina), Thickening *301* (Grünau) and an emulsion or semi-emulsion thickening (based on 'Dispersol' *PR* with 'Manutex' *F* or 'Indalca' *PA/3* as film former).
(2) If steaming conditions are particularly dry and low yields of 'Procinyl' dye are experienced, additions of from 50–100 parts

162

urea/1 000 parts of print paste, will prove beneficial. However, under moist steaming conditions loss of definition in the print may occur if urea is present in too large a quantity.

(3)   'Procinyl' dyes prepared by this recipe may be stored for prolonged periods without significant loss in printing strength.

(4)   'Procinyl' dyes are recommended for use in compound shades and form predictable mixtures. Disperse and 'Procinyl' dyes are also compatible with each other.

(5)   'Perminal' *KB* is included in the printing recipe to facilitate wetting-out of the fabric and so give prints of a smoother appearance.

(6)   Resist Salt *L* (sodium *m*-nitrobenzene sulphonate) is a mild oxidising agent. Its function is to safeguard against possible decomposition of dyestuffs by reduction during steaming.

(7)   In order to prevent prints from marking-off during steaming it is advisable to wrap them in grey (greige) cotton cloth. Care should also be taken that no drops of moisture come into contact with the printed cloth during steaming. The grey cloth used in the steaming treatment should be washed regularly to avoid it marking-back onto the printed lengths.

Processing after Printing

The printed and dried fabric may be developed by *either*

(a)   Steaming for 30 min at atmospheric pressure (see notes 2 and 7 above) *or*

(b)   Making an addition of 200 parts urea per 1 000 parts of print paste and steaming for 1 min at 150°C (300°F) using the ICI High Temperature Steaming Process.

After development, the goods are rinsed well in cold water, treated for 3 min at 40°C (105°F) in a solution containing 2 parts of 'Lissapol' *ND* per 1 000 parts of water, rinsed again in cold water, then dried.

Fastness Properties

Disperse dyes enable a good level of fastness to light and washing to be achieved on cellulose acetate. Certain dyes on this fibre are liable to undergo an unusual shade change, to which the term *gas fume fading* has been given. The change in shade, which is irreversible, is most pronounced with some blue disperse dyes and consequently also affects brown and grey mixture shades containing these blues. The causes of the shade changes are nitrogen oxides produced during the combustion

Table 12.1. 'DURANOL', 'DISPERSOL' AND 'PROCINYL' DYES PRINTED ON CELLULOSE ACETATE

'Duranol', 'Dispersol' and 'Procinyl' Dye	Light (daylight) 1/1 Standard depth	Washing I.S.O. Test No. 3 30 min at 60°C (140°F) Effect	Staining of adjacent Acetate	Viscose rayon	Burnt gas fumes
Dispersol Fast Yellow T	7	4	4	5	5
Procinyl Yellow G	5–6	5	5	5	5
Dispersol Fast Yellow T4R	6	4–5	4–5	4–5	5
Dispersol Fast Yellow A	5–6	3	3	3	5
Dispersol Fast Orange B	6–7	4	4	4–5	5
Dispersol Fast Orange A	6.	3Y	2	4–5	5
Procinyl Orange G	5	5	5	5	5
Dispersol Fast Scarlet B	4–5	4	3–4	4–5	5
Procinyl Scarlet G	5	4–5	4–5	5	5
Dispersol Fast Red R	4–5	3	3–4	4–5	5
Dispersol Fast Red TB	5	4–5	5	5	5
Dispersol Fast Red T3B	6–7	4	4	4	5
Procinyl Red G	5–6	5	5	5	5
Duranol Red X3B	5	3	3	4	3Y
Dispersol Fast Rubine BT	6	3	3–4	5	5
Duranol Printing Violet B	5R	2	2	4	3R
Duranol Printing Blue B	5	2	2	4–5	3–4R
Duranol Blue G	5	2	3	4–5	3–4R
Procinyl Blue R	5–6R	4–5	4–5	5	3–4RD
Dispersol Navy P-R	4–5	3	4	4–5	4–5R
Duranol Dark Blue T	4–5R	3	2	4	3–4RD
Duranol Blue Green B	6–7	3	3	4	4–5R
Dispersol Fast Brown T3R	5–6	4–5	4–5	5	5
Dispersol Black PMF	4–5	4	4	5	5
Duranol Direct Black T	5R	3	2	4–5	3–4R

D = duller, R = redder, Y = yellower

of gas, coal, oil, etc., and when air is passed over heated filaments. Since the widespread build up in the air of nitrogen oxides to a concentration sufficient to bring about shade changes in printed disperse blues is fortunately very rare, only sporadic fading occurs which may be localised on a particular piece of fabric.

Typical examples would be exposed folds of cloth in a warehouse where contamination from traffic fumes or persistent foggy weather caused the fabric folds to fade to a different shade than the body of the cloth, which would be protected. A garment hung in a wardrobe near which a gas fire was regularly used would also be liable to this type of fading. The Colour Fastness to Burnt-Gas Fumes (Nitrogen oxides)[1] describes the test apparatus used and produces the nitrogen oxides by mixing a solution of phosphoric acid with sodium nitrite. There are two ways in which difficulties due to gas fume fading may be avoided. Firstly, a 'gas-fume fast' disperse blue may be used in which the chemical structure has been changed to resist attack by nitrogen oxides. These blues are either much more expensive than the average 'Duranol'-type blue, or if azoic derivatives, lack the high light fastness associated with the anthraquinone-based 'Duranol' blues. The 'Dispersol', 'Duranol' and 'Procinyl' dyes recommended for printing cellulose acetate together with details of their more important fastness properties are given in *Table 12.1*.

Fading Due to Ozone in the Atmosphere

It was demonstrated in 1937 that minute quantities of oxides of nitrogen in the atmosphere produced reddening of the shade of certain disperse blue dyes on cellulose acetate. However, in 1955 Salvin[2] reported the fading of a number of gas fume fast-disperse blues to a much larger extent than would have been predicted by the Burnt Gas Fastness test. A detailed investigation uncovered another form of fading due to the presence of minute quantities of ozone in the atmosphere. Dyes were classified according to their sensitivity to *O-fading* on cellulose acetate and also on various fibres including acrylics, polyester nylon and cellulose triacetate. Fibres other than cellulose acetate were much less liable to 'O-fading', particularly if the dye fixation process had included a heat treatment stage giving rise to good penetration of the dye into the fibre. The use of gas fume fading inhibitors on cellulose acetate for protection against burnt gas fumes tended to mask the effect of ozone fading where both gases were present, since the inhibitor afforded a degree of protection against both agents.

Fastness testing for resistance to ozone has been studied in the USA and the current methods are described in the AATCC Technical Manual[3]. These take into account the fact that a greater degree of fading is likely to happen in the presence of ozone when the humidity is high.

THE PRINTING OF CELLULOSE TRIACETATE

The recipe for printing 'Dispersol', 'Duranol' and 'Procinyl' dyes on cellulose triacetate is very similar to that used for cellulose acetate, except that to obtain good yields by steaming at atmospheric pressure the addition of a 'carrier' is necessary. An alternative to the use of a carrier is steaming under pressure. By adjusting the recipe the ICI High-Temperature steaming process may be used.

Printing Recipe

The basic printing recipe is as follows:

10–100 parts	'Dispersol', 'Duranol' or 'Procinyl' dye are dispersed in
360–270 ,,	water.
600 ,,	The dispersion is then stirred into thickening (Note 1) containing (previously dissolved)
10 ,,	Resist Salt L and
20 ,,	'Perminal' KB
1 000 parts.	

Notes
(1) Suitable thickenings include all those listed under the recipe for cellulose acetate.
(2) Adjustments are made to this recipe according to the method chosen for fixing the dyestuffs (see below).

Processing after Printing

A choice of three development methods may be made depending on the available equipment. They are:

(a) Steaming for 30 min at a pressure of 7×10^4 N/m² (10 lbf/in²). If steaming conditions are dry make an addition of from 50 to 100 parts of urea per 1 000 parts of print paste, *or*

(b) For atmospheric steaming it is necessary to add a 'carrier' to the print paste. Neither 'Tumescal' *PH* nor 'Tumescal' *PCA* are currently marketed by ICI, although they were formerly widely used for this purpose. The addition of 30–50 parts 'Glyezin' *PFD* (BASF) per 1 000 parts of print paste is recommended. With this addition good colour yields are obtained by steaming for 30 min under atmospheric pressure, *or*

166

(c)   Making an addition of 200 parts of urea per 1 000 parts of
      print paste and steaming for 1 min at 180°C (355°F) using the
      ICI High Temperature Steaming Process.

After development the fabric should be rinsed well in cold water
and then treated for 5 min at 50°C (120°F) in a solution containing
2 parts 'Lissapol' *ND* per 1 000 parts. This is followed by a further
rinse in cold water and drying.

Dye Selection

The main fastness properties of 'Procinyl', 'Dispersol' and 'Duranol'
dyestuffs are given in *Table 12.2*. In addition, the dyes recommended
by Courtaulds for use on *S*-finish 'Tricel' for their 'Tricel' labelling
scheme are indicated. The dyes recommended by Amcel Europe SA
for the printing of 'Arnel' cellulose triacetate are also noted.

Printing with Acid Dyestuffs

Around 1965 there was considerable interest among dye and fibre
makers in processes which enabled selected acid dyes to be fixed on
'Arnel' and 'Tricel'. Many years earlier, printing processes for acid
dyes on cellulose acetate had been investigated. The cellulose acetate
processes used swelling agents which enabled the acid dye to penetrate
the fibre during steaming, where it remained after the swelling agent
had been removed. Attempts to evolve new processes for cellulose
triacetate were faced with similar problems, e.g. the swelling agent
must be powerful enough to allow the dye to penetrate the fibre but
not so powerful that the fibre is damaged. A second condition was
that a sufficient number of dyes were compatible with the swelling
agents used. Acid dyes and 1:2 premetallised dyes (i.e. acid dyes
where two molecules are bridged by a metal atom) formed the basis of
a range, but in addition work was done with water-insoluble 1:2 premetallised dyes. A technical bulletin published in December, 1965, by
the Celanese Fibres Marketing Company, USA[4] summarises the position
and gives details of five processes. These processes which are
distinguished by the name of the dye makers or fibre maker who
originated them are listed in *Table 12.3*.
      The technical bulletin referred to in Reference 4 also contains a
summary of the advantages and disadvantages of printing acid and
premetallised dyes compared with disperse dyes. These will now be
briefly described.

167

Table 12.2 'PROCINYL', 'DISPERSOL' AND 'DURANOL' DYES PRINTED ON CELLULOSE TRIACETATE

| | Light (daylight) 1/1 Standard depth | Washing I.S.O. Test No. 3 30 min at 60°C (140°F) | | | Burnt gas fumes | | 'Tricel' label (Courtaulds) | 'Arnel' label (Amcel, Europe) |
		Effect	Staining of adjacent Tri-acetate	Viscose rayon	Normal	S–Finish		
Dispersol Fast Yellow T	7	4–5	5	5	5	5	Rec	Rec
Procinyl Yellow G	5	5	5	5	5	5	Rec	Rec
Dispersol Fast Yellow T4R	6	4–5	4–5	4–5	5	5	Rec	Rec
Dispersol Fast Yellow A	6	4	4–5	5	5	5	Rec	Rec
Dispersol Fast Orange B	6–7	3–4	5	5	5	5	Rec	Rec
Dispersol Fast Orange A	6	4Y	4–5	4–5	4Y	5	Rec	Rec
Procinyl Orange G	4	5	5	5	5	5	Rec	Rec, ½ D
Dispersol Fast Scarlet B	4	4–5	4	5	5	5	Rec	Rec
Procinyl Scarlet G	5	5	5	5	5	5	Rec	N
Dispersol Fast Red R	3–4	4–5	5	5	5	5	Rec	Rec
Dispersol Fast Red TB	5	4–5	5	5	5	5	Rec	Rec
Dispersol Fast Red T3B	6–7	4–5	5	5	5	5	Rec	Rec
Procinyl Red G	4	4–5	5	5	4Y	5	Rec	Rec
Duranol Red X3B	5	4–5	4	4–5	2Y	4–5Y	Rec	Rec, F

Dispersol Fast Rubine BT	6	4–5	5	5	4–5	5	Rec	Rec
Duranol Printing Violet B	5R1	4	4	5	2RD	5	Rec	N
Duranol Printing Blue B	5R	3–4	5	5	1RD	4–5R	Rec	Rec
Duranol Blue G	5–6R	3–4	3–4	4–5	2RD	5	Rec	Rec, $\frac{1}{2}$ D
Procinyl Blue R	4–5R	5	5	5	2R	4R	Rec	Rec
Dispersol Navy P-R	4–5	4	5	4–5	4R	4–5	Rec	Rec
Duranol Dark Blue T	4R	4	4–5	4–5	3RD	4–5R	Rec	N
Duranol Blue Green B	6	3WG	4	4	3RD	4R	Rec	Rec, $\frac{1}{4}$ D
Dispersol Fast Brown T3R	5	4–5	5	4	5	5	Rec	Rec, $\frac{1}{2}$ D
Dispersol Black P-MF	4–5	4–5	5	5	5	5	Rec	Rec
Duranol Direct Black T	3–4R	4–5	4	4	3–4R	4R	Rec	N

D = duller, G = greener, R = redder, W = weaker, Y = yellower, Rec = recommended, N= not recommended, $\frac{1}{2}$ D = suitable up to half I.S.O. standard depth, F = requires addition of gas fume inhibitor.

Table 12.3. ACID AND PREMETALLISED DYE PRINTING PROCESSES FOR TRIACETATE AND TRIACETATE/NYLON FABRICS

Process	Dyes	Swelling agents	Penetrating agents	Fixation methods
BASF	'Vialon' 'Ortolan' (selected dyes only)	Thiourea	'Solvocine' PFD* 'Solvocine' A†	Steaming at atmospheric pressure at 100°C (212°F) for 15–20 min, *or* pressure steaming at 1 x 10⁵ N/m² (15 lbf/in²) for 10–15 min
Celanese	61 dyes from 8 manu-facturers	Zinc thio-cyanate Urea	'Solvocine' PFD*	Steaming at atmospheric pressure at 100°C (212°F) for 15–20 min
CIBA (Triacid process)	'Avilon' Fast Benzyl Fast 'Cibalan' 'Kiton'	Thiourea sodium salicylate phenyl cellosolve	None	Steaming at atmospheric pressure at 100°C (212°F) for 8–10 min, *or* flash ageing at 120°C (250°F) for 30–60 s.
Francolor	'Amichrome' Light	Urea or thiourea	'Solutene' CI‡ (thiodiethyl-ene glycol)	Steaming at atmospheric pressure at 100°C (212°F) for 15–20 min, *or* pressure steaming at 1 x 10⁵ N/m² (15 lbf/in²) for 10 min
Geigy (Irgatril process)	'Erico' 'Irgalan' 'Irganol'	Thiourea resorcinol and Solvent SW	Thiodiethyl-ene glycol	Steaming at atmospheric pressure 100°C (212°F) for 15–20 min, *or* pressure steaming

*'Solvocine' PFD is sold in Europe as 'Glyezin' PFD (BASF)
†'Solvocine' A is sold in Europe as 'Glyezin' A (BASF)
‡'Solutene' CI (thiodiethylene glycol) is sold under several names including 'Glydote' BN (ICI) and 'Glyezin' A (BASF)

Advantages of Acid and Premetallised Dyes

1. Improved wet fastness and less staining on white backgrounds.
2. Reduced steaming times and temperature.

170

3. Improved sublimation fastness which is important for pleating applications.
4. Better union shades on cellulose triacetate/nylon blended fabrics over a wide range of fibre content ratios.
5. Good fastness to sea water and chlorinated water making the dyes highly suited for bathing costume fabrics.

Disadvantages of Acid and Premetallised Dyes

1. More limited dye selection.
2. Difficulty in obtaining a few bright shades.
3. Limited penetration into tightly woven fabrics.
4. In roller printing deep engravings are preferred. (This is to ensure the deposition of sufficient swelling and penetrating agent on the fabric.) The engraving depths and scales quoted, i.e. 0·18—0·35 mm deep and 11·0—13·4 lines per centimetre (0·007—0·010 in and 28—34 lines per inch) would make the printing of intricate patterns on a hydrophobic (and hence low absorbency) fabric extremely difficult. In screen printing, care would need to be taken that the print paste did not attack either the screen lacquer or the screen gauze itself.

Printing of Cellulose Triacetate Blends

Two main types of blend incorporating cellulose triacetate are encountered. They are cellulose triacetate/viscose rayon and cellulose triacetate/nylon. These two blends will be dealt with separately since the approach to printing them is different.

Cellulose Triacetate Viscose Rayon 67/33 Blends

In considering a printing blend of this type it should be established whether or not a single range of dyes is capable of colouring both fibres to a satisfactory level of fastness. By printing selected 'Caledon',and 'Durindone' vat dyes together with a swelling agent (p-hydroxy diphenyl) coloration of both fibres is achieved.

The alternative procedure is to choose a separate class of dye for each of the two fibres in the blend. Mixtures of 'Dispersol' and 'Duranol' disperse dyes with 'Procion' dyes will colour the cellulose triacetate and viscose rayon fibres respectively. The use of acid or premetallised dyes would give wet fastness on the viscose rayon of a much lower order than on the cellulose triacetate, and so the method is not used.

Printing with Vat Dyes. A print paste is prepared as follows:

50–200 parts		Dyestuff are pasted with
200– 50 ,,		thin neutralised thickening
		and stirred into
500 ,,		thickening (Note 1) containing
50 ,,		anhydrous sodium carbonate and
100 ,,		sodium sulphoxylate formaldehyde.
		Finally
50 ,,		p-hydroxy diphenyl dispersed in
50 ,,		water (Note 2) are added
Bulk to 1 000 parts.		

Notes
(1)   A suitable thickening is 'Nafka' Crystal Gum Supra (Scholtens).
(2)   Aggregation of dye may occur if print pastes containing p- hydroxy diphenyl are stored. To prevent this such additions should only be made when the print pastes are ready for use.

Processing after Printing. The printed and dried goods are steamed for 30 min at atmospheric pressure. Steaming is followed by rinsing in cold water and then an oxidation treatment is given comprising 10 min at 40°C (105°F) in a solution containing 30 parts of hydrogen peroxide (20 volumes) and 5 parts of ammonia (Sp. Gr. 0·88) per 1 000 parts of water. Finally, the goods are treated for 5 min at the boil in a solution of 2 parts 'Lissapol' *ND* and 0·5 parts soda ash per 1 000 parts of water, rinsed again in water and dried. An oxidation treatment of the type just described is more vigorous than that normally used on 100% cellulosic fabrics. Nevertheless it does not convert the vat dye inside the cellulose triacetate fibre into a sufficiently stable physical form to withstand steam pleating without a change in shade. This defect may be easily overcome by carrying out a 10 min steaming treatment on the oxidised, washed and dried print. Such a treatment produces a print which will withstand steam pleating for 15 min at 1×10^5 N/m^2 (15 lbf/in^2) with little or no shade change or staining.

Dyestuff Selection. Recommended *QF* brands of the 'Caledon' and 'Durindone' ranges together with details of their more important fastness properties are given in *Table 12.4.*

Printing with 'Dispersol', 'Duranol' and 'Procion' Dye Mixtures. The method involves printing 'Procion' *H* dyes by the sodium bicarbonate

172

Table 12.4. FASTNESS PROPERTIES OF 'CALEDON' AND 'DURINDONE' VAT DYESTUFFS PRINTED ON CELLULOSE TRIACETATE/VISCOSE RAYON /67:33 BLEND

'Caledon' and 'Durindone' vat dyestuffs	Light (Xenon-arc) standard 1/1 standard depth	Washing I.S.O. Wash No. 1 30 min at 40°C (160°F)			Burnt gas fumes
		Effect on print	Staining of		
			tri-acetate	viscose rayon	
QF Caledon Printing Yellow 5G	5	5	5	5	5
QF Caledon Printing Yellow GK	4	5	5	5	5
QF Durindone Printing Orange RN	6	5	5	5	5
QF Durindone Printing Scarlet 2B	6	5	5	5	5
QF Durindone Printing Pink FF	6	5	5	5	5
QF Durindone Printing Magenta B	6	5	5	5	5
QF Caledon Printing Purple 4R	6	5	5	5	5
QF Durindone Printing Blue 4BC	6	5	5	5	5
QF Caledon Printing Jade Green XBN	6	5	5	5	5
QF Caledon Printing Jade Green 2G	6	5	5	5	5
QF Durindone Printing Brown G	6	5	5	5	5
QF Durindone Printing Black TL	6	5	5	5	5

recipe in admixture with selected disperse dyes of similar shade. A thickening based on 'Manutex' *F* or an emulsion thickening based on 'Dispersol' *PR* is used. Fixation involves a 30 min steaming treatment at a pressure of 7×10^4 N/m² (10 lbf/in²). Further details are given in Reference 5 which also includes fastness properties of typical mixtures.

Cellulose Triacetate/Nylon Blends

A 65/35 blend of 'Tricel' (Courtaulds) and 'Celon' nylon 6 (Courtaulds) is marketed as 'Tricelon'. Before printing it is recommended that the fabric is given an S-Finish. A wide range of shades which meet the fastness requirements of the 'Tricelon' labelling scheme is obtainable using selected 'Procinyl', 'Dispersol' and 'Duranol' dyes. An alternative method involves the use of acid and premetallised dyes by one of the special processes described earlier in this chapter. There is no difficulty in fixing these dyes on nylon and no recipe modifications are required.

Unlike 'Tricel'/viscose blends 'Tricelon' is not printed satisfactorily by vat dyes. The nylon fibres are not readily penetrated by vat dyes and furthermore the resulting shades often differ considerably from those obtained on cellulosic fibres. Many vat dyes are so finely dispersed in nylon that their light fastness is much lower than normal. Re-steaming after oxidation and soaping causes aggregation of the vat dye but some occurs at or near the surface. The net result is that the light fastness is raised but the rubbing fastness of the print is lowered and the process is impractical.

Printing with 'Procinyl', 'Dispersol' and 'Duranol' Dyes. The recommended printing recipe is:

10—100 parts	'Procinyl', 'Dispersol' or 'Duranol' dye are dispersed in
100 ,,	urea dissolved in
260—170 ,,	water. The dispersion is then stirred into
600 ,,	thickening (Note 1) containing previously dissolved
10 ,,	sodium chlorate (Note 2) and
20 ,,	'Perminal' *KB*
1 000 parts.	

Notes
(1)   Suitable thickenings include 'Manutex' *F* (Alginate Industries), 'Nafka' Crystal Gum Supra (Scholtens), 'Meyprogum' *AC* (Meyhall), 'Indalca' *U* (Cesalpinia) and Thickening *301* (Grünau).
(2)   The presence of nylon in the blend precludes the use of Resist Salt *L* since this is retained by this fibre. The use of sodium chlorate as an oxidising agent is a necessary alternative to minimise dye reduction during steaming.

Processing after Printing. The printed and dried fabric is steamed for 30 min at a pressure of 7×10^4 N/m² (10 lbf/in²). This is followed by rinsing in cold water and treating for 5 min at 50°C (120°F) in a solution containing 2 parts of 'Lissapol' *ND* per 1 000 parts of water. Finally, a further rinse in cold water is followed by drying.

174

Dye Selection. Those members of the 'Procinyl', 'Dispersol' and 'Duranol' ranges which meet the requirements of the 'Tricelon' labelling scheme when printed on 'Tricelon' are listed in *Table 12.5.*

Table 12.5. DISPERSE AND REACTIVE DISPERSE DYES RECOMMENDED FOR PRINTING 'TRICELON'

Dye	Light 1/1 Standard depth (xenon)	Washing I.S.O. No. 2 (45 min at 50°C (120°F))			Burnt gas fumes
		Effect on print	Stain on 'Celon'	Stain on 'Tricel'	
* Dispersol Fast Yellow T	6–7	4	5	5	5
† Procinyl Yellow G	5–6	5	4–5	5	5
* Dispersol Fast Yellow T3R	6	4–5	5	5	5
* Dispersol Fast Yellow T4R	5–6	4–5	3–4	5	5
† Procinyl Orange G	4	5	4–5	5	5
* Dispersol Fast Orange B	5–6	4–5	3	4–5	5
† Procinyl Scarlet G	4	5	4–5	5	5
* Dispersol Fast Scarlet TR	5	4–5	4	4	5
† Procinyl Red G	4	5	4–5	5	5
* Dispersol Fast Red TB	6	4–5	5	5	5
‡ Duranol Brilliant Red T2B	5–6	4–5	4	4–5	5
* Dispersol Fast Rubine BT	5	4–5	4–5	5	5
* Duranol Fast Blue T2R	6	4–5	4–5	5	4–5
‡ Dispersol Fast Blue GFD	3	4	5	5	5
* Duranol Blue G	5	4	3–4	4	4–5
† Procinyl Blue R	6	5	4	5	4R
* Dispersol Fast Navy T2G	4–5	4–5	4–5	4–5	4–5
* Duranol Blue Green B	5–6	4–5	4	5	4R
† Duranol Black P-MF	4	4	4	4–5	4–5

Available brands: * = Liquid brand, † = *PQ* Paste brand, ‡ = 300 Powder Fine brand. R = redder.

REFERENCES

1. *Standard Methods for the Determination of the Colour Fastness of Textiles,* 3rd edn., The Society of Dyers and Colourists, Bradford, England (1962)
2. SALVIN, V. S. and WALKER, R. A., *Textile Research Journal,* **25,** 571–585 (1955)
3. *Technical Manual of the American Association of Textile Chemists and Colourists,* **45,** 144–146 (1969)
4. Technical Bulletin TD69 NB-65-38, Dec. 1965, *Printing Triacetate and Triacetate/nylon Fabrics with Acid and Premetallised Dyes,* Celanese Fibres Marketing Co., Charlotte, N.C., USA
5. Technical Information Dyehouse No. 770, *Printing of Cellulose Triacetate/ viscose Rayon 67/33 Blends,* ICI Dyestuffs Division, Issued 13 Aug. 64

13

The Printing of Acrylic Fibres

The chemistry involved in the preparation of this group of fibres allows some variations which give end products whose printing and dyeing properties may vary from one manufacturer to another. The monomeric unit of the polymer chain is acrylonitrile, and when this is present in the fibre in excess of 85% by weight the fibre is classified as an acrylic fibre. By polymerising acrylonitrile in the presence of varying amounts of vinyl and vinylidine chloride so that the end product contains more than 35% but less than 85% of acrylonitrile, modified fibres are formed. These modified fibres were defined as *modacrylics* in 1960 by the USA Federal Trade Commission, and now this term is frequently encountered in the literature.

Fibre trademarks for both groups include:

Acrylic fibres	*Modacrylic fibres*
'Acrilan' (Monsanto)	'Dynel' (Union Carbide)
'Courtelle' (Courtaulds)	'Teklan' (Courtaulds)
'Creslan' (American Cyanamid)	'Verel' (Tennessee Eastman)
'Dralon' (Bayer)	
'Orlon' (Du Pont)	

In preparing the unmodified acrylic fibres it is usual to incorporate small quantities of other monomers to alter the crystalline structure of the fibre, thus giving it the necessary thermoplasticity. A third additional comonomer may be added to modify the dyeing properties. The manufacturers usually distinguish between such modifications by using the same trademark followed by a number, e.g. 'Orlon' *81*, 'Orlon' *41* and 'Orlon' *42*. Thus when planning to dye or print an acrylic fibre it is advisable to seek advice from the supplier or the manufacturer as to which specific type of acrylic fibre is involved. Further details of the chemical and physical background relating to acrylic fibres are available in Reference 1. The commercially available types in the USA in 1970, together with their suppliers and an indication of their end uses is to be found in Reference 2.

176

Outlets for printed 100% acrylic fabrics include blankets, dress goods, woven and knitted goods and also pile fabrics. These fabrics are characterised by their soft handle and good abrasion resistance and may be printed by conventional techniques. The behaviour of various classes of dyes of potential interest for printing 'Acrilan', 'Courtelle' and 'Orlon' is summarised in *Table 13.1*.

Table 13.1. SUMMARY OF DYE CLASSES OF INTEREST FOR PRINTING 'ACRILAN', 'COURTELLE' AND 'ORLON'

Class of dye	Light fastness	Washing fastness	Steam pleating	Remarks
Acid	Moderate – good	Moderate – good	Good	Only of interest on 'Acrilan'. Careful dye selection necessary. Steamed at atmospheric pressure
Basic	Moderate – good	Moderate – good	Moderate – good	Build-up to full bright shades. Most widely used range on acrylics. Steamed at atmospheric pressure
Disperse	Moderate – good	Good	Good	Pale to medium shades only obtained by steaming at atmospheric pressure. Wide range of full shades obtained by pressure steaming
Vat	Good – very good	Good	Good	Wide range of pale to medium shades obtained. Steamed at atmospheric pressure

PRINTING WITH BASIC DYES

Some of the older synthetic dyes are included in this group and they are not identified by a specific trademark, e.g. 'Rhodamine' *B*, 'Malachite' Green *AN*. With the advent of acrylic fibres and the realisation that basic dyes would probably be the best range for their coloration, dye makers carried out further research on basic dyes. This led to the appearance of new basic dyes which were 'modified' to give improved

177

properties on acrylic fibres. These 'modified' basic dyes are available under a number of trademarks which include 'Astrazone' (F. Bayer), 'Maxilon' (Geigy), 'Sevron' (Du Pont) and 'Synacril' (ICI).

Printing Recipe

The general printing recipe is:

10–25 parts	'Synacril' dye are dissolved in
30 ,,	'Glydote' *BN*
30 ,,	glacial acetic acid and
290–275 ,,	hot water. When solution is complete add to
600 ,,	thickening (see note). Finally, add
40 ,,	'Glyezin' *PFD* (BASF)
1 000 parts.	

Note
Suitable thickenings include 'Indalca' *PA/3* (Cesalpinia), Nafka Crystal Gum Supra (Scholtens) — not recommended for high temperature steaming — and an emulsion based on 'Dispersol' *PR* (but avoid using sodium alginate as film former).

Processing after Printing

The printed and dried fabric is developed by *either*
(a) Steaming for 20–30 min at a pressure not exceeding 3.5×10^4 N/m^2 (5 lbf/in^2) *or*
(b) Steaming for 90 s at 150°C (300°F) using the ICI High Temperature Steaming Process. In this case the printing recipe should be amended as follows: the 'Glyezin' *PFD* is omitted and an addition of 200 parts urea, per 1 000 parts of print paste is made.

After development the goods are rinsed well in cold water and then treated for 5 min at 60°C (140°F) in a solution containing 2 parts of 'Lissapol' *ND* per 1 000 parts of water, rinsed again in cold water and dried.
It should be noted during any wet processing of acrylic fabric that the fibre becomes thermoplastic above about 90°C and that any subsequent quick cooling will set the fabric in creases and folds. For this reason the 'Lissapol' *ND* treatment recommended for prints should

not be given at above 60°C. If by accident a print is immersed in a bath of water or detergent at 90°C or above, creasing may be minimised by adopting the technique used in dyeing, viz. allowing the bath to cool slowly down to 60°C. This is very much more effective than removing the fabric from the hot solution and plunging it into cold water.

Fastness Properties

The main fastness properties of the 'Synacril' dyes printed on three representative acrylic fibres are given in *Table 13.2*; a wider range of fastness properties is listed in Reference 3. This shows the 'Synacril' Fast dyes to have excellent resistance to burnt gas fumes and very good fastness to chlorinated water, sea-water, perspiration and steam pleating. Where brilliance of shade and maximum economy are of greater importance than higher fastness, a selection of ordinary basic dyes may be considered suitable. By comparing the fastness properties of 'Synacril' dyes in *Table 13.2* with those of basic dyes in *Table 13.3* the differences may be assessed in relation to the end use requirements. In the range of faster 'Synacril' dyes there is a lack of a chocolate brown and a black. This does not present any problem in printing, since 'Synacril' dyes are readily miscible with each other. A basis for a dark brown in roller printing is:

17 parts 'Synacril' Fast Yellow *R* ⎫
56 ,, 'Synacril' Fast Red *2G* ⎬ per 1 000 parts print paste.
7 ,, 'Synacril' Blue *5G* ⎭

This mixture would be too strong for screen printing so the proportions would be kept constant and the strength reduced appropriately by about 30%. Blacks which are invariably mixtures in this class of dye are usually prepared by the dyemaker. 'Synacril' Fast Black *R* and 'Synacril' Black *A* are available for this purpose, the former dye possessing the better fastness properties.

PRINTING WITH VAT DYES

Not all vat dyes can be printed satisfactorily on acrylic fibres, but it is possible to print a selected number using the conventional alkali-carbonate-sodium sulphoxylate formaldehyde (all-in) process. The selection of dyes to be used and the efficiency of the washing-off process are of great importance if optimum fastness to rubbing is to be obtained.

179

Table 13.2. FASTNESS PROPERTIES OF 'SYNACRIL' DYES PRINTED ON ACRYLIC FIBRES

'Synacril' Dye	Light (1/1 Standard depth)			Washing – I.S.O. Test No. 3 (30 min at 60°C (140°F))								
				'Courtelle'			'Acrilan' 16			'Orlon' 42		
	'Courtelle'	'Acrilan' 16	'Orlon' 42	Effect on print	Stain on 'Courtelle'	Stain on wool	Effect on print	Stain on 'Acrilan'	Stain on wool	Effect on print	Stain on 'Orlon'	Stain on wool
Synacril Fast Yellow 8G	6–7	6–7	6–7	5	5	5	5	5	5	5	5	5
Synacril Fast Yellow Brown G	6	6	6–7	4–5	5	5	5	5	5	4–5	5	5
Synacril Fast Scarlet G	5–6	5–6	5–6	5	5	5	5	5	5	4–5	5	5
Synacril Brilliant Red 4G	3–4	3–4	3–4	5	5	5	5	5	5	5	5	5
Synacril Fast Red 2G	5–6	5–6	6	4–5	5	5	5	5	5	4–5	5	5
Synacril Fast Red 5B	5–6	5–6	6	5	5	5	5	5	5	5	5	5
Synacril Fast Blue R	6–7	6–7	7	5	5	5	5	5	5	5	5	5

Table 13.3. FASTNESS PROPERTIES OF BASIC DYES PRINTED ON ACRYLIC FIBRES

Basic Dye	Light (1/1 Standard depth)			Washing – I.S.O. Test No. 2 (45 min at 50°C (120°F))								
				'Courtelle'			'Acrilan' 16			'Orlon' 42		
	'Courtelle'	'Acrilan' 16	'Orlon' 42	Effect on print	Stain on 'Courtelle'	Stain on wool	Effect on print	Stain on 'Acrilan'	Stain on wool	Effect on print	Stain on 'Orlon'	Stain on wool
Bismarck Brown RLN	3	3	4	3YBr	4–5	5	3	5	5	3	5	4–5
Rhodamine BN	3	3	3	4	5	5	3	5	5	4–5	5	4–5
Magenta PN	3	4D	3D	4	5	5	4–5	5	4–5	4	5	5
Acronol Sky Blue 3G*	3	3	4	5	5	5	4–5	5	4–5	4	5	5
Brilliant Green YN	4	4B1	4	4	5	5	4–5	5	4–5	4	5	5
Malachite Green AN	4B1	4–5	4D	4	5	5	4–5	5	4–5	4	5	5

*Now available as Synacril Blue 5G. Abbreviations: Bl = bluer, Br = brighter, D = duller and Y = yellower.

Printing Recipe

The general printing recipe is as follows:

50–200 parts		dyestuff paste are thoroughly stirred with
200–100	,,	thin neutralised thickening then added with constant stirring to
600–500	,,	thickening into which has been incorporated
0–50	,,	glycerine
50–50	,,	anhydrous sodium carbonate (soda ash) and
100	,,	sodium sulphoxylate formaldehyde
1 000 parts.		

Note

To assist in retaining the printed mark it is advisable to use a thickening of high solids content such as 'Nafka' Crystal Gum Supra (Scholtens). A reduction of the glycerine content of the print paste and the use of the less hygroscopic sodium carbonate in preference to potassium carbonate are recommended, to prevent flushing of the print.

Processing after Printing

The printed and dried fabric is steamed at atmospheric pressure for 10 min, which will generally be found to be an adequate period of time. Steaming is followed by a washing-off sequence which commences with a more vigorous oxidation than is necessary for cellulosic fibres. A bath containing 5 parts of hydrogen peroxide (20 volumes) and 3 parts ammonia (sp. gr. 0·880) per 1 000 parts is raised to 90°C (195°F) and maintained at this temperature for 5 min, or until oxidation is complete. After oxidation the prints are treated for 5–10 min at or as near to the boil as facilities permit, in a solution containing 2 parts of 'Lissapol' *ND* per 1 000 parts of water. This is followed by a final cold water rinse and drying.

Dye Selection

The following vat dyes have given satisfactory shades and fastness properties on 'Acrilan' *16*, 'Courtelle' and 'Orlon' *42*:

QF Caledon Printing Yellow 5G Paste	QF Caledon Printing Yellow GK Paste

QF Caledon Printing Orange
  6R Paste
QF Durindone Printing Orange
  RN Paste
QF Durindone Printing Brown
  G Paste
QF Durindone Printing Scarlet
  2B Paste
QF Durindone Printing Pink
  FF Paste

QF Durindone Printing Magenta
  B Paste
QF Durindone Printing Blue
  4BC Paste
QF Caledon Printing Jade Green
  XBN Paste
QF Durindone Printing Black TL

PRINTING WITH DISPERSE DYES

These dyes give satisifactory pale to medium shades on acrylic fibres
when steamed at atmospheric pressure. A few members of the range
will build-up under these conditions above medium depth. Much
improved yields are obtained however if steaming at pressures of from
$3.5 \times 10^4 - 7 \times 10^4$ N/m^2 (5–10 lbf/in^2) are possible on available
equipment.

Printing Recipe

The general printing recipe is as follows:

30–100 parts	'Dispersol' or 'Duranol' Liquids or
20–50 ,,	'Dispersol' or 'Duranol' Grains or Powder are diluted with
310–240 ,,	water and the suspension is stirred into
600 ,,	thickening containing
50 ,,	'Perminal' *KB* and
10 ,,	Resist Salt *L*
Bulk to <u>1 000</u> parts.	

Notes
(1)   When using Grain or Powder Fine brands, care should be taken to
      ensure that the dispersion properties are such that specks are not
      apparent at the depth of shade required.
(2)   A crystal gum, e.g. 'Nafka' Crystal Gum Supra (Scholtens) has
      been found to give the most level prints coupled with good
      definition and high colour yield. Alternatively, an emulsion
      thickening may be employed.

Process after Printing

After printing the goods are dried and steamed, preferably for 30 min at a pressure of $3.5 \times 10^4 - 7 \times 10^4$ N/m² (5–10 lbf/in²). The higher pressure is essential to obtain medium to full depths of shade with the majority of dyes. Medium depths may be obtained with some dyes by steaming at atmospheric pressure for 30–45 min.

Steaming is followed by a thorough rinse in cold water, then a treatment at 60°C (140°F) for 15 min in a solution containing 2 parts of 'Lissapol' *ND* per 1 000 parts of water. Finally, a further rinse in cold water is given and then the fabric is dried.

Use of 'Carriers' in the Print Paste

Experimental work has been carried out which indicates that an addition of 10% of urea or 5% of resorcinol to the recommended printing recipe, leads to an increase in colour value of disperse dyes printed on 'Orlon' and 'Courtelle' ('Acrilan' appears more receptive to disperse dyes than the other two fibres). While resorcinol (2:4 di-hydroxybenzene) is considerably more effective than urea it is also much more difficult to remove from the fabric afterwards. Removal is essential because resorcinol left on the fibre darkens noticeably on exposure to light and adversely affects the light fastness of the final print. Under laboratory conditions it has been shown that a treatment of 15 min at 90°C (195°F) in 2 parts 'Lissapol' *ND* per 1 000 parts of water is needed to remove all the resorcinol. These fairly severe washing-off conditions may give rise to staining of the unprinted grounds with some dye combinations. Urea, while less effective than resorcinol, does not give rise to difficulties in removing it from the fibre. However, since urea is hygroscopic and acrylic fibres are hydrophobic, it may prove impossible to use the agent if steaming conditions are excessively moist. Trials should be carried out to determine the optimum amount of urea that may be included in the print paste without the resulting print losing definition during steaming.

Dye Selection

The following members of the 'Dispersol' and 'Duranol' disperse ranges are recommended for printing 'Acrilan' *16*, 'Courtelle' and 'Orlon' *42*:

* Dispersol Printing Yellow 3GS Paste   † Dispersol Fast Yellow A Liquid

† Dispersol Fast Yellow G Liquid

Dispersol Fast Yellow GR Grains

* Dispersol Fast Orange A Liquid

Dispersol Fast Orange B Liquid

Dispersol Fast Orange Brown RN 150 Powder Fine

* Duranol Printing Brown G Paste

* Dispersol Fast Crimson B 150 Powder Fine

Dispersol Fast Scarlet B Liquid

† Duranol Red X3B Liquid

* Duranol Brilliant Violet BR 300 Powder Fine

† Duranol Printing Violet B 300 Paste

Duranol Blue G Liquid

* Duranol Printing Blue B 200 Paste

† Duranol Brilliant Blue CB 300 Powder Fine

Duranol Blue TR 300 Powder Fine

* Duranol Dark Blue T Liquid

Duranol Blue Green B Liquid

* These dyes together with those marked † build up more readily on 'Acrilan' than the remainder.
† These dyes build-up more readily by atmospheric steaming on 'Courtelle' and 'Orlon' than the remainder.

Fastness data relating to vat and disperse dyes printed on acrylic fibres is available in Reference 4. Although this publication refers in its title to 'Dralon' as well as three other acrylic fibres, it does not contain detailed fastness properties or recommendations in respect of this Bayer fibre. It is, however, explained that although a full investigation of 'Dralon' has not been carried out, preliminary indications are that the printing behaviour of this fibre is similar to that of 'Courtelle'.

PRINTING WITH 2:1 PREMETALLISED DYES

Chemstrand, the makers of 'Acrilan' have pointed out[5] that this class of dyestuff can give reasonable yields on 'Acrilan' giving shades of a subdued tone. However, not all dyes of this class give a satisfactory build-up, although light and wet fastness are good and rub fastness is adequate. Premetallised dyes are of particular interest in printing 'Acrilan' wool blends.

It appears[6] that although experience is somewhat limited, a number of premetallised dyes are also suitable for application to 'Courtelle'.

Recipes

The recipes given by the two fibre makers are similar both in components and quantities:

'Acrilan'		dyestuff	'Courtelle'	
x parts				x parts
30	,,	'Glydote' *BN*	−	,,
−	,,	urea	10	,,
370−x	,,	hot water	360−x	,,
550	,,	thickening	600	,,
50	,,	'Glyezin' *PFD* (BASF)	30	,,
1 000 parts.			1 000 parts.	

PIGMENT PRINTING

Acrylic fibres whose appeal includes an attractive soft handle and ease of care properties, are a particularly exacting test for pigment printing compositions. In addition, the baking treatment needed to polymerise the resin binder should not be allowed to exceed 120°C (245°F) with 'Courtelle' or 140°C (285°F) with 'Acrilan' otherwise yellowing of the fibre may occur. Both fibre makers draw attention [5, 6] to the advisability of carrying out preliminary trials with pigment printing compositions. These trials should have regard to the difficulties that sometimes arise in achieving adequate fastness to rubbing and mechanical washing. Such properties must be combined with an acceptably soft handle in the finished fabric, or alternatively the process must only be used for end products where such properties are not an important consideration.

PRINTING OF ACRYLIC FIBRE BLENDS

The acrylic-based blended fabrics that have so far appeared fall into two main groups:
  (1)   acrylic-wool blends
  (2)   acrylic-cellulose blends.
Blends of acrylics with nylon or cellulose triacetate are less frequently encountered.

Printing of Acrylic-Wool Blends

As with other fibre blends, the final choice of dye class or classes to be used is determined by a number of factors. The most important of these in this case is whether the dyes which colour the acrylic fibre satis-factorily behave equally well on the wool. The dye classes described for use on 100% acrylic fibres and their behaviour on wool may be summarised as follows:

Dye used for acrylic fibre	Behaviour on wool
Basics	Wet fastness lower than on acrylics
* Vats	Applicable by a modified recipe
Disperse	Of no value on wool
* Premetallised dyes	Suitable for both fibres
† Pigments	Limitations on 100% acrylic fibres also apply to the blend with wool

* Suitable and of interest   † Suitable but little used

From the above it will be seen that only two classes of dye are suitable but this is adequate and there is no need to resort to printing two classes of dye, i.e. one for each fibre in the blend.

Vat Dyes on Acrylic/Wool Blends

If vat dyes were applied to a wool fabric by the 'all-in' recipe the alkali carbonate present would severely damage the wool. Vat dyes may be applied to wool and also to acrylic/wool blends by using a special reducing agent called 'Manofast' (Hardman and Holden). This product is a white stable crystalline solid. It is a reducing agent with a slightly acid reaction and will reduce many vat dyes to their free acid leuco compounds. These in many cases have affinity for wool and also for acrylic fibres. Because of the slight acidity it is possible to obtain good colour yields with minimum degradation of the wool in the blend. Detailed information on dye selection and recipe variations may be obtained from References 5 and 7.

Printing Recipe

A typical print paste recipe is:

50–150 parts	vat dyestuff paste are diluted with
200–100 ,,	water or diluted thickening and stirred into
590 ,,	thickening (Note 1) into which
50 ,,	'Glydote' BN
50 ,,	'Glyezin' PFD (BASF) and
60 ,,	'Manofast' (Note 2) have been incorporated
__1 000__ parts.	

Notes
(1) Suitable thickenings include those based on British Gum, Gum Tragacanth and 'Nafka' Crystal Gum (Scholtens).
(2) If possible, the 'Manofast' should be dispersed by high speed stirring and the colour homogenised.

Processing after Printing

The printed goods are dried and then steamed for 15–20 min at atmospheric pressure. Steaming is followed by rinsing in cold water and then oxidation with hydrogen peroxide and ammonia at a temperature of 60°C (140°F). Oxidation is followed by a treatment in 2 parts of 'Lissapol' *ND* solution per 1 000 parts of water at 60°C (140°F), to remove unfixed vat dyestuff and to ensure good rubbing fastness.

Premetallised Dyes on Acrylic/Wool Blends

The recipes given for the printing of 100% 'Acrilan' or 'Courtelle' with these dyestuffs are suitable for printing acrylic-wool blends as well.

It is pointed out[6] that premetallised dyes are also of value in printing 'Courtelle'/nylon blends. In choosing appropriate premetallised dyes for acrylic blends attention must be paid to finding dyes which give similar build-up on both fibres. The technical service departments of the fibre makers are usually able to supply on request detailed information in respect of their own fibres.

Printing of Acrylic/Cellulosic Blends

Applying the reasoning used for the acrylic-wool blends to the acrylic-cellulosic type the following picture emerges:

Dye used for acrylic fibre	Behaviour on cellulosic fibre (cotton and viscose rayon)
Basic	No affinity for cellulosic fibres without mordant and poor fastness when one is used
Vat	Applicable by 'all-in' process and by 'flash-ageing'
Disperse	Of no value on cellulosics
Premetallised	Of no value on cellulosics
Pigment	Limited by end-use requirements

187

This last list suggests that only vat dyes and pigment printing compositions are of potential interest. However, it is also possible to use disperse dyes in conjunction with reactive dyes, e.g. 'Procion' dyes. It is not possible to use mixtures of basic dyes and reactive dyes, firstly because the dyes tend to precipitate each other, and secondly because the reactive dyes need alkali to fix on cellulose while the basic dyes need acid conditions to fix on the acrylic fibre.

Vat Dyes on Acrylic-Cellulosic Blends

The printing recipe and processing conditions already described for 100% acrylic fibres apply to these blends. The alkali-carbonate-sodium sulphoxylate formaldehyde recipe is therefore used. (The 'Manofast' recipe would not allow fixation to occur on the cellulosic portion and so must be avoided.) Because of the presence of cellulosic fibres it is also possible to apply vat dyes by flash-ageing. With 100% acrylic fabrics the process would be liable to cause creasing and distortion in view of the warp-wise tension involved. Printing recipes and processing details will be as already given for cotton, but the number of suitable vat dyes will be lower. Oxidation will need to be carried out with warm alkaline hydrogen peroxide.

By forming a blend of 'Courtelle' with 'Tricel' Courtaulds have produced a mixture fabric to which a wide range of disperse dyes may be applied.

REFERENCES

1. *Man Made Fibres Science and Technology*, 3, 135–243, Interscience, New York (1968)
2. *Modern Textiles*, 33–48, March (1970)
3. *Synacril Dyes for the Printing of Acrylic Fibres*, Technical Information D 992, ICI Dyestuffs Division, Jan. (1968)
4. *Printing of 'Orlon' (Type 42), 'Courtelle', 'Acrilan' and 'Dralon' Acrylic Fibres*, Technical Information D 762, ICI Dyestuffs Division, July 2nd (1964)
5. Technical Bulletin entitled *Acrilan 16 Printing (1964)* and Technical Bulletin A67/17 entitiled *Printing of Acrilan and its Blends*, Chemstrand Ltd., Leicester, England
6. 'Courtelle' Technical Service Bulletin No. 14 entitled *Printing*, 1st edn (1962) and Bulletin 1/3 entitled *General Properties*, 3rd edn (1966), Courtaulds Ltd., Synthetic Fibres Division, Coventry, England
7. Technical Service Bulletin entitled *'Manofast' Processes Direct and Discharge Printing on Wool*, Hardman and Holden, Manchester, England

14

Discharge Styles

A discharge printing style is one in which the printing operation takes place on a previously dyed fabric often called the 'ground' shade. The dyes used for the ground shade have to be carefully selected so that by applying a suitable print paste the dyed fabric will be permanently decolorised locally giving a 'white' discharge patterned effect. By using other dyes in the print paste which are not decolorised by the compounds used to destroy the ground shade, the simultaneous fixation of these dyes may be achieved while the ground shade is destroyed. Such effects are termed *illuminated discharges* and the dyes used to produce them *illuminating colours*.

Many attractive effects may be produced by discharging suitable dyed ground shades, but to avoid disappointments it is important to appreciate the background principles involved. These styles have always required the printer to exercise a great degree of process control and use a good deal of skill and initiative in choice of dyes and printing recipes.

Historical

Taking indigo as an example of a long established vat dyestuff, it is possible to trace in some detail the methods used as early as 1826 to discharge cotton dyed with it. Diserens has done this[1] and shows how the methods used may be classified into oxidation and reduction processes. The oxidation processes used such products as sodium bichromate (in conjunction with oxalic acid) and sodium chlorate plus sodium ferricyanide (in conjunction with caustic soda). Although these and similar products were used for many years, there was always a danger of oxidation not only of the indigo but also of the cotton itself. The cotton was also liable to be attacked by acid conditions. Not surprisingly, considerable interest was shown in the reduction processes. These resulted from the discovery of new compounds, especially hydrosulphites. The most valuable hydrosulphite derivative was that formed with formaldehyde, viz. sodium-hydrosulphite-formaldehyde, first marketed by BASF in 1905 as 'Eradit' *C*. This is more commonly known by BASF's current name 'Rongalite' *C* as well as other names including 'Formosul' (ACC). This compound forms the basis of the majority of reduction discharge recipes.

The effect of a 'Formosul'-containing print paste on a dyed indigo ground shade is to reduce it to the sodium leuco compound. Since some of this reduced indigo could re-oxidise *in situ* it was liable to soil the purity of the white. The problem was overcome by the introduction in 1910 of 'Leucotrope' *W*. This compound is capable of combining with a leuco compound to form an oxidation resistant ether which is soluble in alkali. Consequently, it was possible to effect white discharges on indigo of greater purity than before.

Apart from indigo, very few other vat dyes are dischargeable to a satisfactory degree, even in the presence of 'Leucotrope' *W*. Indeed, vat dyes are among the most suitable dyes for use as illuminating colours in discharge styles. With printers well aware of the wide variety of methods tried as discharges for indigo, it is not surprising that this previous work formed the basis of tests on new dyes that were emerging from dyemaking factories in the early part of the 20th century. Oxidation discharges proved to be of little or no value on dyes other than indigo. On the other hand, reduction discharges were very widely applicable.

Chemical Principles

The reasons for the wide use of reduction discharges were two-fold. Firstly, the wide use of the azo linkage ($-N=N-$) as a chromophoric (i.e. colour conferring) group in synthetic dyes, and secondly the susceptibility of this group to reduction. If a simple azoic dye is represented as $A-N=N-B$ then reduction gives two fragments, viz. $A-NH_2$ and $B-NH_2$, neither of which possess very much colour.

Reduction occurs during steaming and the dye fragments must be efficiently removed by a thorough wash-off treatment. Failure to carry out this removal properly will give a white discharge which although initially satisfactory, slowly darkens on exposure to light. This appears due to the oxidation of residual traces of $A-NH_2$ or $B-NH_2$ compounds.

CLASSES OF DYESTUFFS POTENTIALLY SUITABLE FOR GROUND SHADES IN DISCHARGE PRINTING

It must be appreciated that for dyestuffs within a class covered by one trademark and showing similar dyeing properties, there are often individual members of the range which have quite different chemical structures. These differences may be such as to give either a dye of excellent discharge properties or one which is virtually impossible to discharge. In dyemakers dyeing pattern cards it is customary to indicate the ease of dischargeability at a range of depths.

Acid Dyes

These dyes are not used on cellulosic fibres, but are applicable to wool, natural silk and nylon. Some acid dyes have azo linkages and are thus potentially capable of being discharged. In discharge printing wool and natural silk, care must be taken not to damage the fibre by using strongly alkaline pastes. Other acid dyes, often in the blue and green part of the range, are anthraquinone derivatives. Such products invariably fail to discharge even enough to allow coloured discharges to be produced.

'Chlorazol' and 'Durazol' Dyes

These are two ranges of direct dyestuffs primarily used on cellulosic fibres. In general the 'Durazol' dyes have the better light fastness and sometimes better wet fastness. Only dyes containing appropriately placed azo groups may be discharged satisfactorily. The main drawback of direct dyes is their relatively low wet fastness which is often much less than the illuminating dyestuffs used in coloured discharge printing.

'Chlorazol' Diazo Dyes

This is a range whose importance is decreasing, largely due to the availability of 'Procion' and other reactive dyes. The dyes are applied as ordinary direct dyes and then treated with a sodium nitrite-hydrochloric acid mixture. This diazotises an amino ($-NH_2$) group on the dye. In a second operation, the diazotised dye on the fibre is treated with a developer. The developer couples with the diazotised dye and a larger dye molecule is formed on the fibre of lower solubility and hence higher wet fastness. This operation forms a further $-N=N-$ group in the fibre, but this does not usually prevent satisfactory discharging operations being carried out.

Insoluble Azoic Combinations

These are formed by the coupling of 'Brentamine' Fast Salts (or diazotised bases) with 'Brenthols'. The reaction is carried out *in situ* and the resulting dye has at least one azo ($-N=N-$) group. A few 'Brenthols', e.g. 'Brenthol' *AT* which produces mainly yellows, do not give dischargeable dyeings. Many other Brenthols do discharge, but not all are equally satisfactory, probably due in part to the varying degrees to which the discharged dye fragments are removable from the fabric. These dyes contain no water-solubilising groups and hence possess very good wash fastness.

Reactive Dyes

A number of 'Procion' *M* and *H* dyes contain azo groups and so are potentially dischargeable. There is a difference in that either $A-NH_2$ or $B-NH_2$ may still be chemically bound to the cellulose, i.e. Cell$-A-$ NH_2. In some cases, especially if the dye residue is large, there may be darkening on exposure to light or an incomplete discharge. This type of behaviour applies to the majority of reactive dyes, except those where a vinyl sulphone grouping is involved in bonding to the cellulose. Such bonds may be broken by strong alkali, and this widens the degree of dischargeability of, for example, the 'Remazol' (FH) dyes. The wet fastness of all reactive dyes to washing is much better than that of the direct, and diazotised and developed ('D and D') direct dyes. The dischargeable shade range is wider than may be obtained with insoluble azoic dyes, notably among the yellows.

IMITATION 'DISCHARGE' EFFECTS

Imitation discharge effects are sometimes achieved by printing an adequate amount of a heavily pigmented paste containing zinc oxide, or titanium dioxide and a resin binder. A printing method applying a relatively thick film is required, e.g. screen printing or stencil printing. No reducing agent is present and hence no destruction of the ground shade is involved since the white 'discharge' effect is due entirely to the pigmented white paste masking the ground shade.

Where a ground shade is relatively pale and it is required to print illuminating colours on it, there are times when discharging may be avoided. This depends on the ground shade and the illuminating colours not being in violently contrasting shades. For example, a pale yellow ground shade to be illuminated with an orange, brown, red and black would merely be overprinted with these colours since the ground shade would usefully contribute to all of them. This technique would be unworkable if a green dye ground was required to show a bright scarlet as well. A straight overprint with a soluble scarlet dye would be unacceptable since it would be dulled by the green and a true discharge would be necessary. The only alternative would be to try and mask the green using a pigment scarlet, but only trials would confirm that this was possible.

CLASSES OF DYESTUFFS POTENTIALLY SUITABLE FOR ILLUMINATING COLOURS IN DISCHARGE STYLES

Vat Dyestuffs

'Caledon' and 'Durindone' dyes are well suited for illuminating colours on cellulosic fibres applied by the alkali-carbonate-sodium sulphoxylate formaldehyde ('all-in') process. This process requires too much alkali to permit its use on wool and silk. By using the 'Manofast' process selected vat dyes may be discharge-printed on wool and natural silk under mildly acidic conditions.

Basic Dyestuffs

These dyes withstand reducing agents such as 'Formosul' but do not have sufficient fastness to be of interest today on cellulosic fibres. They are used for certain specialised styles on wool and natural silk.

DYEING OF COTTON, LINEN AND VISCOSE RAYON FOR DISCHARGE PRINTING

It has been stressed in the earlier part of this chapter that care must be taken to select dyestuffs on the basis of good discharge properties from the appropriate ranges. This has been done in the case of the dyes appearing in the four tables in this chapter which list dischargeable dyes and fastness properties.

It is assumed that only relatively small amounts of fabric are to be dyed, that is, pieces up to about 10 m (30 ft) in length. Longer pieces require special equipment to obtain satisfactory results, and in such cases it is advisable to have the goods dyed by a firm of commission dyers. However, excellent results may be obtained by using small dye vessels with suitable heating arrangements, always taking the precaution that such vessels as are used shall easily accommodate the material, since it is difficult to obtain good results if tight packing is practised. In fact, for the dyeing of piece goods a minimum working ratio of 30:1, that is, 33 g of fabric per litre of water (3 lb per 10 gal) is desirable. The goods should always be submerged as much as possible without packing, during the dyeing operation, but it is uneconomic to use too high a liquor ratio as relatively poor exhaustion of the dyestuff may be obtained under such conditions.

The vessels used for dyeing may be of glass, wood, enamelled iron, stainless steel or Monel metal. Of these materials the last two are to be preferred, since they are strong, resistant to acid and alkali, and are easy to clean. Glass apparatus is quite suitable but is fragile, and enamelled pans are useless when the enamel becomes chipped. Wood is difficult to keep clean as the dye is absorbed by wood, and this makes the dyeing of pale and bright shades impossible. Suitable rods are also necessary for working the materials and these must be kept clean. They should also be perfectly smooth and have rounded ends to prevent damage to delicate materials.

During the dyeing operation the fabric should always be well worked in the dyeliquor for the first 15 min as it is generally during this initial period that most of the dyeing occurs, and on this, the levelness of the result depends to a great extent. After the lapse of this time only occasional working is necessary.

Preparation of Dyestuff Solution

Dry dyestuff should never be added to a dyebath; it should always be dissolved first, using the methods described in the appropriate section. If this is not done there is always a tendency for the dyestuff to form small balls or aggregates which float to the surface of the liquor and which are difficult to dissolve. Insoluble dyestuffs such as 'Brenthol' or 'Caledon' dyes should always be pasted thoroughly, by carefully stirring with water until all the powder is completely wetted and a smooth even paste produced, before proceeding with the preparation of the solution of the dyestuff. This pasting process is made much easier by the addition to the water of a suitable wetting agent such as methylated spirit or Turkey Red Oil *PO*. Suspensions prepared in this manner will easily dissolve to give perfect solutions on further treatment.

Dyeing of Direct Cotton Dyestuffs on Cotton, Linen and Viscose Rayon

'Chlorazol' and 'Durazol' Dyestuffs

Weigh the material and scour it (see chapter 5) and then rinse. Make up the dyebath as follows:

(1) Water (preferably soft) of a quantity at least 30—40 times the weight of the fabric. To this is added the solution of

(2) Dyestuff (the percentage being calculated on the dry weight of the fabric). This should be made into a smooth paste with cold water, and boiling water then poured on until it is dissolved. The solution is then added to the dyebath.

(3) Enter the fabric into the warm dyebath, at about 40°C (105°F). Raise the temperature slowly (over 10 min) to just below the boil. The fabric must be worked well during this period.

(4) Add slowly 10—40% of Glauber's salt crystals or common salt (calculated on the weight of fabric). This should be divided into four portions, successive portions being added at 5 min intervals. The smaller amount of the suggested range is required for light shades and the maximum amount for deep shades. The addition of salt will exhaust the dyestuff, and the fabric should be worked well just below the boil until all (or practically all) the dyestuff has been exhausted.

(5) Rinse and dry.

The fastness properties of 'Chlorazol' and 'Durazol' dyestuffs suitable for the production of dischargeable ground shades on cotton are listed in *Table 14.1.*

'Chlorazol' Diazo Dyestuffs

The dyestuffs are applied in the manner described for 'Chlorazol' and 'Durazol' dyestuffs. After dyeing, the fabric is rinsed and diazotised for 20 min in a cold bath containing (according to depth of shade):

10—30	parts	sodium nitrite and
60—80	„	hydrochloric acid at
or		20° Bé (32° Tw)
20—30	„	sulphuric acid at 66° Bé (168°Tw)
per	1000	parts of material.

Table 14.1. FASTNESS PROPERTIES OF 'CHLORAZOL' AND 'DURAZOL' DYESTUFFS DYED ON COTTON

'Chlorazol' or 'Durazol' Dye	*Light* (Medium depth)	*Washing* Once at $40^{\circ}C$ $(105^{\circ}F)$ Effect on dyeing
Durazol Yellow 6GS	4–5	3–4
Durazol Yellow 4GS	4	2–3
C.R. Durazol Flavine RS	5	2–3
Durazol Brown BR150	4–5	2–3
C.R. Durazol Brilliant Red BS	4–5	2–3
C.R. Durazol Red 6BS	5	2–3
Chlorazol Fast Red F125	3	3–4
Chlorazol Fast Pink BK200	4	3–4
Chlorazol Bordeaux BS	2–3	3–4
Chlorazol Fast Helio 2RK200	2–3	3
Durazol Helio B200	3	2–3
Durazol Blue G200	4	3–4
C.R. Durazol Blue 2R150	4–5	2–3
C.R. Durazol Blue 3RS	4	3–4
C.R. Durazol Blue 4R200	4–5	3–4
C.R. Durazol Grey VG150	5–6	4
C.R. Chlorazol Black GFS	2	3
Chlorazol Black E300	2	3–4

Great care must be taken to avoid breathing the nitrous fumes that are liberated; these are harmful to health, and the above treatment should be carried out in a well-ventilated atmosphere.

The material is then rinsed in acidulated water and immediately treated for 20 min in a fresh liquor containing 1–3% of the required developer calculated on the weight of the goods. Stock solutions at a concentration of 5% developer can be conveniently prepared as follows:

β-naphthol

50	parts	β-naphthol are dissolved in
62·5	,,	caustic soda at 38° Bé (70° Tw) and diluted to
$\overline{1\,000}$	parts	with boiling water.

Direct Developer Z

50 parts	Direct Developer *Z* are dissolved in
1 000 ,,	hot water. The developed material is then well washed and dried.

Table 14.2 lists suitable 'Chlorazol' diazo dyestuffs for the production of dischargeable ground shades or cotton.

Table 14.2. SUITABLE 'CHLORAZOL' DIAZO DYESTUFFS FOR COTTON

Dischargeable 'Chlorazol' Diazo Dye	*Light* (Medium depth)	*Washing* Once at 40°C (105°F) Effect on dyeing
Chlorazol Diazo Blue BR 175 (developed in β-naphthol)	5	5
Chlorazol Diazo Green BD 150 (developed in Direct Developer *Z*)	4–5	5

Dyeing of 'Brenthol' As Combinations on Cotton, Linen and Viscose Rayon

The 'Brenthol' *AS* solution is prepared as follows:

15	parts	'Brenthol' *AS* are pasted with
15	,,	methylated spirit, followed by the addition of
9	,,	caustic soda at 38° Bé (70° Tw);
22·5	,,	of cold soft water are then carefully stirred in and stirring is continued until a clear solution is obtained;
920	,,	cold soft water containing
12·5	,,	Turkey Red Oil *PO* are then added.

Bulk to 1 000 parts.

'Brenthol' solution so prepared should be perfectly clear.

The scoured (and preferably dry) material to be padded should be soaked in this solution (cold or warm) for 20–30 s, using for economy the smallest amount of liquor that is convenient. When thoroughly impregnated, the material should be opened out to full width with the minimum of handling and then passed through the rubber rollers of a household wringer that have been screwed down as tightly as possible. There should be no creases in the material. Development of the shade is then carried out as soon as possible, with or without preliminary drying, by padding the material exactly as above in a cold solution of the required 'Brentamine' Fast Salt prepared as follows:

The solutions of 'Brentamine' Fast Salts are prepared by slowly adding 1 part of the powder with vigorous stirring to 5 parts of cold water. This solution or fine suspension (the Fast Salt may not be completely dissolved) should be sieved into the remainder of the

197

required cold water to give the requisite concentration, when complete solution should be attained. Common salt, to the extent of 25 g/litre of the solution should then be added and dissolved, except in the case of 'Brentamine' Fast Black *K* Salt where this addition is omitted.

Table 14.3 lists the fastness properties of azoic combinations suitable for the production of dischargeable ground shades on cotton.

Table 14.3. FASTNESS PROPERTIES OF AZOIC COMBINATIONS ON COTTON

'Brenthol' *AS* coupled with:	Shade given	Concentration of bath (Parts per 1 000)	*Light* (Medium depth)	*Washing* 5 times at 100° C (212°F) Effect on dyeing
Brentamine Fast Yellow GC Salt	Orange	40	3	2
Brentamine Fast Orange GR Salt	Orange	35	3–4	3
Brentamine Fast Red B Salt	Bluish red	45	2	4
Brentamine Fast Red 3GL Salt	Red	45	4	4–5
Brentamine Fast Red TR Salt	Red	50	2	2
Brentamine Fast Scarlet GG Salt	Scarlet	45	5	4

When development of the shade is complete the material should be well rinsed in water acidulated with a little hydrochloric acid, washed acid-free and then soaped at the boil for 20 min in a solution containing 3 parts 'Lissapol' *ND* and 2 parts soda ash per 1 000 parts of water.

'Procion' Dyestuffs: Preparation of Cotton, Linen and Viscose Rayon for Discharging

Ground shades having fastness properties superior to those of dischargeable direct colours can be prepared very simply using a selected range of 'Procion' dyestuffs. The cloth is padded through a solution of dyestuff, squeezed through a mangle and dried. Fixation takes place during the steaming operation used in the subsequent discharge printing process.

When using this process it is important that during the drying stage the cloth be hung straight and free from creases; otherwise the dyeing will be uneven.

The solution of 'Procion' dye is prepared as follows:

3– 20 parts	dye are mixed with
50 ,,	urea and the mixture is dissolved in
900 ,,	warm water at 40°C (105°F).
	To the solution are added
15 ,,	common salt or Glauber's salt crystals and
10 ,,	Resist Salt L and
15 ,,	sodium bicarbonate
Bulk to 1 000 parts.	

The following 'Procion' dyestuffs are suitable for the preparation of dischargeable ground shades:

Procion Brilliant Yellow M-6G	Procion Dark Brown H-B
Procion Brilliant Yellow H-5G	* Procion Brilliant Blue H-7G
Procion Brilliant Yellow H-4G	* Procion Brilliant Blue H-5G
† Procion Yellow H-A	* Procion Printing Green H-5G
Procion Brilliant Orange H-GR	† Procion Black H-N

* In pale depths are dischargeable by Recipe 1, but at depths above 5 parts of dye per 1 000 parts of padding solution, Recipe 2 should be used (see page 202).
† Recommended for discharging in pale and medium depths only.

WHITE DISCHARGES

'Chlorazol', 'Durazol' and 'Chlorazol' Diazo Dyestuffs Dyed on Cotton, Linen and Viscose Rayon

The properties and behaviour of sodium sulphoxylate formaldehyde ('Formosul') should be appreciated before starting on this type of printing. 'Formosul' is stable when dry but decomposes when exposed to air under damp conditions. Prints containing 'Formosul' should therefore be dried as quickly as possible after printing, e.g. by the use of hot air driers over the screen printing table. Where tables are not fitted with hot air blowers, an ordinary electric fan or a domestic hair drier is quite effective. The prints should not be left exposed to air for long periods before steaming, especially in a moist atmosphere. If steaming cannot be carried out immediately after printing, the cloth should be thoroughly dried, wrapped and stored in a dry place. A polythene bag is useful for storage of dried prints before steaming. It sometimes happens that during steaming a coloured discharge becomes surrounded by a thin white halo owing to the migration of the discharging agent. This trouble can be minimised by padding the goods before printing through an aqueous solution of 5–10 parts of Resist Salt L per 1 000 parts while a reduction in the quantity of discharging agent may also be advantageous.

Discharge Recipe (Neutral Discharge)

150 parts	'Formosul' and
50 ,,	glycerine are dissolved in
200 ,,	cold water. The resulting solution is added to
600 ,,	thickening (Note 1)
Bulk to 1 000 parts.	

Notes
(1) Suitable thickenings include Gum Tragacanth, a mixture of 1 part 'Solvitose' OFC10 and 3 parts of 'Solvitose' C5 (Scholtens).
(2) In any white discharge pastes for cellulosic fibres, the purity of the white may be enhanced by including an optical brightening agent in the print paste. These products are invariably discharge-resistant and do not suffer from being included in the discharge paste. An addition of 1 part of 'Fluolite' C per 1 000 parts of print paste is suggested as a basis for trials.

After printing the goods are dried, steamed for 5 min in steam that is as air free as possible and then finally washed in cold water. With diazotised and developed ('D & D') direct dyes and a few other direct dyes which will withstand the treatment, a light soaping is given for 1–2 min at 40°C (105°F) in 2 parts of 'Lissapol' ND per 1 000 parts water. 'Fixanol' PN is often used as an aftertreating agent in conjunction with discharge printing on direct dyed ground shades. The product is classed as a cationic (i.e. positively charged) dye fixing agent. It reacts with negatively charged ('anionic') dyes such as direct dyes to form a complex which is faster to water washing and perspiration than the untreated dye.

The revised procedure when 'Fixanol' PN is used is to follow the steaming treatment with cold water rinsing as previously described. A treatment is then given in a solution containing 2 parts of 'Fixanol' PN per 1 000 parts of water at 40°C (105°F) for 15 min, followed by drying without intermediate rinsing. 'Fixanol' *PN* will form a precipitate with anionic detergents and so should not be used in conjunction with 'Lissapol' *ND*. No such precipitation occurs with non-ionic detergents, e.g. 'Lissapol' *N*, which should therefore be used if any combined treatment is attempted.

White Discharges on Grounds Dyed with 'Brenthol' *AS* – 'Brentamine' Fast Salts

These insoluble azoic combinations need a stronger reducing recipe for discharge printing. Not only is the 'Formosul' concentration raised, but an addition of alkali is also made together with a reduction catalyst. This is the function of the 'Caledon' Developer *AQ* paste (anthraquinone) which is included in the following recipe.

Alkaline Discharge Recipe No. 1

200 parts		'Formosul' and
40 ,,		Soda ash are dissolved in
140 ,,		cold water. The solution obtained is stirred into
600 ,,		Thickening (Note 1) in which
20 ,,		'Caledon' Developer *AQ* paste have been incorporated

Bulk to 1 000 parts.

Notes
(1) A medium to high solids content thickening is recommended. Suitable thickenings include British Gum, Gum Tragacanth, 'Nafka' Crystal Gum Supra (Scholtens) and a mixture of 'Solvitose' *OFC/10* and 'Solvitose' *C5* (Scholtens).
(2) An optical brightening agent may be included if required (see neutral discharge recipe).

After printing and drying the fabric is steamed for 5 min in a steamer which should be as air-free as possible. In order to obtain the best white it is important to wash-off as soon as possible after steaming. After a preliminary rinse in cold water, a treatment is given in a liquor containing 3 parts 'Lissapol' *ND* and 2 parts soda ash per 1 000 parts of water for 5 min at, or near, the boil.

201

White Discharges on 'Procion' Dyed Cellulosic Grounds

Neutral Discharge Recipe No. 1

150 parts	'Formosul' are dissolved in
200 ,,	water and added to
650 ,,	Gum Tragacanth 7% thickening (Note 1)

Bulk to 1 000 parts.

Notes
(1) Or the other thickenings recommended in the neutral discharge recipe for direct dyed grounds.
(2) An optical brightening agent, e.g. 'Fluolite' *C* may prove beneficial added at the rate of 1 part/1 000 parts discharge, paste.

Alkaline Discharge Recipe No. 2

This is the same as recipe no. 1 except that an addition of 50 parts/ 1 000 parts of sodium carbonate (soda ash) is made with appropriate adjustments to the water and/or thickening.

Alkaline Discharge Recipe No. 3 ('Metabol' WS Discharge)

This recipe is a modified version of recipe no. 2 and is used on more difficult to discharge ground shades. It includes 'Metabol' *W* ('Leucotrope' *W* (GDC)) and Solution Salt *BN200* (sodium benzyl sulphanilate) a dispersing and penetrating agent. Finally, an addition of finely dispersed zinc oxide is made which fills the yarn spaces and assists in improving the appearance of the white pattern.

Alkaline Discharge Recipe No. 3 (Alkaline Solution Salt BN/'Metabol' WS)

This consists of:

150 parts	'Formosul'
25 ,,	sodium carbonate
50 ,,	Solution Salt *BN200*
50 ,,	'Metabol' *WS* ('Leucotrope' *W*) are dissolved in
125 ,,	water and stirred into
500 ,,	thickening (Note 1) in which
100 ,,	zinc oxide (1:1) paste, finely ground (Note 2) has previously been incorporated.

Bulk to 1 000 parts.

202

Notes
(1) The thickenings recommended for the two earlier discharge recipes are equally suitable here.
(2) A 1:1 zinc oxide paste in water is usually milled in industry to avoid the presence of particles large enough to cause screen blockages or 'sticking on' with engraved rollers. In the absence of small scale milling equipment it is suggested that a mortar and pestle are used. The ground paste should then be rubbed through a fine mesh sieve.
(3) 'Fluolite' C added at the rate of 1 part/1 000 parts of print paste will enhance the purity of the white.

The discharge properties of 'Procion' dyes have been related to the depth (Standard Depth (%) $\frac{1}{3}$, $\frac{1}{6}$ and $\frac{1}{24}$) using either a neutral or alkaline printing recipe on cotton and viscose rayon[2]. It is often found that the dischargeability of a dye on viscose rayon is inferior to cotton. The response to neutral or alkaline discharge varies for individual dyes, and in the majority of cases the dischargeability rating falls-off rapidly with increasing depth of shade.

Dischargeability Ratings
  A = readily dischargeable to a good white
  B = readily dischargeable to a white suitable for normal discharge patterns in pale-medium depths of shade
  C = not suitable for white discharges; recommended for coloured discharges
  D = unsuitable for either white or coloured discharges owing to heavy residual stain.

'Procion' Dyes Dischargeability on Cotton
Rated *A* at $\frac{1}{3}$ standard depth:
  Procion Brilliant Yellow H-5G (*n, a*)
  Procion Brilliant Yellow H-4G (*n, a*)
  Procion Dark Brown H-B (*n*)
  Procion Brilliant Yellow M-4G (*n, a*)
  Procion Yellow M-4R (*n*)
  Procion Supra Yellow H-8GP (*n, a*)
  Procion Supra Yellow H-4GP (*n*)
  Procion Supra Yellow H-2RP (*n, a*)
Rated *B* at $\frac{1}{3}$ standard depth:
  Procion Golden Yellow H-R (*n, a*)
  Procion Brilliant Orange H-2R (*n, a*)
  Procion Brilliant Red H-3BN (*n*)

Rated C at $\frac{1}{3}$ standard depth:
 Procion Scarlet H-RN (n, a)
 Procion Orange H-4R (n, a)
 Procion Red H-B (n, a)
 Procion Supra Black H-LP (n, a)
Note
 n = neutral discharge (recipe no. 1)
 a = alkaline discharge (recipe nos. 2 or 3, better result quoted).

After printing and drying the fabric is steamed for 5–10 min in steam as air-free as possible and treated at the boil in a solution of 3 parts 'Lissapol' *ND* per 1 000 parts of water, rinsed and dried.

Aniline Black 'Discharges'

This is a misnomer since aniline black once oxidised on the fibre is discharge-resistant. The term is used to distinguish between two styles, which are the Aniline Black *resist* style and the Aniline Black *discharge* style.

In the resist style proper, the normal sequence of print-white and coloured resists-pad aniline black is followed. The 'discharge' style depends on the fact that an aniline black padding liquor, which is colourless, may be padded on to white cloth and if the cloth is dried extremely carefully it remains unoxidised. Success depends absolutely on being able to dry the cloth so that it remains white. Any tendency to form a pale green is the result of over-drying, and will ruin the process. The aniline-padded but unoxidised cloth is then printed with white and coloured resists and processed in the normal way. This technique was used very successfully for finely detailed patterns, often consisting only of black and white, which were used for traditional 'half-mourning' attire, e.g. in Italy. If such patterns were printed first and then padded with aniline black there was always a possibility that the finer portions of the resist would be 'flooded', i.e. the black would encroach into these areas.

Coloured Discharges with Vat Dyestuffs on Cellulosic Fibres

Fabrics used in this style are mainly cotton, viscose rayon and linen, which must of course have been fully bleached. Only relatively minor modifications are needed to the 'all-in' vat printing process already described in Chapter 8, since the reducing agent used to fix the vat dye also discharges the ground shade. The production of good coloured discharges depends on adjusting the printing recipe to give a complete discharge of the ground without 'haloes'. When a coloured discharge area is surrounded by a white halo the effect is due to the bleeding out of excess reducing agent (see later for remedial action). The following points require consideration when adjusting the printing recipe. The concentration of 'Formosul' should not fall below 10% based on the weight of the print paste since lower concentrations, although often adequate to discharge the ground shade, may result in incomplete fixation of the vat dyestuff. With deep ground shades it may be necessary to increase the 'Formosul' to 15% or even to 20%. The most usual cause of white haloes is due to the fabric being too wet in the steamer. This results from steaming under excessively damp conditions, and the hygroscopic nature of 'Formosul' also contributes as does the presence of glycerine in the vat printing recipe. Drier conditions on the print can be produced by decreasing the quantity of glycerine in the print paste (or omitting it altogether if QF printing brands are used), and by using 6% of soda ash as the alkali in place of the potassium carbonate recommended for normal vat printing. If these measures fail to produce the desired improvement then consideration should be given to the feasibility of increasing the steamer temperature a few degrees. If the incoming steam is bubbled through a water bath, drain it and inject the steam directly. Where the steam is piped from a low pressure supply, increase the supply and try to get a slight pressure in the steamer, e.g. $7 \times 10^3 - 1.4 \times 10^4 \text{N/m}^2$ $(1-2 \text{ lbf/in}^2)$. Appropriate safety precautions must be taken, preferably the use of a safety valve set to blow-off at $1.4 \times 10^4 \text{ N/m}^2$ (2 lbf/in^2). If the steam is generated in the steamer itself and the steamer body will not withstand a slight pressure, there is little practical that can be done, and discharge printing experiments will have to be abandoned. There may be the possibility that even though cotton and viscose rayon show haloing, woollen fabrics may not. This is due to the much greater moisture uptake of wool. Suitable dyes for dyeing wool grounds and printing illuminating colours are discussed in the next section.

DYEING OF WOOL WITH ACID DYESTUFFS FOR DISCHARGE PRINTING

Weigh the fabric and scour it (see Chapter 5) and then rinse. Make up the dyebath as follows:

(1) Water (preferably soft) in a quantity of at least 30–40 times the weight of the fabric. To this is added the solution of
(2) Dyestuff (the percentage being calculated on the dry weight of the fabric). This should be made into a smooth paste with cold water and then boiling water poured on with stirring until it is completely dissolved.

In general, the dyebath should be lukewarm when the fabric is entered, raised slowly to the boil and dyeing continued at the boil for 1 h. The method of dyeing depends on the dyestuff used. After dyeing, the fabric should be rinsed and dried. In all methods the percentage additions are calculated on the fabric weight.

Method 1
   Dye with the addition of
   10—15% Glauber's salt crystals,
   3— 5% sulphuric acid at 66° Bé (168° Tw).

Method 2
   Start with
   10—15% Glauber's salt crystals and
   2— 4% acetic acid (40%) in the dyebath.
   Boil for 30—45 min; then exhaust the dyebath by carefully adding 1—2% of acetic acid (40%).

Method 3
   Dye with the addition of
   2—4% ammonium sulphate.
   Boil for 30 min and, if necessary, exhaust the dyebath with a further 2% of ammonium sulphate.

Method 4
   Dye with the addition of
   8% sulphuric acid at 66° Bé (168° Tw).
   Boil for 75 min and then wash-off well.

DYEING OF SILK WITH ACID DYESTUFFS FOR DISCHARGE PRINTING

Weigh the fabric and treat for 1 h at 95°C (205°F) in a bath containing 10 parts of olive oil soap per 1 000 parts. Rinse. Make up the dyebath as follows:

(1)   Water (preferably soft) in a quantity of at least 30—40 times the weight of the fabric. To this is added the solution of

206

(2)   Dyestuff (the percentage being calculated on the dry weight of the fabric). This should be made into a smooth paste with cold water and then boiling water poured on with stirring until it is completely dissolved.

The material is entered into the dyebath at a temperature of 40–50°C (105–120°F) and the bath is heated slowly to 95°C (205°F) and dyed for approximately 1 h. The dyeing method depends on the particular dyes used. After dyeing, rinse and dry. Percentage dyebath additions are calculated on the fabric weight.

Method 1 or 4
   Dye with the addition of
   10% Glauber's salt crystals and
   4% acetic acid (40%)
   Exhaust with 1–3% sulphuric acid at 66° Bé (168° Tw).

Method 2
   Dye with the addition of
   10% Glauber's salt crystals and
   2% acetic acid (40%).

Method 3
   Dye with
   40% Glauber's salt crystals.

Table 14.4 lists the fastness properties of the acid dyestuffs which are suitable for producing dischargeable ground shades on wool.

WHITE DISCHARGES ON WOOL AND SILK DYED WITH ACID DYESTUFFS

It is usual to incorporate up to 20% of zinc oxide or titanium dioxide in the discharge paste, to improve the quality of the discharge effect on dyed ground shades on silk and especially on wool. Both these agents must be very finely dispersed, and this is achieved by grinding them, together with a small proportion of the water and thickening agent, before adding to the remainder of the print paste.

Table 14.4. FASTNESS PROPERTIES OF ACID DYESTUFFS ON WOOL

Acid Dyestuff	Dyeing method	Light (Medium depth)	Washing Once at 55°C (130°F) Effect on dyeing
Carbolan Yellow 4GS	3	5	4
Lissamine Fast Yellow 2GS	1	6–7	1
Tartrazine NS	1	4	1
Carbolan Yellow RS	3	5–6	4
Coomassie Yellow R 200	2	4–5	5
Naphthalene Fast Orange 2GS	1	5	1
Naphthalene Orange GS	1	4	1
Coomassie Milling Scarlet G 150	2	4	4–5
Naphthalene Scarlet 4RS	1	4	1
Coomassie Red PG 150	2	5	4
Naphthalene Red JS	2	3	2
Lissamine Fast Red B 200	1	5–6	1
Azo Geranine 2G 200	1	5	1
Carmoisine LS	1	3	1

Discharge Recipe

250 parts	'Redusol' Z (Note 1) are pasted with
100 „	blood albumen (40% solution (Note 2)),
80 „	glycerine and
200 „	titanium dioxide (50% paste). This mixture is stirred into
370 „	Gum Tragacanth 7% thickening (Note 3).

Bulk to $\overline{1\,000}$ parts.

Notes
(1) 'Redusol' Z (ACC) is the primary zinc salt of formaldehyde sulphoxylate. It is also sold as 'Decroline' Sol. Conc. (GDC).
(2) Blood albumen, which is coagulated by heat, is added to fix titanium dioxide pigment on the fibre. The 40% solution must be made without heating by allowing the product to swell and dissolve in cold water.
(3) Gum Tragacanth may be replaced by a mixture of 1 part 'Solvitose' OFC10 and 3 parts 'Solvitose' C5 (Scholtens).

After printing, the goods are dried, steamed for 10–15 min in steam that is as air-free as possible, then washed well in cold water. The goods should not be allowed to lie about wet because of the risk of staining the discharged portions consequent upon slight bleeding of the ground shades.

COLOURED DISCHARGES WITH BASIC DYESTUFFS ON WOOL AND SILK DYED GROUNDS

Discharge Recipe

20 parts	basic dyestuff are pasted with
50 ,,	'Glydote' *BN* and to this are added
250 ,,	hot water. When cool,
150 ,,	'Formosul' are added. The mixture is stirred into
530 ,,	Gum Tragacanth 7% thickening (see Note).

Bulk to 1 000 parts.

Note
If required, the Gum Tragacanth may be replaced by the same thickening mixture given in the previous recipe.

The cloth is printed, dried lightly in a hot air stove and steamed for 10 min at 100°C (212°F). It is then rinsed, soaped lightly, rinsed again and dried.

In cases where ingredients are difficult to dissolve, part of the water may with advantage be replaced by methylated spirit. *No acetic acid should be added for solvent purposes to pastes in which 'Formosul' is used.*

The 'Formosul' content of the paste can be varied according to the depth of the ground shade to be discharged.

The following basic dyestuffs are suitable for coloured discharges:

Acronol Yellow TC 180	Rhodamine 6GBN 500
Rhodamine 6GDN 500	Rhodamine BN 450

Note
These dyestuffs have, in general, low fastness to light and washing.

WHITE AND COLOURED DISCHARGES ON CELLULOSE ACETATE, CELLULOSE TRIACETATE AND NYLON

The production of white and coloured discharges on cellulose acetate, cellulose triacetate and nylon is considerably more difficult than on cellulosic fibres, wool and silk. While specialist firms can, and do, produce good results, these are only achieved by accurate process control, particularly at the steaming stage. Difficulties to be overcome include the following.

(1)　The hydrophobic nature of the fibres.
(2)　The need to use swelling agents to allow the reducing agent to penetrate the fibre and destroy the ground shade.
(3)　The tendency of soluble reducing agents to give haloes around a coloured pattern.
(4)　The restricted number of discharge resistant dyes that colour the fibres sufficiently well to justify their use.

The problem was first tackled using insoluble reducing agents. One of these is 'Brotasul' (ACC) which is the calcium salt of formaldehyde sulphoxylate prepared in the form of a fine talc-like powder. The background work on this compound has been described by Hannay[3,4]. While this work was in progress, Bernady and Wirth[5] were experimenting with a product called 'Rongalite' H (BASF) in connection with the production of pigment-illuminated discharges. The two products appear very similar to each other.

An alternative insoluble reducing agent is 'Manofast' (Hardman & Holden) which is thiourea dioxide. The use of this product in conjunction with a zinc salt has been described in Reference 6. The zinc salt should be one that is incapable of discharging the ground shade, and zinc sulphate is preferred. Zinc oxide should be replaced by titanium dioxide since the former product reacts with the thiourea dioxide.

Vat dyes may be applied with either 'Brotasul' or 'Manofast' and in both cases they fix as their acid leuco compounds. The range of vat dyes that fix efficiently is somewhat restricted, probably due to their relatively large molecular size preventing fibre penetration.

The recipes which follow will serve as a basis for the production of white discharges.

'Brotasul' White Discharges on Nylon, Cellulose Acetate and Cellulose Triacetate

The general recipes are as follows:

	Nylon	Cellulose acetate	Cellulose triacetate
Gum Tragacanth (6·5%)	360 parts	360 parts	265 parts
British Gum (1:1)	—	—	100 „
Titanium dioxide	70 „	70 „	70 „
Water	140 „	165 „	140 „
Urea	50 „	50 „	—
Polyethylene glycol 200 (see Note)	100 „	100 „	100 „
'Glydote' BN	—	—	20 „
Zinc sulphate	100 „	100 „	100 „
'Brotasul'	175 „	150 „	200 „
'Lissapol' D	5 „	5 „	5 „
		1 000 parts.	

Note

The figure after the polyethylene glycol refers to the molecular weight of the polymer. A variety of weights is available.

Steaming times of from 15–30 min are required, after which the fabric is rinsed thoroughly in cold water, treated in 5 parts 'Lissapol' *ND* per 1 000 parts of water for 5 min at 50°C (120°F), rinsed and dried.

'Manofast' White Discharges

The recipes are as follows:

	Cellulose acetate	Cellulose triacetate
'Manofast'	50 parts	80 parts
Zinc thiocyanate	100 „	—
Zinc sulphate	—	100 „
Polyethylene glycol 200	—	100 „
Water	150 „	120 „
British Gum (1:1)	700 „	—
'Nafka' Crystal Gum Supra (20%)	—	600 „
	1 000 parts.	

Processing after printing is the same as for the recipes using 'Brotasul'.
In view of the restricted number of vat dyes that may be used as illuminating colours, products made by several firms may be required to obtain a range. It is suggested that the makers of the reducing agents are approached for their latest recommendations before attempting this style in practice[7,8].

Polyester Fibres

There do not appear to be any commercially produced white or coloured discharges on polyester fibres. The difficulty of obtaining penetration into the fibre by a reducing agent constitutes a primary barrier to such a process. In addition, the removal of the discharged fragments of dye-stuff from the fibre would be difficult. The most effective way to obtain a discharge effect on a polyester fabric would be to use the imitation discharge effect which has been described earlier in this chapter. Limitations already described in respect of depth of ground shade and its colour relative to the illuminating colour would apply.

REFERENCES

1. DISERENS, L., *The Chemical Technology of Dyeing and Printing*, 83–102, Rheinhold Publishing Corp., New York, USA (1948)
2. *Pattern Card Procion Dyes Printing*, ICI Dyestuffs Division, Ref. 14570
3. HANNAY and FURNESS, *Journal of the Society of Dyers and Colourists*, 69, 596 (1953)
4. HANNAY, *Journal of the Society of Dyers and Colourists*, 76, 11–15 (1960)
5. BERNARDY and WIRTH, *Melliand Textilberichte*, 38, 1044 (1957)
6. HARDMAN and HOLDEN LTD., U.K. Pat. 719 089 (12.12.51)
7. The makers of 'Manofast' are Hardman & Holden Ltd., Manox House, Miles Platting, Manchester 10, UK
8. The makers of 'Brotasul' are Associated Chemical Companies Ltd., P.O. Box No. 6, Brotherton House, Westgate, Leeds 1, UK

15

Batik Printing

'Batik' is an Indonesian word describing a form of resist printing which, although known and practised as a native craft in south-east India, Europe and parts of Africa, has achieved an unrivalled degree of crafts-manship in the Island of Java.

It is a characteristic of the Java batik that the resist is obtained by applying wax to both sides of the fabric. Dyeing is then carried out in the cold to avoid melting the wax, thus confining the coloration to the unwaxed area. Selective further waxing and re-dyeing allows a variety of colourings of increasing depth to be built up additively. Where complete colour changes are required the wax is completely removed in boiling water and the washed and dried cloth rewaxed to cover those areas that it is desired to protect from further dyeing.

The equipment required to produce batiks consists of:

The 'Tjap': This is a specially made block composed of copper strips, hand-worked and fitted into a copper lattice, and held in place by solder. The all-metal construction allows its use in hot wax and the method of construction allows a completed block to be carefully sawn in two, thus forming a pair of mirror image 'tjaps'. Printing on both sides of the fabric, essential in high-class work, is thus not only possible, but also achieves a high degree of precision even in intricate designs. It may take a skilled craftsman up to a month to make a pair of 'tjaps'. These blocks are seldom seen outside Java.

The 'Tjanting': This is a small cup made of thin copper sheet which carries a tubular spout at one end and is fitted into a short bamboo rod at the other by means of a rolled extension of the copper sheet which forms a fang. The joints are brazed and the spout, which decreases slightly in diameter to the delivery end, has a brazed seam. A skilled metal worker could fairly easily make a 'tjanting' for handicraft work, provided an authentic specimen were first examined and used to prepare a template. The diameter of the spout is varied to accord with the width of the line it is desired to trace and the very small bore 'tjantings' are naturally the most difficult to make and use.

Classical batiks were originally prepared by the daughters of Javanese nobility who worked diligently for many months on a single sarong using only the 'tjanting'. Batiks produced in this way were outstanding examples of technique, comparable in pride of workmanship with the hand embroideries of their European sisters of former times.

The commercial production of batiks still occupies a considerable number of people in modern Java. The basic design is normally applied by 'tjap' and the 'tjanting' used to complete the later stages and dyeing operation. Batiks produced in this way normally have rich but sombre colourings with brown and oranges predominating. Indigo is used as a basis for deep shades of brown or blacks.

An alternative type of batik is characterised by striking designs of birds, animals or floral motifs executed in very bright colourings. These are produced in central Java (especially Pekalongan) by a slightly different technique. First the basic design is either stamped on by 'tjap' or hand drawn by 'tjanting'. Afterwards, dyestuff solution is painted over suitable areas using a small piece of bamboo fanned-out at one end to form a type of brush. In this way a design whose outlines were defined in wax, may receive a large number of different colours without a separate dyeing operation for each. When painting is completed the whole design area is covered with wax on both sides of the fabric using a fairly coarse-spouted 'tjanting'. A background colouring to the whole design is then applied by dipping the fabric in a dye solution which penetrates all unwaxed areas.

Java batiks are normally marketed either in large oblong pieces which form the 'sarong', or in smaller square pieces to form a headcloth, 'kain kapella'. Their designs, especially the use of border areas, have this end use predominantly in mind. Attractive European garments such as dresses, beach shirts, dressing-gowns and even ties can be made from sarong lengths.

The attraction of the batik technique in craft work is that by the exercise of patience and ingenuity excellent results can be obtained with little more than a 'tjanting'. The choice of dyestuff is all-important or otherwise hours of work on the wax resist may be wasted. Particular attention has been given to choice of dye in the sections that follow.

APPLICATION OF THE WAX RESIST

In making Java batiks, the cloth to be printed is first treated with a thin starch solution and ironed; this preliminary process improves the results and tends to prevent undue penetration of the wax into the cloth. Usually, the wax is printed on both the face and the back of the fabric, and the results are better if the wax is not allowed to penetrate the cloth but rather to form layers on the two surfaces. In this way the edges of the objects appear sharper in the final result.

Choice of Wax

In the production of Java batiks the nature of the wax used is varied according to type of final effect desired. If a batik showing a 'crackle effect' is required, a resist consisting of a mixture of paraffin wax and resin is used. A suitable mixture is one of 4 parts of rosin with 1 part of paraffin wax, or 3 parts of rosin with 1 part of paraffin wax should the rosin be a high-melting variety. The higher the proportion of paraffin wax in the mixture the more brittle becomes the print and the more pronounced the 'cracking'. The wax-printed goods are allowed to hang for a few days and during this time the wax hardens and becomes more brittle. Should the hardening be incomplete the final 'crackle' effect will lack the characteristically fine veined effect which is the hall-mark of a high-class batik of this type. To increase the crackle effect the printed and dried pattern is sometimes worked for a short time under cold water to intensify the 'crazing' of the wax. Batiks showing a crackle effect are not normally required in Java. They are more popular outside Java than on the island itself and are often deliberately imitated by mechanical means for the West African market by European roller printers.

The usual Java batik has a clear resist showing no 'crackle' effects, and the wax used is different from that employed for a batik showing a 'crackle' effect. The Java batik is produced by block printing the designs on both sides of the fabric using two types of wax, each of which may have several components whose exact proportions differ from one batik printing establishment to another. The two main types are a light easily removed type consisting essentially of paraffin wax, and a darker more adhesive type consisting essentially of beeswax with some paraffin wax and an animal fat. By the use on the same fabric of waxes having varying adhesive characteristics, different resist effects can be produced. For example, the printed and dried goods can be indigo dipped (described later) and then the light wax carefully shaved-off. This operation is performed by hand with the sarong suspended on a bamboo pole above the operative's head. A crude scraper is used, often consisting of a hacksaw blade sharpened on the non-serrated edge. This is bent double and held in one hand, scraping being performed by the small piece of metal forming the bend. Knowing the basic design required, the operative scrapes away the small areas subsequently to be overdyed. Next the goods are dyed

215

in, for example, a direct cotton dyestuff using the 'gosok' technique and coupled in a suitable developer. At this stage the batik is examined and the hard wax printed areas repaired. Alternatively, further wax designs may be added by means of the 'tjanting', and the sarong overdyed again.

Printing Equipment

The cloth to be printed with the wax is stretched out on a table covered with layers of cloth; to prevent the hot wax from soaking into them the tablecloth is sprinkled with an even layer of china clay or fine sand. In Java, banana leaves previously soaked in dilute caustic soda are used as the wax will neither adhere to these nor penetrate into them.

The wax is applied from a special form of printing block. The wax is kept molten in a simple waxing vessel which is a shallow dish of sufficent size to hold the block. A piece of felt is placed in the bottom of this vessel, wax is poured over the felt and the whole is kept heated throughout the printing operation by a small kerosene lamp. The metal block, which retains its heat throughout the printing operation, is furnished as required from the surface of the felt saturated with molten wax.

Removal of Wax

The final operation in the production of a Java batik is the complete removal of the wax used as the resisting agent. This is carried out, after the dyeing operations described in the following pages have been completed, by immersing the cloth in a bath of very hot or boiling water to remove as much as possible of the surface-held wax, followed by a treatment in a hot solution of soda ash to remove the remainder. The wax that is removed by hot water is skimmed-off, collected, recast into blocks of suitable size and used again. That removed by the alkaline solution will be emulsified and cannot be recovered. Since the total amount of wax used in a batikery represents a quite considerable capital outlay, no attempt is made to use alkali until as much wax as possible has been recovered. This is one reason why a genuine Java batik has a characteristic smell of wax and rosin when first purchased, and this is retained for a considerable period after repeated washings.

216

DYESTUFFS SUITABLE FOR USE IN BATIK PRINTING

Dyestuffs suitable for this work must be capable of being applied from
a cold dyebath, since a heated dyebath would remove the wax resist.
The following classes of dyes are of interest:

(1) Indigo and other cold-dyeing vat dyestuffs
(2) Azoic 'Brenthol' dyestuffs
(3) 'Procion' dyestuffs
(4) 'Soledon' dyestuffs.

Apparatus Required

With dyestuffs other than indigo, batiks are dyed in shallow flat
troughs of suitable size to accommodate a sarong, that is, about
3 m x 1·3 m x 150 mm deep (10 ft x 4½ ft x 6 in deep). The fabric is
placed in the trough and dyeliquor poured over it, and then it is rubbed
gently by hand to aid penetration. When thoroughly moistened the
sarong is removed and either placed flat in another similar trough or
allowed to drain over a bamboo rod. In this way a large pile of sarongs
accumulates and the pile is turned from time to time (the 'gosok'
method). These troughs are also used for local application or azoics by
brush where only the border of the sarong may be treated. An alternative
method uses a shallow concrete trough inclined at a slight angle towards
the operative. Dyeliquor is poured through into the 'V' made by the
incline, and the sarong is plaited into the liquor in folds. The folds are
opened and the sarong may again be rubbed gently by hand on the
slope of the trough. The wetted fabric is then hung on a rail over the
trough and surplus dyeliquor drains on to the sloping trough surface
and collects in the base of the 'V'. Approximate dimensions of such
a device would be 1·3 m wide x 0·9—1·2 m long (4½ ft wide x 3—4 ft
long) and tilted so that the end nearest the operator is about 220 mm (9 in)
lower than the end farthest away from him. The height is adjusted to
allow for comfortable working from a standing position.

In a few areas of Java a simple dipping technique is practised which
requires a shallow wooden box of sarong width (about 1·3 m (4½ ft)).
The maximum depth of these boxes is 220—290 mm (9—12 in) and
their cross-section is that of a truncated cone with the wider section
uppermost. Near the base of the trough one (or sometimes two)
wooden rods are fixed in simple wooden bearings to allow free
rotation. Strings are attached to the corners of the sarong and threaded
under the rollers. Dyeliquor is poured into the trough and the fabric
is passed through the liquor several times by pulling on the strings.
Again the fabric is hung over a rod to drain and dry. The last mentioned

217

type of dye trough is the easiest and cheapest to construct but may not give adequate penetration with heavily waxed batiks unless aided by gentle hand rubbing.

Indigo dipping is carried out in very deep tanks so that the sarongs, which are about 3 m (10 ft) long, can hang straight downwards in the liquor and still leave a space in which sediment can collect. In such cases the object is to have a standing bath that can be used to dye succeeding lots of goods for months, or even for years, without cleaning out. Such considerations as this do not arise, of course, in handicraft work. It should be stressed, however, that it is particularly difficult to prepare small-scale indigo vats for batik dyeing without using alkalis that can attack the wax resists. Unless there is some specific reason why indigo should be used, it is suggested that navy shades be obtained by using azoic 'Brenthol' dyes, which are simpler and far quicker to use. Alternatively, 'Soledon' Indigo *LL* may be applied by the nitrite method, preferably by brushing. Once developed this 'Soledon' gives indigo on the fibre. It will not build-up to heavy shades unlike the parent vat, since it is not practical to apply the dip—oxidise—re-dip—re-oxidise, etc. sequence used with indigo itself.

Indigo and Cold-Dyeing 'Caledon' Vat Dyestuffs

Indigo is a vat dyestuff traditionally used in batiks. It has not got outstanding fastness properties on cotton, but it is cheap and easy to apply in bulk dyeing once the dyebath has been brought into the correct condition by an experienced dyer. Before being made synthetically by processes patented in 1891 and 1901 by BASF in Germany, indigo was extracted from two plants. One was a plant of the genus indigofera, which grew in India and other parts of the tropics. The second plant which was woad (isatis tinctoria) grew in central and southern Europe as well as in the Orient. Woad gave only about half the yield of indigo obtainable from the Indian plant, and so was more expensive. Synthetic indigo replaced the natural product from both sources but it was used in batikeries by the same long established techniques. The 'Caledon' dyestuffs are faster modern vat dyes. They are insoluble in water and are sold as:

Liquids— consisting of a dispersion of the dyestuff in water and generally containing from 10 to 20% of pure dyestuff and a small quantity of dispersing agent to prevent settling.

Powders— The *FD* Powders Fine have now been replaced by the Grains form.

218

Grains— The rapidly dispersing grains now available represent a further improvement on the *FDN* Grains which they have replaced. The grains consist of dyestuff mixed with a solid diluent and some dispersing agent. The content of pure dye varies considerably, Indigo is available as grains but differs from the 'Caledon' grains since it is in the reduced form.

The strength of a powder brand as compared with the paste is usually denoted by a number appended to the dyestuff name; thus a *300* powder is three times as strong as the single-strength paste.

In order to dye vat dyestuffs on cotton it is first necessary to convert them to a form in which they are soluble in water and possess affinity for the cotton. This conversion is brought about by a chemical reaction involving a certain part of the dyestuff molecule that is common to all vat dyestuffs. This particular part of the molecule is reduced by means of sodium hydrosulphite (hydros) into the form of an organic acid, which is then neutralised with sodium hydroxide (caustic soda) to form a salt, which is soluble in water and has affinity for cotton. The actual solubility and affinity varies from dyestuff to dyestuff and may necessitate variations in the quantities of hydrosulphite and caustic soda used to dissolve the dyestuff in preparation for dyeing.

The process of converting the insoluble vat dyestuff into the soluble compound used for dyeing is termed *vatting,* and the solution so produced is called a *vat.* The reduced or vatted dyestuff is often spoken of as the *leuco compound.* Owing to the chemical change that takes place during the vatting of the dyestuff, the colour of the vat or leuco product may be very different from that of the original dyestuff. Fully vatted indigo is yellow, but excess reducing agent slows down the rate at which the shade can be built up, and vats that are a yellow-green colour are usually preferred. In the 'Caledon' series this colour change may be from yellow to blue, from orange to violet, or may be barely noticeable.

Indigo is more readily reduced than vat dyestuffs of the 'Caledon' class, and in native craft-dyeing, caustic soda and sodium hydrosulphite have never become established in certain areas. Reduction may be brought about by fermentation induced by fruits or syrups in the presence of alkalis such as wood ashes, soda ash or lime. Alternatively, ferrous sulphate or zinc dust may be used as a reducing agent with lime as the alkali. Certain of these indigo vats have less destructive action on the various resist pastes employed in batik work. The establishment and control of such vats on a handicraft scale is so tedious and so liable to cause disappointment and unsatisfactory results that it is not recommended that such attempts be made.

To apply indigo, a solution for dyeing a medium shade using the caustic soda and sodium hydrosulphite vat is prepared as follows:

3 parts	caustic soda at 38° Bé (70° Tw) and
1 "	sodium hydrosulphite are dissolved in
950 "	cold water. Into this solution is stirred gently
7 "	Indigo Vat 60% Grains, avoiding as far as possible aeration of the solution.

Bulk to 1 000 parts.

The solution should be yellowish-green and, when all the indigo is dissolved, dyeing can be started. If, during the course of the dyeing, the dyebath becomes bluer, this indicates that the indigo is becoming oxidised and the bath requires further reducing agent. The addition of 1 part of caustic soda at 38° Bé (70° Tw) and 1 part of sodium hydro-sulphite should be sufficient to bring the bath back to its required reduced state.

The material to be dyed is entered and dyed for 10 min. It is then removed, squeezed or mangled and allowed to oxidise in air for 5 min. To build up the required depth of shade it is necessary to re-immerse for 2–3 min and then remove, re-squeeze and re-oxidise. These operations must be repeated in this sequence until the desired shade is obtained. For many purposes three to four sequences of 'dips' will be found to give a sufficiently deep shade. The dyed fabric is then rinsed thoroughly in cold water and dried.

'Dip Dyeing'

'Caledon' dyestuffs are normally dyed by one of three well-established dyeing methods, but for batik work only Methods 2 and 3 are recommended. These methods are similar in that caustic soda and sodium hydrosulphite are the vatting agents employed in each case. They differ in respect of the relative amounts that are used, as shown in *Table 15.1*.

The following procedure is used for the dip-dyeing application of 'Caledon' vat dyestuffs:

The required quantity of the vat dyestuff liquid or rapidly dispersing grains is weighed into the dye vessel, then diluted with the weight of soft water shown in the table, before heating to the correct vatting temperature, usually 40–60°C (100–140°F). The requisite amounts of caustic soda and sodium hydrosulphite are added in the order given, and the dyestuff is allowed to vat for 5–10 min with gentle stirring. At the

Table 15.1. QUANTITIES OF CHEMICALS FOR DISSOLVING 'CALEDON' DYESTUFFS OPEN VAT (30:1)

Vatting Solutions	Method 2							Method 3						
	100 g of Material in 3 litres of Dyeliquor													
Dyestuff, single-strength (g)	2	5	10	15	20	30	40	2	5	10	15	20	30	40
Water (cc)	20	50	100	150	200	300	400	20	50	100	150	200	300	400
Caustic soda at 38° Bé (cc)	1·25	3	6·25	9·5	12·5	18·75	25	1·25	2·5	5	6·25	7·25	8·75	10
Sodium hydrosulphite (g)	0·5	1·25	2·5	3·75	5	7·5	10	0·5	1·25	2·5	3·75	5	7·5	10
Additions: Caustic soda at 38° Bé (cc)	5	5	5	5	5	5	5	2·5	2·5	2·5	2·5	2·5	2·5	2·5
Sodium hydrosulphite (g)	2	2	2	2	2	2	2	2	2	2	2	2	2	2
Sodium sulphate anhydrous or common salt* (g)	5	10	20	25	30	35	40	10	20	40	50	60	70	80

* In place of anhydrous sodium sulphate, double the quantity of Glauber's salt may be used.

N.B. – The amounts of caustic soda and sodium hydrosulphite required depend on the amount of liquor used. For example, 6 litres of liquor would require double the amount specified, and so on. If there is any sign of the dyestuff coming out of solution or oxidising in the vat, the vat should be 'sharpened' by the addition of small amounts of caustic soda and sodium hydrosulphite and allowed to stand until the dyestuff is re-vatted. Note also that 38° Bé $\equiv$ 70° Tw.

end of this time the dyestuff is fully reduced and the dyebath is then carefully diluted to the required liquor length (1 part by weight of material in 20 parts of weight of dyeliquor) with cold soft water, in which the weights of adjuvants shown in the table have been dissolved.

Dyeing is carried out by dipping the material and working well for a few minutes. The material is then removed and allowed to oxidise in the air for 10–20 min and the process is repeated until the required depth of shade is obtained, after which the cloth is thoroughly washed in warm water until free from alkali. It is then dried.

The vatted dyestuff may also be applied by brushing the solution on to the fabric. Nylon brushes are recommended for this purpose as natural bristle is attacked by caustic soda.

After brushing, the fabric must be allowed to oxidise in the air for 10–20 min before thoroughly washing. The use of common salt in the dyebath is not absolutely necessary for dip dyeing and should be omitted for brush work. It is only used when maximum colour value is required from the vat and should then be added gradually during dyeing.

Vat dyestuffs, which are especially recommended for this purpose, are reduced at 50°C (120°F) and dyed cold (*Table 15.2*).

Table 15.2. THE FASTNESS PROPERTIES OF 'CALEDON' DYESTUFFS ON COTTON

'Caledon' Dyestuff	Method of dyeing	Light (Full depth)	Washing 5 times at 100°C (212°F) Effect on dyeing
Caledon Gold Orange 3G Grains	2	6–7	5
Caledon Brilliant Orange 6R Grains	2	7–8	3–4 B
Caledon Brilliant Violet 3R Grains	2	7	4
Caledon Brilliant Blue 3G Grains	2	7–8	4
Caledon Jade Green XBN Grains	2	7	4–5
Caledon Olive R Grains	2	7	3–4WG
Caledon Brown R Grains	2	7–8	4–5

Table 15.3. STRENGTHS OF LIQUID AND GRAIN BRANDS OF 'CALEDON' DYESTUFFS LISTED IN TABLE 15.2.

Vat Dye	Grains strength	Liquid strength
Caledon Gold Orange 3G	400	200
Caledon Brilliant Orange 6R	325	250
Caledon Brilliant Violet 3R	450	250
Caledon Brilliant Blue 3G	450	Not available
Caledon Jade Green XBN	1500	600

Table 15.3 shows the strengths of the Liquid and Grains brands of those vat dyestuffs whose fastness properties are given in *Table 15.2.* (Single strength = 100)

Azoic 'Brenthol' Dyestuffs*

The 'Brenthols' are a series of products which, in conjunction with the 'Brentamine' Fast Salts, are used to produce shades of remarkable brilliancy, depth and, in many cases, extremely high fastness. The more substanstive 'Brenthols' are to be preferred for batik printing because they give the best rubbing fastness. The recommended range of combinations is given in *Table 15.4.*

Table 15.4. RECOMMENDED RANGE OF COMBINATIONS OF AZOIC DYESTUFFS

Combination	Shade
Brenthol CT – Brentamine Fast Red TR Salt	Turkey red
Brenthol AT – Brentamine Fast Scarlet GG Salt	Yellow
Brenthol CT – Brentamine Fast Red B Salt	Bluish red
Brenthol CT – Brentamine Fast Bordeaux GP Salt	Bordeaux
Brenthol CT – Brentamine Fast Garnet GBC Salt	Garnet
Brenthol CT – Brentamine Fast Orange GC Salt	Orange

The 'Brenthol' solutions are carefully prepared in soft water as follows:

'Brenthol' AT

15 parts	'Brenthol' *AT* are pasted with
15 "	methylated spirit followed by the addition of
9 "	caustic soda at 38° Bé (70° Tw);
30 "	of cold water are carefully stirred in and stirring is continued until a clear solution is obtained. This is poured into the dyebath, set with
910 "	cold soft water containing
20 "	Turkey Red Oil *PO*.
Bulk to 1 000 parts.	

*No longer sold by ICI. See Appendix 2 for alternative suppliers.

'Brenthol' CT

15 parts		'Brenthol' *CT* are pasted with a mixture of
22	,,	methylated spirit,
30	,,	cold water and
6	,,	caustic soda at 38° Bé (70° Tw). Stirring is continued until a clear solution is obtained. This is poured into a dyebath containing
900	,,	cold soft water,
20	,,	Turkey Red Oil *PO* and
2	,,	caustic soda at 30° Bé (70° Tw).

Bulk to   1 000 parts.

The wax-printed cloth is dipped into the cold 'Brenthol' solution made up as detailed above. It is worked for a short while, allowed to drain and then dried, if possible in the dark but certainly away from direct sunlight. The material is then developed by immersing it in a liquor containing the 'Brentamine' Fast Salt. Alternatively, where localised application is required, e.g. an azoic dyed border – the 'Brenthol' solution may be brushed-on with a 1–2 in paint brush. The 'Brenthol' liquor may be thickened slightly in this case by replacing part of the water with Gum Tragacanth thickening. A short time is given for the 'Brenthol' to penetrate, and then, using a clean brush, the solution of 'Brentamine' Fast Salt is similarly applied. Brushes used for this purpose should be thoroughly washed after use if made from natural bristle, so as to minimise attack by caustic soda. Rubber gloves should be worn whenever the cloth is being treated in either a 'Brenthol' or a 'Brentamine' Fast Salt Solution, in order to protect the hands from attack by caustic soda, or staining due to dyestuff formation on the skin.

'Brentamine' Fast Salt solutions are prepared as follows:

40 parts		'Brentamine' Fast Salt are pasted with
300	,,	water at a maximum temperature of 30°C (85°F). A smooth paste should be formed which will then easily dissolve in the remaining
725	,,	water which is then added, followed by
25	,,	common salt (10 g (1 lb) in the case of 'Brentamine' Fast Garnet *GBC* Salt).

Bulk to   1 000 parts.

In the case of 'Brentamine' Fast Red *B* Salt, it is better to sprinkle the Fast Salt into the whole of the water with vigorous stirring. When 'Brentamine' Fast Scarlet *GG* Salt is used in combination with 'Brenthol' *AT*, 4 parts of 40% acetic acid per 1 000 parts should be added to the developing bath before use. When the shade is completely developed the material should be well washed in water containing 3·5 parts of 20° Bé (32° Tw) hydrochloric acid per 1 000 parts, followed by a thorough rinsing in cold water.

'Procion' Dyestuffs

The 'Procion' dyestuffs offer considerable scope for batik work in handicraft applications but only those of the cold-dyeing type ('Procion' *M* dyes) are sufficiently reactive to fix under air drying conditions. It is important to appreciate that, whereas for other forms of printing both *H* and *M* dyes are satisfactory, for batik work only 'Procion' *M* dyes are suitable.

'Procion' dyestuffs possess in general fairly low substantivity and for very heavy shades it may be necessary to build up the shade with several dips. The dye uptake on unmercerised cloth is fairly low, but on both mercerised cotton and viscose rayon deeper shades are obtained with fewer dips, and the use of unmercerised cotton should be avoided where possible.

By the use of a dip-dyeing technique or by brush painting locally over waxed areas, a series of bright novel shades is produced with 'Procion' dyestuffs. Another unusual property of 'Procion' dyes is also of interest in batik work. The majority of 'Procion' dyes will react with a very limited number of 'Brentamine' Fast Salts to produce rich dark-brown shades similar to those frequently seen in Java batiks. Outstanding in this respect is the reaction product between a dyed 'Procion' dyestuff and 'Brentamine' Fast Black *K* Salt. It is recommended that batik dyeings based on this reaction be limited to this particular 'Brentamine' Fast Salt. Other members of the 'Brentamine' range either do not react with 'Procion' dyes at all, or give shades similar to 'Brentamine' Fast Black *K* Salt, but of much lower intensity. Typical examples of the shades obtained by reaction with 'Brentamine' Fast Black *K* Salt are:

Normal shade	*Reacted shade*
Procion Brilliant Red M-2B	Reddish brown
Procion Yellow M-R	Yellowish brown
Procion Blue M-3G	Chocolate brown

Alternative effects may be produced by introducing a further waxing operation after dyeing in a 'Procion' dyestuff and then developing in 'Brentamine' Fast Black *K* Salt. The portions protected by the over-waxing do not react, while the remainder of the unwaxed pattern does and the bright 'Procion' shades stand out very effectively against a deep, usually brownish, developed shade as background.

The following 'Procion' dyestuffs are of interest in batik dyeing and may be mixed with one another in any proportion:

Procion Brilliant Yellow M-6G	Procion Brilliant Red M-5B
Procion Yellow M-R	Procion Red M-G
Procion Brilliant Orange M-G	Procion Brilliant Blue M-R
Procion Brilliant Red M-2B	Procion Blue M-3G

The dyebaths are prepared as follows:

25 parts	urea are dissolved in
300 ,,	boiling water and allowed to cool to 60°–70°C (140°–160°F). This solution is then added portionwise to
10– 50 ,,	'Procion' dyestuff with stirring and, finally,
565–525 ,,	cold water.
Bulk to 900 parts.	

Immediately prior to dyeing a previously prepared alkaline solution containing:

4 parts	anhydrous sodium carbonate and
8 ,,	sodium bicarbonate dissolved in
88 ,,	cold water and bulked to 100 parts

is stirred into the dyebath described above. Once the alkali has been added the dyebath is only suitable for use for 2–3 h. The dye solution without added alkali may be stored for 2–3 days and it is thus possible by adding a proportionate amount of alkali to portions of the dyeliquor to conduct several dipping operations from one batch of dyeliquor. The residue after each dipping is discarded. It is not possible to distinguish visually between dyestuff solution that has decomposed owing to being in contact with alkali too long, and one that is fit for use. The observed result after dyeing from a decomposed dyebath after removal of the wax is a very pale shade. At this stage it is, of course, too late to rectify matters, so the instructions with regard to dyebath stability in the presence of alkali should be strictly followed, and dyeliquors outside the time limits suggested discarded regardless of appearance.

226

In order that the reaction between a 'Procion' dyestuff and a cotton fibre shall proceed satisfactorily, heat, moisture and alkali must be present. Efficient batik dyeing requires a proper control of all these factors, but fortunately this is a simple procedure. At room temperature, fixation may proceed on the fabric for several hours but the rate of fixation is speeded up in warm humid atmospheres, and optimum fixation may be achieved in 2–3 h. In a drying cupboard to which steam could be introduced intermittently, e.g. from an electric kettle, excellent fixation may be obtained in even shorter periods. The method to be adopted will depend on local equipment and conditions, but can easily be established by trials.

'Procion' dyestuffs while undergoing fixation in this manner are not susceptible to sunlight, but are seriously affected by acid fumes, which prevent proper development. Several of the 'Procion' dyes are also affected in shade, even when fixed, by the nitrous acid development baths used for 'Soledon' dyes, and the use of these two classes of dye alongside each other is not recommended.

'Soledon' Dyestuffs

The 'Soledon' dyestuffs are water-soluble derivatives of vat dyestuffs, and the more substantive members of the range are ideally suited to batik dyeing. They are soluble in water and may be applied cold. 'Soledon' dyestuffs of low substantivity may be used, however, if more highly concentrated solutions are employed. The material is dipped in a cold solution of dyestuff containing 5 parts of sodium nitrite per 1 000 parts, squeezed out and then developed by a short treatment in a solution containing 2 parts by volume of sulphuric acid at 66°Bé (168° Tw) per 100 parts of water. The majority of the 'Soledon' dyestuffs may be developed cold, but others require a treatment at 60°–80°C (140°–175°F).

The acid treatment should not be unduly prolonged because of the possibility of chemical damage to the fabric and also because of the noxious nitrous fumes that are evolved during the treatment. Efficient ventilation should be maintained. The sodium nitrite may be omitted from the dyebath and added instead (as a solution) to the acid treatment bath, in which case rather more fumes may be evolved.

The range of 'Soledon' dyestuffs that can be used for the above process is shown in *Table 15.5*. After the shade of the 'Soledon' dyestuff has been developed, the printed material should be well washed in cold or warm water, taking care that no acid is left in the goods.

'Soledon' dyestuffs are also suitable for application by brushing and are often so used in the Pekalongan area of central Java. In this type

227

of batik, floral or bird motifs are first printed by 'tjap' or painted by 'tjanting' in wax. Small sticks of bamboo with fanned-out ends are used, and 'Soledon' solutions are painted on to appropriate parts of the design. 'Brentogen' dyestuffs may also be used alongside the 'Soledons' and development may be brought about either by hanging in strong sunlight or in an acid bath. The whole design area is then completely covered by wax on both sides, and then dipped again into a 'Soledon' solution to dye up the background shade.

Table 15.5. FASTNESS PROPERTIES OF THE RANGE OF 'SOLEDON' DYESTUFFS THAT CAN BE USED FOR PRINTING ON COTTON

	'Soledon' Dyestuff	*Light* (Full shade)	*Washing* 5 times at $100°C$ ($212°F$) Effect on dyeing
	Soledon Golden Yellow RKS	5–6	4–5
	Soledon Golden Yellow GKS	4–5	2
	Soledon Yellow 3RS	6–7	4–5
	Soledon Brown RS	7	4–5
	Soledon Dark Brown 3RS	7	4–5
* †	Soledon Pink FFS	4	4–5
	Soledon Red 2BS .	6	4
* †	Soledon Blue 4BC 125	4	3–4
† ‡	Soledon Blue 2RCX	7	4–5
	Soledon Indigo LLS	3	1
	Soledon Jade Green XS	6–7	4
*	Soledon Grey BS	5	3–4

* These dyestuffs are developed at $60°–80°C$ ($140°–175°F$).
† These 'Soledons' are of low affinity.
‡ This should be developed using half the normal amount of sodium nitrite.

WEST AFRICAN WAX PRINTS

These have long been exported from Europe to west Africa, but now there remains only one British and one Dutch firm active in this field. These two firms have been involved with others in the establishment of local firms in west African territories to carry out this highly specialised work. The wearing of expensive wax prints is regarded as a status symbol in west Africa, and with growing prosperity the demand for them is expected to increase.

Few details of the process involved in printing west African wax prints have been published, since the firms involved regard such 'know-how' as a very important part of their business. There is one significant difference between Javanese batiks and west African batiks.

228

In a Javanese batik, wax printing is carried out on cloth already torn into sarong lengths for ease of processing. In a west African batik a continuous roll of cloth is fed into a duplex roller printing machine. Arrangements are made for the colour boxes containing the wax to be heated so that the wax remains molten in them. Both sides of the cloth are thus coated with a wax in a patterned design in one operation. The waxed cloth, usually after several days storage to harden the wax, is then submitted to a 'cracking' operation. This is the basis of the production of fine blue veins in the final product. Several methods of producing a 'crackle' or veining effect are probably in operation. One method is to pile the cloth into cold water by dropping it from a high overhead winch-roller. Cracking is followed by indigo dyeing where the appropriate number of dips are given to produce the desired depth of ground. Wax removal follows and in some cases this is done very skillfully so as to leave small blobs of wax on the cloth to form resists for the next process.

A number of wax prints show, in addition to indigo, a yellow and a red. The production of the yellow and the red, if they are insoluble azoic dyes, requires two separate printing cycles. For example, pad the fabric in 'Brenthol' AT then print with a suitable 'Brentamine' Fast Salt (e.g. 'Brentamine' Fast Corinth V), dry and wash-off to remove surplus 'Brenthol'. Next, pad the cloth in 'Brenthol' AS and print with a red forming 'Brentamine' Fast Salt (such as 'Brentamine' Fast Bordeaux GP), dry and finally wash away the residual 'Brenthol' AS. This description is deceptively simple because after indigo dyeing and washing-off, the cloth carries the basic design. Since it was wax printed, the cloth has been subjected to dyeing, washing and drying. The fabric dimensions are therefore different from when it was first printed and so is the design repeat. To overprint on the 'Brenthol' AT prepared using a roller printing machine would give rise to serious progressive mis-fitting. One way by which this dilemma could be overcome is to fill in the yellow areas by hand-block printing. The penetration obtainable by block printing is a desirable feature since it approaches the duplex effect of the dyed indigo. The hand block printing operation has to be repeated to obtain the red. Such processes are time consuming and expensive industrially, and much effort was devoted to evolving a machine capable of giving a printed effect comparable to a hand block print. The essential feature of such a machine is that the pattern 'fit' can be adjusted continually to compensate for fabric dimension changes.

Instead of producing an insoluble azoic dye *in situ*, a characteristic orange shade is produced by printing an aluminium mordant, drying and then winch dyeing in 'Alizarine' Orange AS. In former times, the rich brown shades seen in west African wax prints were produced using mordant dyes, some of which were obtained from natural dye-woods. Large numbers of west African prints were formerly produced in Europe and Japan which did not involve wax printing, although some of the patterns deliberately set out to show the features of a genuine batik print. Not surprisingly, such prints were called *imitation* wax prints and were easily distinguishable from the genuine article by being paler on the unprinted side than on the face side. These back to face differences are most clearly seen if an attempt has been made to imitate fine veining. To do this, the part of the blue roller printing the veining will carry a shallower engraving than the rest of the roller. These shallow areas will fail to penetrate to the back of the cloth to the same extent as the rest.

In addition to imitation wax prints, a whole series of other west African prints are produced to which the collective name of *fancies* is applied. These are bold in design and striking in colouring and are produced to an increasing extent by the various west African countries themselves. On the grounds of price, insoluble azoic colours predominate, e.g. 'Brenthol' *AS* and 'Brenthol' *AT* prepared fabric printed with 'Brentamine' Fast Bases and Salts. There is an increasing tendency to supplement the azoic combinations with 'Procion' and other reactive dyes to give shades not obtainable on a single 'Brenthol'.

'Alcian' dyes used either alone or in admixture with 'Brentamine' Fast Bases and Salts may also be used to obtain novel shades on 'Brenthol' prepares.

16

Special Methods of Textile Printing

A description of some of the more unusual forms of textile printing is being included for the benefit of the reader who may come across them elsewhere, not accompanied by any details.

In general, these methods are applied to textiles other than those in fabric form. Variations or adaptations of conventional printing methods form the basis of these special methods. The variation in machine size is quite remarkable. A hank printing machine is small by textile fabric printing standards, while a machine capable of printing tufted carpet 5 m (15 ft) wide is understandably extremely large. The methods to be discussed are: carpet printing, Melange or Vigoureux printing, warp printing, flock printing, yarn or hank printing and transfer printing.

CARPET PRINTING

The most usual way of obtaining a patterned effect on traditional carpets of the Axminster and Wilton types is by weaving the design with dyed yarns. Tufted carpets are of more recent origin, and are produced much more rapidly in widths of 5 m (15 ft). To produce single colour effects, tufted carpet may be yarn-dyed before tufting, dyed in the piece on the winch (a discontinuous process) or dyed in continuous form. Since the tufting machine cannot produce patterned effects, unlike a carpet loom, any patterned effects must be produced by printing either the carpet itself or the yarns to be used for tufting.

The yarn printing of carpet yarns is also termed *space-dyeing* and *random-dyeing,* the former term being more widely encountered. The method consists of leading a flat web of yarn through a pair of rollers, the lower one being immersed in a trough containing low viscosity printing paste. The nature of the rollers differs depending on the system used. In the Laing Controlled Area Dyeing Plant[1,2] there are four sets of embossed solid rubber application rollers each normally carrying lateral stripes which may differ in width and distance apart. The upper rollers are of slightly different diameters to the lower ones and embossed in such a way that completely random application is attained while maintaining a uniform appearance in hue of the yarn.

An alternative system, the Stalwart Unit[1,2] has much in common with the Laing plant but differs in the colour application system. A flexible foam-covered roller runs with its lower section in the print paste. Colour transfer is achieved by an upper metal roller which intermittently presses the yarn web on the lower roller when activated by pneumatic pistons. The colour sequence is governed by an electro-pneumatic control unit which can readily be set to produce a wide range of patterns, random or otherwise. The present unit is equipped with a steamer but no pre-dryer.

With both the Laing and Stalwart units the printing and steaming operations are followed by washing-off, drying and re-winding. The printed yarns are then used in the carpet tufting machine. Many novel effects can be produced, ranging from multicolour mottled designs to large patterned areas.

In addition to the printing of carpet yarn, several firms have produced machines to print the tufted carpet itself. These machines have many of the features of conventional textile printing machines, but being designed to handle a substrate 5 m (15 ft) wide are more robustly constructed at all stages. A machine patented by the Bradford Dyers' Association (BDA is now part of Viyella International) is described in detail in Reference 3. A unique feature of this machine is that when the colour is applied to the flat screen, a section box below the carpet sucks it down to the bottom of the pile. The same firm[4] also patented a steamer for use with tufted carpet, which includes a preheating chamber through which the carpet travels horizontally before entering the steamer proper, through which it passes in loops (i.e. a festoon-type steamer). In carpet printing, unlike fabric printing, it is not the practice to dry the print before it enters the steamer.

Another carpet printing machine which uses the flat screen method is that made by the firm of P. Zimmer[5]. Here the squeegee is replaced by two metal rollers and print paste is pumped into the space between the roller from a perforated overhead pipe. Below the screen are powerful electromagnets, arranged so that they move across the screen in a longitudinal direction and pull the two metal rollers along, while at the same time causing them to revolve. This system functions as a very efficient method of forcing the print paste through the screen mesh and down the carpet pile. Screen printing using the Aljaba rotary screen principle has also been applied to carpet printing. The circular screens are arranged around a central cylinder but there are some modifications over the normal Aljaba machine necessitated by the much greater operating width. The Stork rotary screen printing machine, in which the screens are arranged in-line along a horizontal printing surface, has also proved adaptable to printing tufted carpets.

The Stalwart Pickering system and the British Tufting Machinery (BTM) system[2, 6, 7] both have their designs raised in relief on rollers. To increase the amount of print paste which is picked up from the colour box and transferred to the carpet, the printing surface has a layer of sponge-like material attached to it. The main difference between the two systems is that the carpet travels vertically in the Stalwart system and horizontally in the BTM machine. Small scale application of a design to tufted carpet for experimental purposes is best achieved using a flat block which has been coated with polyurethane foam and cut to an appropriate design. This is easier than using a screen and gives better penetration into the carpet.

The Deep Dye Process is different to all the previously mentioned processes (developed by Deep Dye Processes, USA). The carpet is processed pile downwards, and in this form is pressed into a printing shape. This shape, which may be for example 1 m x 1 m (3ft x 3ft), has a flat surface and is split up into compartments representing all the colours in the design, and each separate area of the individual colours. These compartments are fed with the different colours from below and once the carpet has been pressed into place the compartment walls prevent colour mixing. Refilling of the printing form calls for very exact metering and pumping of the individual colourings. The relatively small size of the printing area also calls for very accurate fitting in two directions to enable the pattern repeats to be printed-off without spoiling the continuous appearance of the pattern.

A recent patent[8] issued to Singer Cobble Ltd. describes a carpet printing system in which the liquor is fed to the interior of the printing rollers and is caused to move outwards through the porous shell by means of vacuum suction boxes. Sections of the roller are made impervious to the passage of the liquor and so enable a patterned effect to be produced.

MELANGE OR VIGOUREUX PRINTING

Patents were granted in 1863 to S. Vigoureux in Britain and France for a machine which allowed the production of mixture yarns of much improved appearance. Prior to this invention, mixed or blended yarns normally of wool were produced by dyeing the wool at the slubbing stage and then blending-in a suitable proportion of white before spinning. The mixing of white and coloured wool was achieved by passing both through a gill box simultaneously.

The Vigoureux machine was designed to print a wide web of slubbing with diagonal, or less frequently, lateral stripes of colour. Part of the slubbing was left uncoloured so that during subsequent gilling and combing operations (which followed steaming to fix the dye and washing-off) a very uniform yarn was produced. These yarns enabled a much superior fabric to be woven than was possible from mixed-dyed and white wool blends. The depth of shade of the fabric produced from melange printed slubbing is determined more by the printed area than by the concentration of the dye in the print paste. The printing machine is similar in design to a rotary block or surface printing machine. One roller dips into the colour box and furnishes print paste to a felt covered intermediate roller. The printing roller, or sometimes two printing rollers, form a nip through which the thin web of sliver passes. Where the printing roller has the design raised in relief the pressure causes transfer of the print paste from the felt roller to the sliver. Where there is no pattern in relief on the printing roller there is no pressure and hence no colour transfer.

The designs on the rollers print diagonal stripes of varying width and to do this they carry the design in a spiral. This spiral may be either right handed or left handed. Using one of each on a two-printing roller unit it is possible to fill-in increasing areas of the web of slubbing because although some 'falling-on' will occur, the second roller will always print in some of the white areas left by the first roller. The French firm SACM[9] produce rollers in four standard stripe printing sizes and using these either singly or in pairs on their machine, eight combinations are possible giving 18, 27, 40, 50, 60, 70, 78 and 85% coverage. Further details of these designs and illustrations of the mechanics of the operation are available in References 10 and 11.

After printing, the slubbing is not dried but is taken to a discontinuous steamer and steamed in batches usually for two consecutive periods of 1 h. The interrupted steaming is claimed to give better results in terms of dye yield. The dyestuffs used are generally the faster acid and metal complex dyes, and with the latter there is always the possibility that the steaming time may be reduced.

Melange printing is predominantly applied to wool, but there have been sporadic attempts to use the method for viscose rayon, staple, regenerated protein fibres, nylon and 'Terylene' polyester fibre. None of these has reached significant proportions to date. After steaming the slubbing is passed through a four to five bowl back washing machine. This terminology, which is somewhat alien to the textile printing technician, describes a machine which is very similar to a 4–5 tank open soaper with a mangle (bowl) between each tank. The machine used for slubbing has a drying range on the exit side and also gives a first gilling operation after printing in the gill box.

WARP PRINTING

This form of printing, which may be done using a surface printing machine, by screen printing or with engraved copper rollers, calls for practically no mechanical modifications. In place of fabric, warp from one or even two beams is fed into the printing machine. The dyes used for printing must be capable of developing satisfactorily even if this operation is delayed for some considerable time. It would not be satisfactory to print the warp and develop and wash it off in warp form, since the warp threads would be displaced and the pattern would fail to keep in fit when being woven. Dyestuffs ideal for warp printing, particularly where high light fastness demands must be met, are 'Caledon' dyes applied by the pad-steam or flash-age process. The printed warps after drying are not plaited-down in the normal way, but wound back on to warp beams.

The most used outlet for warp printing is the production of furnishing fabrics. After weaving the printed warp with an uncoloured weft, the original design is equally visible on both sides of the fabric, i.e. it becomes a duplex print because of the alternative raising and lowering of the warp threads in the loom. Furthermore, the design assumes a soft, almost dissolving character in place of the crisp, precise, multi-colour print which would have resulted from printing on an already woven suface. At one stage when warp printing was very popular, attempts were made to imitate the effect by engraving rollers as nearly as possible to the final pattern. Such imitations are easily detected by their lack of reversibility, or if duplex-printed, by the almost inevitable appearance of small pattern areas which do not correspond exactly. This is the best established by picking out a small motif on one side and pushing a pin through it. When the cloth is reversed, the pin will not exactly pierce the corresponding piece of the design.

FLOCK PRINTING

Flock may be prepared from many synthetic fibres by cutting them accurately into pre-determined lengths using a suitable machine. With cotton and wool fibres, flock is usually prepared by grinding and lengths may be as short as 0·3 mm (0·013 in). The flock may be dyed or uncoloured. A suitable material is chosen to form the base fabric for the flock and the base material, and the flock may be composed of the same or different fibres. The base fabric may be either coated all over on one side with a suitable adhesive resin, or the resin applied locally in a printed design. When printing is used a method which transfers a reasonably

235

thick film gives the best results, e.g. rotary screen printing by the Aljaba or the Stork system or on a smaller scale, flat-screen printing.

The resin adhesive used must be one which adheres firmly to the substrate being printed, but equally so, must be capable of anchoring the flock firmly once it is attached. The resin film must be flexible, have a soft handle and possess a good resistance to washing.

Methods of Flock Application

The flocking operation may be carried out in at least three different ways, which will now be described.

Flock Application Using Compressed Air

This method uses special flock spray guns and is simple to apply. Various sizes of spray guns are available and they are used mainly by handicraft workers as well as painters and decorators. When applied by a spray gun, the flocks lie in a completely disordered state and will never produce a clear velvet-like effect.

Flock Application by the Shaking Process

In this method the flocks are applied merely by shaking, dusting or sprinkling the flock either directly by hand or through a fine sieve. The fabric may be shaken at the same time as the block is being sprinkled. This may be done in the case of small areas of fabric by attaching a wooden rod of hexagonal cross section to the shaft of a small electric motor, and allowing this to come into contact with the reverse side of the printed cloth. As with the previous method, shaking produces a flocked effect on which the individual flocks are attached in a random fashion.

The Electrostatic Method

A lot of development work on this system has been carried out in W. Germany. In principle, a high voltage is generated and connected to two pole-plates, one of which is earthed the other being effectively insulated. Flocks between these pole-plates will endeavour to close the circuit and spring from one plate to the other in an intense to and fro motion which results in them becoming aligned vertically. When the

236

resin printed fabric is introduced, the flocks are effectively 'shot' into it vertically and adhere in the printed areas. Because of the vertical adhesion of the flocks, the desired velvet-like appearance is achieved. A collection device removes excess flock from the treatment area and returns it to the machine for re-use.

Special resin binders have been evolved for flock printing, e.g. 'Printofix' *PD* and *PF* (Sandoz) and 'Orafix' *PF* (CIBA). In Reference 12, a method patented by Heberlein, a well known Swiss firm of speciality printers, of preparing a resin which was capable of dissolving both the flock and the fabric being printed, is described. This method involved dissolving viscose rayon scrap in solvents such as zinc chloride, sodium zincate or benzyl-trimethyl ammonium hydroxide. Good fibre to flock bonding was claimed. D. G. Kale[13, 14] has a short article on flock printing in his book which also includes illustrations on machines used, plus a mounted example of a flock print.

The present state of the flock industry is well described by P. Green[15] in an article entitled *The Fall and Rise of the Flock Industry*. This exemplifies the many and varied domestic uses and other outlets for all over and patterned flocked articles. In the same journal, the following article is entitled *New End Uses and the Diversification of the Flock Industry*[16]. Also a well illustrated and comprehensive article appeared in the Bayer Farbenreview[17]

YARN (OR HANK) PRINTING

It is possible, but laborious, to take a hank of yarn and form a mechanical resist by tying-up selected areas with wax thread and then dyeing to obtain local coloration of the hank. By repeating this operation several times, a multicoloured hank is produced. Such a slow operation must of necessity be expensive. A very similar effect may be produced by the use of a hank printing machine[14]

First, the hank or hanks are opened out and maintained in this condition by two carrier reels which may be adjusted to maintain the necessary tension. The frame containing the hanks and reels is then pulled past the printing head and through the nip formed by the two printing rollers. These two rollers are furnished with printing colour from a tray below them. The yarn passing through this nip is printed on both sides simultaneously and receives a further printing as the frame is returned to its original position. Transverse bands of colour are thus printed on a portion of the hank. More than one colour may be printed simultaneously by dividing the colour-containing tray into compartments. To print the remainder of the hank, it is turned

237

around by moving the reels so that an unprinted portion comes upper-most and the to-and-fro operation repeated. This cycle of operations is continued until all the hank has been printed, after which it is taken for further processing. Drying may not be required. These printed hanks differ from melange printed slubbing, since in the hanks the stripe is printed laterally while slubbing is printed with the stripes at an angle of 45°. Printed and processed hanks are used to form warp or weft yarns, or in some cases both warp and weft yarns, for the same fabric. The fabrics woven from printed yarns have a characteristic speckled effect and irregular areas of one or more colours, depending whether single coloured or multi-coloured hanks were printed.

REFERENCES

1. *Technical Information Dyehouse No. 918,* ICI Dyestuffs Division (10.10.66)
2. 'Carpet Printing', *Bayer Farben Revue,* **14,** 28–40 (1968E)
3. UK Pat. 895 706 (9.5.62)
4. UK Pat. 1 125 183 (28.8.68)
5. P. Zimmer Ltd., Kufstein, Tyrol, Austria
6. Stalwart Pickering system manufactured by E. Pickering Ltd., Blackburn, Lancs., UK
7. British Tufting Machinery (BTM) machine manufactured by Singer Cobble Ltd., Blackburn, Lancs., UK
8. SINGER COBBLE LTD., UK Pat. 1 121 084 (24.7.68)
9. Société Alsacienne de Constructions Mechaniques de Mulhouse
10. BUXTORF, F. & WIAZMITNOWA, *J.S.D.C.,* **69,** 550–556 (1953)
11. POTTER, J. A., *J.S.D.C.,* 71, 645–652 (1955)
12. HEBERLEIN & CO., UK Pat. 662 452 (5.12.51)
13. KALE, D. G., *Principles of Cotton Printing,* 405–410, Publication Committee for Prof. Kale's book on Cotton Printing, Ahmedabad, India (1957)
14. KALE, D. G., Principles of Cotton Printing, 340, Publication Committee for Prof. Kale's book on Cotton Printing, Ahmedabad, India (1957)
15. GREENE, P., *American Dyestuffs Reporter,* **58,** 11–13 (1969)
16. GREENE, P., *American Dyestuffs Reporter,* **58,** 14–15 (1969)
17. *Bayer Farbenreview,* Special Edition No. 2 (In English)

Transfer Printing

The bulk of this chapter is concerned with sublimation transfer printing which utilises disperse dyes and forms a major industrial growth area. Before considering this main topic, some of the earlier processes and a few of their more important modern descendants will be described.

Transfer Printing from 'Plastic' Rollers

Unless the term *transfer printing* carries some further description it does not adequately describe a process. Thus the Sark[1], Tschekonin, Orbis[2], Hyne-Devin, Chromostyle, Polychrome and Dynascope processes rely on a system in which the design is built up in malleable material containing dye around the surface of a roller. By mixing dyestuffs with dampened thickening-agent powders a putty-like 'plastic' is formed in as many different colours as desired[3,4]. Marble or mosaic patterns are particularly effective, but plain shades are also useful. The surface of the printing roller forms a continuous design; this is left to harden and finally trimmed on a lathe. In use the roller is accurately pressed against a second resilient roller with the previously dampened cloth to be printed passing through the nip formed by the two rollers[5]. These processes allow a wide variety of fabrics to be coloured by a transfer process and several classes of dye to be employed. It is important to realise that the transfer of the pattern from the 'plastic' roller to the damp fabric is not the end of the operation[6]. The dye must next be fixed by conventional methods appropriate to its class, e.g. steaming, followed by a final washing-off treatment.

'Heat-Melt' Transfer Printing

A relatively small number of firms have specialised in this process. Little data have been published on the ink compositions used, but p.v.c. is employed in some instances. The most successful areas in which heat-melt transfers appear are labels, motifs for T-shirts and similar outlets. At least one manufacturer offers continous designs. The transfers are supplied either on paper

or transparent plastic film. The common features of this type of transfer
are that colouring is by pigments, the printed ink is thermoplastic and so a
heat pressing causes the pattern to adhere to the fabric. The paper or plasti
sheet in the non-printed areas does not adhere and is peeled off leaving the
pattern. No further treatment is necessary to fix the transferred pigments
and no washing-off process is required.

'Star', 'Fastran' and Other Wet-transfer Processes

Both the 'Star'[7] and 'Fastran'[8] processes use conventional paper-printing
machinery to print a variety of ranges of textile dyes on to paper. The
paper, which may be stored until it is convenient to process it further, is
then used to effect a transfer on to fabric. Some form of dye fixation and
washing off is required. The 'Star' process was named after the pioneering
Italian firm Stampa Tessuti Artistici of Milan and it is the earlier of the tw
A feature of the 'Star' system is to use inks and papers so that when cloth
and transfer paper are passed through the nip formed by a heated metal
calender bowl and a cotton-covered one, a large proportion of the dye is
physically transferred to the fabric. Both dye fixation and washing-off
operations are needed to complete the process. The 'Fastran' process was
originally developed for printing woollen garments such as fully-fashioned
sweaters. Because the latter require a flat-bed non-continuous press, most
development work has been along these lines. The garment is first padded
in a special fixer. A sheet of transfer paper is then placed on each side of tl
garment, printed side to the fibre surface, and a sandwich formed by placii
the composite between two sheets of silicone rubber. Depending on the
press size, a number of such sandwiches may be loaded in. When the press
head is lowered the garments and transfer are securely held. The 'Interthei
press which generates heat by radio-frequency heating is recommended foi
this type of transfer printing. Two related processes have been operated in
Japan since the early 1970s, they are the 'Max-Spielio' and 'Plus-Max' met
The term *wet*-transfer is often applied to all four of these processes, but
there are differences between them. Essentially, in some, e.g. 'Fastran',
transfer and fixation take place in an aqueous medium. In the others heat
and pressure cause the dye to transfer to the fabric and then fixation is
given as a separate treatment. In all cases a washing-off treatment (aqueou:
or solvent) is needed to remove surplus dye, resin binder, etc. from the
fabric.

Sublimation Transfer Printing

This process has been pioneered by the Swiss-based firm Sublistatic S.A. It
became commercially important after an exhibition in Atlantic City in 19(
The invention is claimed by a Frenchman N. de Plasse[11]. He describes the

240

process as 'dry dyeing'. There are now many firms printing paper suitable for sublimation transfer printing and it is common to hear the phrase 'Sublistatic printing'. This is incorrect unless the paper was produced by the Sublistatic Corporation and sold under their trademark. Sublimation transfer printing demands the use of dyes, invariably disperse dyes which will sublime (i.e. form a gas when heated) at temperatures below those which will damage the fabric with which they are in contact. Because the fabric is chosen to be one for which disperse dyes have an affinity, e.g. 'Terylene' polyester fibre, the dye in gaseous form is able to penetrate rapidly into the fibre. Such penetrated dye exhibits the same level of fastness as if it had been fixed by conventional methods. Nothing else sublimes from this type of transfer paper so the 'dry dyeing' operation named by N. de Plasse avoids both a subsequent fixing and a washing-off process. Given a supply of suitably printed sublimation transfer paper all that is needed is a supply of fabric and a heat transfer press. (See page 268 for details of small-scale transfer press suppliers.) On the industrial scale there are several suppliers of both flat bed (intermittent) and continuous presses. Within the UK, Hunt and Moscrop (Middleton, Manchester), Bates (Leicester) and Ibis Engineers (Kendal) have designed machines especially for this method. The German firms of Kannegiesser and Kleinewefer as well as the French firm Lemaire Co. have also been active in this field.

In the remainder of this chapter it is hoped to describe how the thriving industrial process of sublimation transfer printing may be adapted for use in Colleges interested both in design and colour reproduction.

Possibilities in Small-scale Sublimation Transfer Printing

Garment Printing

Transfer printing gives best results on 'Terylene' and other polyester fabrics when selected sublimable disperse dyes are used to print the paper. With the smaller intermittent presses the substrate is normally printed in two main forms either as the knitted garment or garment pieces. Depending on the working area of the press, a knitted garment may be either transfer printed all over, first on one side and then the other, or motifs applied over parts of the garment. If lettering is required for names or slogans there are two methods. Paper previously coloured all over with the desired shade for lettering is cut up or punched out into shapes corresponding to the required letters. The shapes are placed printed-side downwards on top of the garment on the press base. A sheet of plain paper larger than the area of the garment is lowered carefully over it so as not to disturb the letters. At this stage the press head is lowered, e.g. for 30 s at 210 °C (410 °F) and transfer of the dye takes place. The reverse effect, i.e. white letters on a coloured ground, is obtained by cutting-out the required letters in an impervious material. This may be stout paper, thin card or even metal cooking foil. The transfer paper in this method should be slightly larger than the garment, which should be placed on top of a still larger sheet of unprinted white paper. The impervious letters are next arranged on the garment in the desired areas as required, the transfer paper placed gently on top of the letters and the press head lowered as before. When operating a transfer press the padded base or 'buck' should be kept scrupulously clean because any dye marking-off from the transfer paper on to the base will inevitably mark back in a subsequent operation on to the next garment or fabric being processed. The best way to avoid such marking-off difficulties is to use a paper liner over the buck and replace it after each operation. The use of a press head directly on to a garment may lead to damage to the fabric. Thus when applying colour from cut-out letters it is a wise precaution to lay a sheet of white paper over the whole garment.

Printing 'Cut and Sew' Pieces

An alternative to printing directly on knitted garments is to base the procedure on that adopted by the 'cut and sew' trade. Here continuous lengths of material are piled down in layers and cut out, e.g. with a bandsaw into multiple pieces, each multiple corresponding to one of the various parts of a garment. A complete set of garment parts, i.e. one from each multiple pile, is then fitted on the press surface, previously covered with white paper, so as to occupy the minimum area. Transfer paper is placed on top of the pieces and the head lowered for transfer. Clearly this process is easily adapted to small-scale working by cutting-out individual pieces using a 'paper pattern' as used in home dressmaking. If the press working-area is insufficient to allow pieces for a complete garment to be processed in one operation then the amount transferred may be broken down into three or four operations.

Whether working with complete garments or 'cut and sew' pieces it should be remembered that transfer printing gives rise to endless possibilities for illustrating more than one design. Examples include the 'patch-work quilt' effects by cutting portions of several designs and arranging them on white paper with a simple aqueous adhesive. The combined paper then forms the transfer. Another method of adding a touch of exclusivity to a garment is to prepare a motif on white paper, either by hand painting, writing or drawing with suitable crayons*. The motifs so prepared are inserted between the garment

* Crayons incorporating disperse dyes are supplied by Cosmic Crayon Co.

242

and the transfer paper used to form the background, e.g. a simple
stripe or spot design. To prevent the background pattern striking
through the specially prepared motif the latter is best backed with
thin aluminium foil. The description relating to 'cut and sew' garments
is equally applicable to ties, scarves, etc.

Recommended Fibres and Other Polymer Forms

Fabric Preparation

Irrespective of the fabric chosen for transfer printing it should have been
thoroughly scoured before printing and treated, if desired, with an optical
brightening agent. Knitted fabrics which have not been scoured to remove
knitting oils give off objectionable white fumes during the pressing
operation. This is easily avoided by scouring beforehand.

Polyester Fabrics

The reason why polyester fabrics are of prime importance for transfer
printing is that disperse dyes colour the fabric readily and the dyes have
a wash fastness and light fastness acceptable for dress goods. Members
of the disperse ranges, developed in recent years to give optimum
light fastness and heat fastness on 'Terylene', tend to have poor sublimation properties at atmospheric pressure.

Care is needed in extending transfer printing with disperse dyes to
fibres other than polyester. The constraint is not that of dye fixation,
it is that the resulting fastness properties, particularly fastness to washing and perspiration, are lower than on polyester fabrics. The acceptable
level of wet fastness must be related to the end use requirements, e.g.
a nylon carpet should have good light fastness but the wet fastness
criteria will not be as exacting as those for underwear, socks or blouses.

Polyamide Fabrics

Polyamide fabrics are conventionally printed with acid and premetallised
dyes. Neither of these two groups of dyes will sublime so the possibilities
of using disperse dyes have been reinvestigated. Firstly it is necessary
to distinguish between the two main groups of polyamide fibres, viz.
nylon 66 and nylon 6. Not only has nylon 6 a lower melting point than
nylon 66, but the fastness of disperse dyes on nylon 6 is also inferior
to nylon 66. Because nylon 66 itself is only borderline in wet fastness
when disperse dyes are used, this has led transfer printers to concentrate
on nylon 66 and avoid nylon 6. Even on nylon 66 heavy shades are
best avoided, as are dyes which give an undesirable shade shift when
transferred on to nylon and compared with the same dye on polyester
fibre.

243

Acrylic Fabrics

Using conventional methods the most frequently printed class of dye on acrylic fibres are basic dyes, e.g. 'Synacril' dyes. Basic dyes do not sublime sufficiently as a range to be of value for sublimation transfer printing. Within the transfer-printing trade attempts to transfer print disperse dyes on acrylic fibres have been carried out. The resulting wash fastness properties are only moderate. Results have varied, but the main difficulty has been that acrylic fibres from different manufacturers exhibit different properties. Two main problems arise, one group of acrylic fibres go yellow during the pressing operation, especially if the temperature is too high. Sometimes lowering the temperature sufficiently to prevent yellowing seriously reduces the amount of dye transfer that takes place. The second problem is that having evolved an acceptable time and temperature cycle which does not affect the fabric's colour the dye uptake is found to vary considerably between one maker's acrylic fibre and another's. It is virtually impossible to obtain blacks and heavy shades such as dark brown, bottle green and navy on some acrylics, while others will give acceptable results. The result of trying to transfer print acrylic fibres from two sources possessing different properties which have been woven or knitted into the same fabric may be imagined. It is strongly advised that before attempting to transfer print on 'acrylic' fibre the degree of heat yellowing and dye uptake behaviour are checked with small test-pieces.

Secondary Cellulose Acetate and Cellulose Triacetate

Provided care is taken not to exceed the recommended temperature, it is possible to transfer disperse dyes on to secondary acetate without stiffening or otherwise damaging the fibre. The wet fastness properties of the resulting print are only moderate and care must be taken not to use the print for a purpose where better fastness is required. The wet fastness of disperse dyes on cellulose triacetate are better than on secondary acetate, but to obtain a satisfactory transfer on cellulose triacetate the fabric must not have been given an 'S' finish before printing (see p. 161). This treatment forms a ring of cellulose around the fibre and this cellulose acts as a barrier to the subliming disperse dye.

Other Polymer Forms

Transparent or opaque polyester films, e.g. 'Melinex' are printed very successfully by sublimation transfer methods. Polymethylmethacrylate sheet, e.g. 'Perspex' shows considerable promise. P.V.C. sheet has proved more difficult to print satisfactorily and further work is required. Results with some polyurethane-coated fabrics, while initially very promising, proved on storage to be subject to dye migration in the printed layer. Leather in an uncoated state is receptive to subliming disperse dye and possibilities here are being investigated. Fabrics which have been flocked with a suitable material will invariably tranfer print satisfactorily. In this end-use the lack of a wet after-processing stage is all-important.

Press Operating Conditions

The recommended time and temperature conditions for various fibres are given below; these are average values. The temperature is that of the press head and the temperature achieved on the fabric will be influenced by the press pressure and the thickness of paper between the press and the fabric. The thickness of the fabric itself is also an important factor since a thick fabric will require more heat to raise it to a high enough temperature for transfer than a thin fabric. In the list below it is recommended that the first experiments are conducted at the lower temperature and the shortest time. If this is not completely satis-factory then the time should be extended before raising the temperature.

Polyester	200–230 °C (392–446 °F), 20–45 s
Nylon 66	190–210 °C (374–410 °F), 20–40 s
Nylon 6	190–200 °C (374–392 °F), 20–30 s
Secondary acetate	190–200 °C (374–392 °F), 15–30 s
Cellulose triacetate	190–210 °C (374–410 °F), 20–40 s

Acrylics

(1) 'Courtelle'*	190 °C (374 °F), 20–40 s
(2) 'Acrilan'†, 'Orlon†', etc.	200–210 °C (392–410 °F), 15–30 s

It is a wise precaution to make an independent check on the press temperature from time to time using indicator papers (e.g. Peak Temperatures Ltd., Sinfin Lane, Derby) or indicator crayons (e.g. 'Thermochrom' supplied by A. W. Faber Castell, Stein, near Nuremberg, W. Germany). A test paper carrying a range of, say, five temperature-indicating panels is fixed on the back of the transfer paper so that it comes in contact directly with the head of the press. If crayons are used, marks are made on the paper using those crayons covering the expected range of temperatures. Once the press head is lowered, the

---

* Yellows readily above 190 °C (88 ° F). ('Courtelle' *HT* has improved resistance to yellowing.)

† These acrylic types have less tendency to yellow on heating.

indicator papers or crayons will react rapidly and 2–3 s is normally adequate to obtain a positive result.

The other main proviso for press operation is that if the temperature is too high or the pressure excessive then the fabric surface will become glazed. Bulked yarns will be flattened and fabrics produced from them will lose their attractive handle to a greater or lesser degree.

Ink Systems for Transfer Printing

To understand why a variety of ink systems are in use for printing transfer paper, some general background knowledge of the main paper-printing systems is essential. For the majority of Colleges and Schools of Art the screen-printing method using aqueous inks or oil-in-water emulsion inks is undoubtedly the safest. Any experiments with solvent-based systems must be rigorously monitored and appropriate fire precautions put in hand.

The ink system used determines the physical form of the dye which forms the starting material as well as the nature of the ancillary equipment needed to make the ink.

The way the requirements of commercial paper-printing machines have determined the evolution of transfer printing inks is discussed below.

Evolution of Transfer Inks for Paper-Printing Systems

The paper printing industry possesses two categories of wide-width high-speed presses (i.e. continuous printing machines). These are the rotogravure or gravure and the flexographic (flexo) types. The mechanical sophistication of both these basic types of machine is far ahead of that on a textile roller printing machine. The main purpose of mechanical refinements on a gravure machine is to enable very-high-speed printing to be carried out. The consequences of high-speed printing are that the 'ink system' (cf. textile print paste) must dry very quickly. The ink printed on the paper by the first cylinder (engraved roller) must be dry or virtually dry before the paper web receives its impression from the second printing cylinder. Drying is achieved by having a drying chamber in between each printing station. The system is termed *inter-station drying* and the evaporation of relatively large quantities of inflammable solvent in the drying chambers means that very rigorous flame-proofing precautions are necessary in the vicinity of the printing machine. Even the discharge of a static spark from the paper web to the ink-tray has been known to cause a fire. For this reason many machines are fitted with emergency carbon dioxide 'flooding' arrangements which blanket any fire outbreak which is immediately evacuated by the machine operating staff. For college work the typical gravure transfer inks are considered too inflammable for normal student use unless strict safety precautions are followed.

The flexographic machines may either have a central impression cylinder or individual 'back-up' rollers for each printing position. In either event the 'web path' (the route the paper passes on its way through the machine) is much shorter on a flexo machine than on a gravure machine. The main operational difference between the two printing systems is that the cylinder of the gravure machine consists of an electrically deposited copper layer which is etched to a depth of 0·038–0·051 mm (0·0015–0·0020 in) in the design areas and then chromium plated. The design cylinder for a flexo machine carries the pattern raised in relief often in rubber. A mould is prepared into which the rubber may be cast; the resulting 'stereo' is firmly stuck by a powerful adhesive to a smooth-surfaced steel roller. A normal design motif is arranged so that multiple stereo castings form the basis of the design by a given roller. More complicated designs are carved from a solid rubber surface.

Since the flexo roller carries its design in rubber, the ink system must not be based on toluene or similar solvents which would cause swelling and distortion of the design. For this reason a flexo ink is normally based on an alcohol–water mixture. The viscosity characteristics are important too, because the ink has to be accurately furnished to the printing roller via an all-over engraved roller often called an *anilox* roller. Flexo rollers deposit a much thinner layer of ink than a gravure roller, approximately 0·006 mm (0·00025 in) compared with 0·0254 mm (0·001 in). It follows therefore that to get the same final shade after transfer, the dye concentration in a flexo ink must be proportionately higher than in a gravure ink. This led to a preoccupation with dyestuff strengths for transfer-printing inks both by ink makers and dye makers.

When it is considered that the engraving depth for textile roller printing may, for polyester fabrics, lie in the range 0·076–0·152 mm (0·003–0·006 in) then a depth factor of two to four times that of a gravure cylinder depth for paper is involved.

The phrase *100% disperse dyes* has become a common term in transfer-ink making. The 'Dispersol' Conc. *TP* powders were introduced along with others and they were three to four times stronger, on average, than commercial 'Dispersol' Liquid or Grain brands. Such dyes did not contain added diluents or dispersing agents to disperse them in water. To make an ink for gravure printing or flexo printing the *TP* powder is solvent milled and let down with an appropriate dilution medium. This is an operation which carries a considerable fire hazard and it is not recommended for general college use.

247

The commercial paper-screen printer works on principles partly different from his textile counterpart. The difference lies in the fact that a paper-screen printer is set-up to print on a single sheet basis and not for continuous lengths. When an automated paper-printing device is used it is again based on a sheet-fed system. These machines print one colour at a time and the sheets, after drying, are collected and reassembled in the right position. Textile materials are insufficiently dimensionally stable for this to be practicable. A second passage through the machine follows. Alternatively, a hand-printing method is employed but again all the sheets are printed with the first colour, dried and then reprinted with the next colour. Solvent-based inks are used in commercial screen printing; they are inflammable but not quite so readily ignited as a gravure ink. In any case the rate of solvent loss from a gravure ink is too great for screen printing and leads to 'drying in'. Furthermore, a gravure ink has a much lower average viscosity than a screen ink and requires a change of reduction medium at the dilution stage.

The value of the screen-printing method for transfer printing on the small scale lies in two main directions.

1. Screen-printing methods, once an optimum gauze has been selected (e.g. 16T) give prints of acceptable quality while depositing a relatively thick dye-containing layer. Hence concentrated dye brands are not essential.
2. Small-scale hand screen-printing equipment for textiles can be adapted fairly readily for paper printing.

For small-scale screen printing the following points may prove helpful. It is much harder when using paper to print table lengths of acceptable quality compared with textiles. Attempts to stick the paper on to the rubber blanket surface even with a permanent or semi-permanent adhesive have proved unreliable. The paper is too readily creased when ironing down and when removing it it is very easy for small areas of paper to remain stuck to the table and tear strips along the web. A method which has proved practical over short tables is to stretch the paper very tightly over the table top in a lengthways direction. If the paper is available on a reel, sufficient is pulled-off to cover the table and make a loop over the far end. This loop is turned back and firmly fixed with an adhesive tape to the back of the paper. Into the loop, a heavy metal roller, slightly wider than the paper, is introduced. This will form a tensioning device if a braking system is fixed on the paper reel at the other end. If the reel cannot be fitted with a brake then the loop system is duplicated so there is one roller at each end of the table. Provided suitable weights can be added to the spindle ends, a wooden roller may be inserted into the paper instead of a metal roller.

248

Having stretched the paper over the table, printing may commence. Aqueous-based inks are simple to prepare and washing-off the screens is much easier than with solvent inks. One disadvantage with aqueous inks is that once the ink wets the paper, cockling may occur and this persists until the paper is almost dry. Naturally the greater the area printed by a given screen the more severe the cockling. The thinner the paper the more the cockle. Paper is described by its 'grammage' which is the weight in grammes per square metre (g/m^2). A 50–60 g/m^2 paper will cockle with aqueous inks while a paper in the range 80–110 g/m^2 is much less liable to do so. To expedite drying, but only with aqueous inks, a current of warm air is beneficial. A domestic hair dryer is suitable. It must be emphasised that these dryers are not flameproof and they must not be used where solvent inks or emulsion-based inks are in use.

Some firms of ink makers do offer ranges of solvent-based screen inks and suitable dilution media (which corresponds in function to the reduction thickening in textile printing). The advantage of such inks is that being solvent based, they do not cause paper cockling. Jobbing screen printers in the paper trade have taken readily to using such inks, but they are, of course, used to working with solvent-based inks and the fire precautions (including ventilation requirements) that are necessary. In making inks on a solvent basis for screen printing it is not so essential with highly concentrated powders as it is with gravure and flexo inks. The main reason why ink makers prefer the concentrated brands is that the diluents and dispersing agents present in the textile brands are liable to interfere with the solvent milling agents. This interference is usually one of the causes of ink concentrate instability.

Once the system aqueous inks–screen print (hand or semi-automatic) is accepted, the maximum use is possible of the existing Grain or Liquid qualities in the 'Dispersol' range. It must be accepted that not all disperse dyes are suitable for transfer printing. Whether or not a given disperse dyestuff will sublime is partly governed by its molecular weight and partly by the nature of the substituent groups present. In general, the lower the molecular weight the more readily the dyestuff sublimes. The transfer of dye involves subliming it off the paper, and because the non-dyestuff components of the ink do not sublime it is possible to avoid the troublesome washing-off processes entirely. In classifying 'Dispersol' dyes for dyeing 'Terylene' the terms A, B, C and D are used. In this classification, the A dyes have the lowest heat fastness and the D dyes the highest. Sublimation behaviour is the reverse of heat fastness so A class disperse dyes sublime most readily and D class dyes least readily. In practice, only the A and B class dyes (plus an occasional C class dye) are of interest for transfer printing. A slight anomoly is that an occasional disperse dye which is not recommended for 'Terylene' dyeing does

transfer print satisfactorily. For this reason a dye without the initial
A–D appears in the list.

Dyes Recommended for the Preparation of Aqueous Screen Inks for Transfer Printing

Dispersol Yellow A-G Grains* and
 Liquid
Dispersol Yellow B-GR Grains only
†Dispersol Yellow C-5G Grains and
 Liquid
‡Dispersol Orange B-A Grains* and
 Liquid
Dispersol Orange B-2R Grains only
Dispersol Red B-2B Grains only
Dispersol Red B-3B Grains¶ and
 Liquid

Dispersol Violet A-2R Powder
 only
Dispersol Violet B-G Powder only
Dispersol Blue B-2G Grains only
Dispersol Blue G Powder only
Dispersol Navy B-R Grains
Dispersol Navy B-T Grains and
 Liquid
Dispersol Blue BN grains¶ and
 Liquid

A wide range of self shades and mixtures are possible using the above
products. Blacks and browns are seldom homogeneous products in the
disperse range. Existing 'Dispersol' Browns and Black mixtures on the
Selling Range are not properly balanced for transfer printing. Suitable
black mixtures are usually possible by using as a blue component, e.g.
'Dispersol' Blue *BN*, Blue *G*, Navy *B-T* or Navy *B-R*. Any one of these blues
shaded with 'Dispersol' Yellow *A-G* and/or 'Dispersol' Orange *B-2R* and
adjusted if necessary with a red such as 'Dispersol' Red *B-2B* will give a
satisfactory black. It should be remembered that a black or grey suitable
for 'Terylene' seldom gives the same shade if printed on nylon 66. It
may be advisable to reformulate the ink by altering the proportions of
the components when a change of fibre is involved. Suitable browns may
be obtained by using one of the two 'Dispersol' violets in admixture,
say, with 'Dispersol' Orange *B-2R* as a basis and shading bluer or yellower
as required.

Preparation of Aqueous Screen Inks

The principles involved are simple but the successful preparation involves
some attention to detail. When Grain qualities are used they must be

* Grains 1·5 times strength of liquid.
† Dye not recommended for nylon.
‡ Bluer and duller shade on nylon.
¶ Grains 2 times strength of liquid.

introduced into enough water to allow a proper dispersion to be made.
If difficulty is experienced with a heavy shade then some or all of the
made-up thickening agent must be replaced by water. The thickening-
agent powder is then stirred into the dye—water dispersion. The transfer
of dye is hampered if too much thickening agent is present in the dried-
down film. The amount of thickening agent present in the film may be
reduced by replacing part of it by an oil-in-water emulsion. This technique
is limited by the need to leave sufficient room in the recipe for water
in which to disperse the dyestuff.

Stock Emulsion Thickening

The preparation is described in Chapter 3, p. 25. The desired amount
should be mixed with a previously prepared thickening such as 9%
'Indalca' *PA3*. The latter is made up by sprinkling the dry 'Indalca' *PA3*
(9 parts) into cold water (91 parts) with high-speed stirring.

Printing-ink recipe

10–100 parts	'Dispersol' Grains are sprinkled into
490–400 parts	water at 30–40 °C (85–105 °F)
	and stirred thoroughly. The mixture
	is left for up to 15 min to complete
	dye dispersion, and when cool stirred
	into
350 parts	stock emulsion thickening in which
150 parts	'Indalca' *PA3* 9% thickening have
	previously been incorporated.
Bulk to 1000 parts	

Notes
(1) The 'Dispersol' Grains disperse most readily when sprinkled on to
     10–20 times their weight of water. This is not possible in preparing
     the strongest shades in the above recipe. It has proved practical on
     a small scale to prepare satisfactory dispersions provided care is
     taken to avoid lumps.
(2) Where a Liquid brand is available this is simply diluted with cold
     water and added into the thickening.
(3) Where a stock emulsion is not available replace it by a mixture of
     'Indalca' *PA3* and water sufficient to obtain a suitable printing
     viscosity without unduly depressing the yield on transfer.

(4)   The 150 parts of 'Indalca' *PA3* 9% thickening in the above recipe
      contain 13·5 parts of dry thickener and 136·5 parts of water. In
      cases of difficulty in dispersing larger amounts of Grain quality
      this amount of water may be added to that already calculated for
      the recipe above. Once the grains have been dispersed the dry
      thickener quantity is stirred directly into the cooled grain dispersion
      and allowed to dissolve.
(5)   Under no circumstances should stock emulsion thickening be
      mixed with warm-water dye dispersions as the emulsion is liable
      to break and the printing viscosity will be lost.

Printing and Screen Washing Operations

These are carried out as described earlier in the text and the screens
washed with an ample supply of cold water afterwards. Water is perfectly
satisfactory for washing-out both aqueous inks and emulsion-based
(oil-in-water) inks. Should solvent-based inks be employed, then water
is not suitable for washing-down and advice should be sought from the
ink suppliers as to their recommended cleaning solvent and the precaution:
to be observed in using and storing it.

   If the screen lacquer appears to be attacked by either water or solvent
this is probably due to the screen maker being inadequately advised about
the end use requirements. Where there is a possibility that a given screen
is required to be used for both aqueous and solvent-based inks, then a
lacquer capable of resisting both should be requested. A corollary to
this requirement is the screen printer of paper who uses entirely solvent-
based inks and a screen lacquer that is water soluble. Here water is only
used to remove the design from the screen before putting on the next
pattern.

REFERENCES

1. UK Pat. 632 278 (16.5.49) and US Pat. 3 256 102 (14.6.66)
2. German Pats. 614 786 (23.5.35) and 658 437 (17.3.38), and US Pat. 1 999 150
    (23.4.35)
3. UK Pats. 592 484 (19.9.47) and 600 451 (9.4.48)
4. UK Pat. 850 310 (5.10.60)
5. German Pat. 665 524 (30.12.37)
6. BARTL, H., *Innovations in Textile Printing*, Melliand Textilberichte, 1283-1287
    (1955)
7. UK Pat. 754 233 (8.8.56)
8. UK Pat. 1 284 824 (9.8.72)
9. LYNN, J. E., *American Dyestuffs Reporter*, 20-21, 28-30 (1969)
10. GROSS, D., *Knitted Outerwear Times*, 56-59 (1969)
11. French Pat. 1 223 330 (16.6.60)

18

Dyestuff Equivalents and the Use of the Colour Index

A brief mention has been made in Chapter 2 of the *Colour Index*. The second edition of this important reference work was issued in 1956* jointly by the Society of Dyers and Colourists, Bradford, UK, and the American Association of Textile Chemists and Colourists, Lowell, Mass, USA. The first edition was published as long ago as 1924, and its supplement in 1928. The economic depression in the early 1930s prevented work on a revised edition. Plans to commence the work in the late 1930s were prevented by the outbreak of the Second World War. As soon as the war was over however, work commenced in 1945, but such was the magnitude of the task that it was not until 1956, eleven years later that the work appeared, to be followed in 1963 by a supplement. After 1963 smaller paper-backed supplements appeared at regular intervals. The work is divided into three parts.

In Part I all the known commerical names under which a dye is sold are given. In addition to the list of names, Part I also contains details of the method of applying the colouring matters, their usage, their more important fastness properties and certain other basic data.

In Part II the chemical structure of the dye is given, and where known the inventor and the literature including patents. If a dyemaker does not wish to reveal the constitution of a novel product it will not be allocated a Part II reference although it will appear in Part I.

Part III includes lists of abbreviations used in the index, a list of dye and pigment makers with their abbreviations, details of the fastness tests, patents index and commerical names index.

Part I consists of two volumes, and Part II and Part III of one volume each. The 1963 supplement constitutes another large volume. Page references are given as four figure numbers in which the first figure indicates the volume number. The chemical structure is indicated by a five figure number.

Examples of how the Colour Index may be used are as follows:
1. Suppose an American equivalent to 'Caledon' Jade Green was

*The third edition was published in 1971 (see p. 256).

sought. The 'Caledon' name would be looked up in the supplement (whose pages are prefixed by the letter 'S'). On page S 769, five brands of 'Caledon' Jade Green are listed distinguished by different letters, viz. *3B, 3BW, 2G, XBN* and *XN*. Opposite each different brand is given the Part I reference and it will be noted that some of these are the same. Two products are listed as *CI* Vat Green *4*, two as *CI* Vat Green *1* and one as *CI* Vat Green *2*. In addition, the Part II reference again shows that the same chemical structure is assigned to two lots of two products. Now suppose that a recheck on the exact product name showed that 'Caledon' Jade Green *XBN* was involved. This would immediately be seen to correspond to *CI* Vat Green *1*, Part I, page number 2519; Part II reference number 59825.

Turning to page 2519 would give application details for both dyeing and printing, including various fibres and also fastness properties. In addition, all known names and makers of *CI* Vat Green *1* would be found listed together with their makers' initials, code letters or abbreviations. These may be converted to the full name and address of the maker by reference to the preface of the 1963 supplement. Thus 'Ponsol' Jade Green (DuP) is seen to be made by E.I. Du Pont de Nemours & Co. Inc., Wilmington 99, Delaware, USA. The process could be applied similarly to all other manufacturers in the list.

2. A sample labelled 'Nyloquinone' Blue *2J* is received, but the label gives no indication of manufacturer and also it is not known to which class of dye the product belongs. Using the list of trade names in the supplement it is seen that the manufacturer's code letter is Fran, the product *CI* Disperse Blue *7*, the Part I reference is 1716 and the Part II reference 62500. Since the Part I reference starts with a '1' this means that Volume I is required. Turning up page 1716 in the volume a list of equivalents will be found including 'Duranol' Blue Green *B* (ICI), 'Cibacet' Turquoise Blue *G* (CIBA) and also that Fran sell the product under another name, 'Esteroquinone' Light Blue *4JL* as well as 'Nyloquinone' Blue *2J*. The name and country of origin of the manufacturer is obtained by reference to the supplement (page x) where Fran is used to indicate Companie Francaise des Matières Colorantes S.A., Paris, France. Because a Part II reference was given this means the chemical constitution is known. Looking up Part II, reference 62500, it is seen that the dye was discovered in Germany in 1931 and marketed as 'Celliton' Fast Blue Green *B* by the pre-war I.G. chemical combine. Two methods of synthesis are indicated, both starting from leuco-1, 4, 5, 8-tetra hydroxy anthraquinone. In the structural formula

254

given, the $-OH$ groups in positions 5 and 8 in the anthraquinone remain unchanged while those in positions 1 and 4 are replaced by the NHC_2H_4OH group.

The Colour Index is very helpful and informative provided the name of a dyestuff is known and equivalents are being sought. However, if a dyestuff whose name is not known requires identification then this is a much more difficult matter. Most major dyemakers have Dyestuff Identification experts who undertake this work. Generally, a reference collection is kept of all chemically different dyes, but identical products from several manufacturers are not included in the collection.

The colour reactions of dyestuffs in the presence of a number of chemical reagents are documented. The identification usually aims to establish the class of dyestuffs to which the unknown sample belongs first, e.g. acid, direct, reactive or vat, etc. When this has been done an attempt is made to determine which previously recorded dyestuff most closely resembles the unknown product in reactions. This may then be tested side by side with the unknown sample to obtain positive confirmation of the latter's identity. This identity will only indicate the product by reference to a previously recorded sample or one on the identifying dyemaker's selling range. It is not possible to tell by dyestuff identification testing which dyemaker produced the product, except in those few cases where only one manufacturer is known to produce a given dye.

It is possible to have a dyestuff classified by its colour reactions without knowing its chemical structure. Where an exact chemical structure is required, and this is seldom necessary except where a dyemaker is carrying out a check on a competitors' products, then the classical methods of organic analyses are employed. Once a most probable structure has been evolved, this is then tested by synthesis followed by a check that the two products are identical.

The identification of the dyestuffs present on a piece of dyed or printed cloth is sometimes required. This type of work usually falls within the scope of a dyestuff identification specialist. An identification of the fibre or fibres present is a valuable first step. This may be followed by stripping (removing) the dyestuff or dyestuffs present from the fibre. To separate out dyes extracted from the fibre into individual products frequent use is made of either thin layer or column chromatography.

In the case of printed fabrics, a printing technologist can frequently assist the dyestuff identification. He may either recognise a particular printing style and ask only for confirmation that a certain dye or dyes are present, or alternatively, if told what one or two colours in a pattern are as a result of preliminary work by the identification expert, the printing technologist is often able to reason out the various methods by which the print could have been done. A few further dye checks may enable the exact printing method to be deduced. A simple example would be if a direct-dyed ground shade was reported. The suggestion that the pattern could be a discharge print with vat illuminating colours would be rapidly verified. If the vat dye suggestion could not be confirmed then the next possibility, viz. that pigment printing compositions had been used would be investigated. Microscopic examination of the printed fibres at high magnification would confirm the presence of pigment particles on the fibre surface. The identification expert would be well aware that a few discharge resistant pigments are themselves vat dyes and so microscopic examination would confirm by which method such a dye had been applied. if the vat dye has been applied as a pigment, only suface deposition on the fibre and not full penetration in to the fibre would be seen under the microscope.

Published books on dyestuff identification are relatively rare and many of those available have been overtaken by the numbers of new dyestuffs continually appearing on the market. A. G. Green's book[1] on dyestuff analysis was one of the first to set down a series of tables of specific tests and reactions which follow a plan not unlike that adopted today.

In 1971 the third edition of the Colour Index was published. There are now five volumes and the contents have been extensively revised. Howe because the well established background principles have been retained it is possible to carry out the examples in this chapter by changing the volume and page numbers to correspond to the new edition.

REFERENCE

1. GREEN, A. G., *The Analysis of Dyestuffs and their Identification in Dyed and Coloured Materials, Lake-pigments, Foodstuffs, etc.*, 3rd edn, Griffin & Co., London (1920)

Appendix 1

USEFUL INFORMATION

Where it becomes necessary to change working units between the
SI system and Imperial, students are recommended to consult
*Changing to the Metric System – Conversion factors, symbols and
definitions,* by Anderton and Bigg. The second edition was published
by H.M.S.O. in 1967.

Comparative Hydrometer Scales at 15°C (60°F)

Twaddell	Baumé	Specific Gravity	Twaddell	Baumé	Specific Gravity
1	0·7	1·005	33	20·3	1·165
2	1·4	1·01	34	20·9	1·17
3	2·1	1·015	35	21·4	1·175
4	2·7	1·02	36	22	1·18
5	3·4	1·025	37	22·5	1·185
6	4·1	1·03	38	23	1·19
7	4·7	1·035	39	23·5	1·195
8	5·4	1·04	40	24	1·2
9	6	1·045	41	24·5	1·205
10	6·7	1·05	42	25	1·21
11	7·4	1·055	43	25·5	1·215
12	8	1·06	44	26	1·22
13	8·7	1·065	45	26·4	1·225
14	9·4	1·07	46	26·9	1·23
15	10	1·075	47	27·4	1·235
16	10·6	1·08	48	27·9	1·24
17	11·2	1·085	49	28·4	1·245
18	11·9	1·09	50	28·8	1·25
19	12·4	1·095	51	29·3	1·255
20	13	1·1	52	29·7	1·26
21	13·6	1·105	53	30·2	1·265
22	14·2	1·11	54	30·6	1·27
23	14·9	1·115	55	31·1	1·275
24	15·4	1·12	56	31·5	1·28
25	16	1·125	57	32	1·285
26	16·6	1·13	58	32·4	1·29
27	17·1	1·135	59	32·8	1·295
28	17·7	1·14	60	33·3	1·3
29	18·3	1·145	61	33·7	1·305
30	18·8	1·15	62	34·2	1·31
31	19·3	1·155	63	34·6	1·315
32	19·8	1·16	64	35	1·32

Twaddell	Baumé	Specific Gravity	Twaddell	Baumé	Specific Gravity
65	35·4	1·325	89	44·4	1·445
66	35·8	1·33	90	44·8	1·45
67	36·2	1·335	91	45·1	1·455
68	36·6	1·34	92	45·4	1·46
69	37	1·345	93	45·8	1·465
70	37·4	1·35	94	46·1	1·47
71	37·8	1·355	95	46·4	1·475
72	38·2	1·36	96	46·8	1·48
73	38·6	1·365	97	47·1	1·485
74	39	1·37	98	47·4	1·49
75	39·4	1·375	99	47·8	1·495
76	39·8	1·38	100	48·1	1·5
77	40·1	1·385	102	48·7	1·51
78	40·5	1·39	104	49·4	1·52
79	40·8	1·395	106	50	1·53
80	41·2	1·4	108	50·6	1·54
81	41·6	1·405	110	51·2	1·55
82	42	1·41	120	54·1	1·6
83	42·3	1·415	130	56·9	1·65
84	42·7	1·42	140	59·4	1·7
85	43·1	1·425	150	61·8	1·75
86	43·4	1·43	160	64·2	1·8
87	43·8	1·435	165	65·2	1·825
88	44·1	1·44	168	65·9	1·84

258

Solutions of Common Chemicals (grammes per 100 grammes)

°Tw	Acetic acid CH₃COOH	Formic acid HCOOH	Hydrochloric acid HCl	Sulphuric acid H₂SO₄	Tartaric acid C₄H₆O₆	Tannic acid C₁₄H₁₀O₉	Potassium dichromate K₂Cr₂O₇	Sodium dichromate Na₂Cr₂O₇	Caustic soda NaOH	Sodium acetate CH₃COONa	Sodium bisulphite (SO₂ in NaHSO₃)	Sodium carbonate Na₂CO₃	Potassium carbonate K₂CO₃
1	4	2	1	0·8	1·1	1·3	0·7	0·7	0·5	1	0·3	0·5	0·6
2	7·2	4	2	1·6	2·2	2·5	1·3	1·4	0·9	2	0·6	0·9	1·1
3	10·6	6	3	2·3	3·3	3·8	2	2·1	1·3	2·8	0·9	1·4	1·6
4	14	8	4	3	4·4	5	2·6	2·8	1·7	3·8	1·2	1·9	2·2
5	18	10	5	3·8	5·5	6·2	3·3	3·5	2·2	4·8	1·5	2·4	2·7
6	22	12	6	4·5	6·5	7·4	4	4·3	2·6	5·8	1·8	2·8	3·3
7	25	14	7	5·3	7·5	8·6	4·6	5	3	6·7	2·1	3·3	3·8
8	29	16	8	6	8·6	9·9	5·5	5·7	3·5	7·6	2·4	3·8	4·4
9	33	18	9	6·7	9·6	11	6·3	6·4	3·9	8·6	2·7	4·2	4·9
10	38	20	10	7·4	10·7	12·3	7	7·1	4·4	9·6	3	4·7	5·5
11	43/100	22	11	8·2	11·7	13·5	7·7	7·8	4·8	10·6	3·2	5·2	6
12	48/98	24	12	8·9	12·7	14·7	8·3	8·5	5·2	11·5	3·5	5·7	6·5
13	56/94	25	13	9·6	13·8	15·9	9	9·2	5·7	12·4	3·8	6·2	7·2
14	63/90	28	14	10·3	14·8	17	9·5	10	6·2	13·3	4	6·7	7·6
15	75/80	30	15	11	15·8	18·2	10·3	10·7	6·6	14·2	4·3	7·1	8·1
16		32	16	11·7	16·8	19·3	11	11·4	7	15	4·6	7·6	8·6
17	*See Note 1 below*	34	17	12·4	17·7	20·6	11·7	12·1	7·5	16	4·9	8	9·2
18		36	18	13	18·7		12·3	12·8	8	17	5·1	8·5	9·7
19		38	19	13·7	19·6		12·9	13·5	8·4	17·8	5·4	8·9	10·2
20		40	20	14·4	20·5		13·5	14·2	8·8	18·7	5·7	9·3	10·7
21		43	21	15	21·5		14·3	15	9·2	19·6	6·1	9·8	11·2
22		45	22	15·7	22·6		15	15·7	9·6	20·5	6·4	10·3	11·7
23		47	23	16·4	23·6			16·4	10	21·4	6·7	10·8	12·3
24		49	24	17	24·6			17·1	10·5	22·3	7	11·2	12·8
25		51	25	17·7	25·5			17·8	11	23·2	7·3	11·7	13·3
26		53	26	18·4	26·4			18·5	11·5	24	7·6	12·2	13·8
27		55	27	19	27·2			19·2	12	24·8	7·9	12·7	14·3
28		58	28	19·7	28·1			20	12·5	25·6	8·3	13·1	14·8

Continued on page 260.

Note 1. Where the hydrometer reading indicates two possible concentrations, add some water. A rise in the reading indicates that the acid is of the **higher** concentration; a fall indicates the lower strength

259

Solutions of Common Chemicals (continued) (grammes per 100 grammes)

°Tw	Acetic acid CH₃COOH	Formic acid HCOOH	Hydrochloric acid HCl	Sulphuric acid H₂SO₄	Tartaric acid C₄H₆O₆	Tannic acid C₁₄H₁₀O₉	Potassium dichromate K₂Cr₂O₇	Sodium dichromate Na₂Cr₂O₇	Caustic soda NaOH	Sodium acetate CH₃COONa	Sodium bisulphite (SO₂ in NaHSO₃)	Sodium carbonate Na₂CO₃	Sodium carbonate K₂CO₃
29		60	29	20·3	29·2			20·8	13	26·5	8·6	13·5	15·3
30		62	30	21	29·9			21·5	13·4	27·4	8·9	14	15·8
31		64	31	21·6	30·9			22·3	13·8	28·2	9·2	14·4	16·3
32		66	32	22·3	31·7			23·1	14·2	29	9·5		16·8
33		68	33	22·9	32·7			23·9	14·6	29·8	9·8		17·3
34		70	34	23·5	33·5			24·7	15	30·6	10·1		17·8
35		72	35	24·2	34·5			25·5	15·5		10·4		18·3
36		74	36	24·8	35·2			26·3	16		10·8		18·8
37		76	37	25·4	36·2			27	16·5		11·2		19·3
38		78	38	26	36·8			27·7	17		11·5		19·7
39		81	39	26·7	37·8			28·3	17·4		11·9		20·2
40		84	40	27·3	38·5			29	17·8		12·2		20·7
41		87	41	27·9	39·5			29·7	18·2		12·6		21·2
42		90	42	28·5	40·4			30·4	18·7		12·9		21·7
43		93		29·1	41·2			31·1	19·2		13·3		22·2
44		96		29·8	42			31·8	19·7		13·7		22·6
45		100		30·4	42·7			32·5	20·2		14·1		23·1
46				31	43·7			33·2	20·6		14·4		23·6
47				31·6	44·6			33·9	21		14·8		24
48				32·2	45·2			34·5	21·5		15·1		24·5
49				32·8	46·2			35·1	22		15·5		24·9
50				33·4	46·7			35·8	22·4		15·8		25·4
51				34	47·7			36·5	22·9		16·3		25·8
52				34·6	48·6			37·2	23·3		16·7		26·2
53				35·2	49·1			37·9	23·7		17·2		26·7
54				35·8	50			38·6	24·2		17·5		27·1
55				36·4	50·8			39·3	24·6		17·9		27·6
56				36·9	51·5			40	25		18·3		28·1
*				*	*						*		*

* Continued on page 261.

Note 1. Where the hydrometer reading indicates two possible concentrations, add some water. A rise in the reading indicates that the acid is of the higher

Solutions of Common Chemicals (continued)
(grammes per 100 grammes)

°Tw	Sulphuric acid H_2SO_4	Tartaric acid $C_4H_6O_6$	Caustic soda NaOH	Sodium bisulphite (SO_2 in $NaHSO_3$)	Potassium carbonate K_2CO_3
57	37·5	52·3	25·5	18·7	28·6
58	38·1	53	26	19·1	29
59	38·7	53·8	26·4	19·6	29·5
60	39·3	54·7	26·9	20·2	30
61	39·8		27·4	20·8	30·4
62	40·4		27·9	21·4	30·8
63	41		28·3	22	31·2
64	41·5		28·8	22·4	31·6
65	42·1		29·3	22·7	32·1
66	42·6		29·8	22·9	32·5
67	43·2		30·3	23·2	32·9
68	43·8		30·7	23·4	33·3
69	44·3		31·2	23·6	33·8
70	44·8		31·8		34·2
71	45·4		32·3		34·6
72	45·9		32·8		35·1
73	46·5		33·3		35·6
74	47		33·7		36
75	47·5		34·2		36·4
76	48		34·7		36·8
77	48·6		35·2		37·2
78	49·1		35·7		37·6
79	49·6		36·2		38
80	50·1		36·7		38·4
81	50·6		37·2		38·9
82	51·1		37·7		39·4
83	51·6		38·2		39·8
84	52·1		38·7		40·1
85	52·6		39·2		40·5
86	53·1		39·7		40·9
87	53·6		40·2		41·4
88	54·1		40·7		41·8
89	54·6		41·2		42·2
90	55		41·7		42·7
91	55·5		42·2		43·2
92	56		42·8		43·6
93	56·5		43·3		43·9
94	57		43·8		44·3
95	57·4		44·3		44·7
96	57·8		44·9		45·1
97	58·3		45·4		45·6
98	58·8		45·9		46
99	59·3		46·4		46·6
100	59·8		46·9		47·2
102	60·7		48		47·8
104	61·6		49·1		48·3
106	62·5		50·1*		48·9
108	63·4				49·6
110	64·3				51·8*
120	68·7				
168	95				

* not soluble above this concentration at room temperature

Atmospheric Pressure

Pressure in Atmospheres	lbf/in^2	N/m^2
½ atmosphere	7·35	$5·07 \times 10^4$
1 atmosphere	14·70	$1·01 \times 10^5$
1½ atmosphere	22·04	$1·52 \times 10^5$
2 atmosphere	29·39	$2·02 \times 10^5$
2½ atmosphere	36·74	$2·53 \times 10^5$
3 atmosphere	44·09	$3·03 \times 10^5$
3½ atmosphere	51·44	$3·54 \times 10^5$
4 atmosphere	58·78	$4·04 \times 10^5$

Strength of Ammonia Liquor

Specific Gravity of Ammonia Liquor to be Used	Amount needed to Replace 10 Parts of Ammonia Liquor (specific gravity 0·880)
0·880	10·0 parts
0·885	10·5 parts
0·890	11·0 parts
0·895	11·7 parts
0·900	12·4 parts
0·905	13·2 parts
0·910	14·0 parts
0·915	15·0 parts
0·920	16·1 parts
0·925	17·3 parts

262

Conversion between 'grammes per litre' and 'ounces per Imperial and US gallons'

g/litre	oz/US gal	oz/Imp gal	g/litre	oz/US gal	oz/Imp gal
100	13·32	16	10	1·35	1⅝
90	11·97	14⅜	9	1·25	1½
80	10·62	12¾	8	1·04	1¼
75	9·99	12	7	0·94	1⅛
70	9·37	11¼	6	0·73	⅞
60	8·01	9⅝	5	0·67	¾
50	6·66	8	4	0·52	⅝
40	5·31	6⅜	3	0·42	½
30	8·96	4¾	2	0·31	⅜
25	3·33	4	1	0·21	¼
20	2·71	3¼	0·75	0·10	⅛

oz/US gal	g/litre	oz/US gal	g/litre	oz/Imp gal	g/litre	oz/Imp gal	g/litre
16	119·82	6	44·49	16	100	6	37·5
15	112·31	5	37·44	15	93·75	5	31·25
14	104·83	4	29·95	14	87·5	4	25
13	98·59	3	22·46	13	81·25	3	18·75
12	89·85	2	14·98	12	75	2	12·5
11	82·36	1	7·49	11	68·75	1	6·25
10	74·87	¾	5·62	10	62·5	¾	4·68
9	67·39	½	3·74	9	56·25	½	3·12
8	59·90	¼	1·87	8	50	¼	1·56
7	52·41			7	43·75		

Conversion Formulae:

$$\frac{\text{g/litre}}{100} = \text{lb/Imp. gal} \qquad \frac{\text{g/litre}}{120} = \text{lb/US gal}$$

$$\frac{\text{g/litre}}{6·25} = \text{oz/Imp gal}$$

$$7·49 \times \text{oz/US gal} = \text{g/litre}$$
$$6·25 \times \text{oz/Imp gal} = \text{g/litre}$$
$$100 \times \text{lb/Imp gal} = \text{g/litre}$$

Note: The US gallon (used in the USA) is smaller than the British or Imperial gallon. By referring to the table it is possible to convert metric units to and from US gallons.

1 Imp gal = 1·20094 US gal
and 1 US gal = 0·83268 Imp gal

Conversion of 'US gallons to litres', and 'litres to US gallons and US pints'

US gallons	litres	litres	US gallons and US pints	
1	3·7853	1		2·11
2	7·5706	2		4·23
3	11·3559	3		6·34
4	15·1412	4	1	0·45
5	18·9265	5	1	2·56
6	22·7118	6	1	4·68
7	26·4971	7	1	6·79
8	30·2824	8	2	0·91
9	34·0677	9	2	3·02
10	37·853	10	2	5·13
20	75·706	11	2	7·25
30	113·559	12	3	1·36
40	151·412	13	3	3·47
50	189·265	14	3	5·59
60	227·118	15	3	7·70
70	264·971	16	4	1·81
80	302·824	17	4	3·93
90	340·677	18	4	6·04
100	378·530	19	5	0·15
200	757·060	20	5	2·27
300	1135·590	21	5	4·38
400	1514·120	22	5	6·49
500	1892·650	23	6	0·61
1000	3785·300	24	6	2·72
		25	6	4·83
		50	13	1·66
		75	19	6·49
		100	26	3·32

CONCENTRATED BRANDS: PERCENTAGE ADJUSTMENT

In many cases, dyestuffs are marketed in concentrations differing from that of the standard product. In all such cases the strength relationship between the particular product and the standard brand is shown in the product name, for example:

'Chlorazol' Green *BN 125* is 1·25 times as strong as
'Chlorazol' Green *BNS*.
'Chlorazol' Black *EN 200* is twice as strong as 'Chlorazol' Black *ENS*.

The recipes given in our publications usually refer to dyestuffs of normal (standard) concentrations, and the following table indicates the quantities of concentrated brands necessary to replace given percentages of standard products.

For S Brand:	1%	0·9%	0·8%	0·7%	0·6%	0·5%	0·4%	0·3%	0·2%	0·1%
Concentrated brand	%	%	%	%	%	%	%	%	%	%
110	0·91	0·82	0·73	0·64	0·545	0·455	0·365	0·275	0·181	0·091
115	0·87	0·78	0·7	0·61	0·52	0·435	0·35	0·26	0·172	0·087
120	0·83	0·75	0·66	0·58	0·5	0·415	0·335	0·25	0·166	0·083
125	0·8	0·72	0·64	0·56	0·48	0·4	0·32	0·24	0·16	0·08
130	0·77	0·69	0·615	0·54	0·46	0·385	0·315	0·23	0·154	0·077
135	0·74	0·67	0·59	0·52	0·445	0·37	0·297	0·222	0·148	0·074
140	0·71	0·64	0·57	0·5	0·43	0·355	0·285	0·215	0·143	0·071
145	0·69	0·62	0·55	0·48	0·415	0·345	0·275	0·206	0·138	0·069
150	0·67	0·6	0·533	0·466	0·4	0·335	0·265	0·2	0·134	0·067
155	0·645	0·58	0·515	0·45	0·386	0·325	0·26	0·194	0·129	0·064
160	0·625	0·56	0·5	0·436	0·375	0·315	0·25	0·188	0·125	0·062
165	0·605	0·545	0·485	0·425	0·365	0·305	0·245	0·181	0·122	0·06
170	0·59	0·53	0·47	0·41	0·353	0·295	0·235	0·176	0·118	0·059
175	0·57	0·51	0·46	0·4	0·345	0·285	0·23	0·172	0·114	0·057
180	0·555	0·5	0·445	0·39	0·335	0·28	0·225	0·166	0·111	0·055
185	0·54	0·486	0·43	0·38	0·325	0·27	0·215	0·162	0·108	0·054
190	0·526	0·473	0·42	0·37	0·315	0·263	0·21	0·158	0·106	0·052
195	0·512	0·46	0·41	0·36	0·31	0·256	0·205	0·154	0·103	0·051
200	0·5	0·45	0·4	0·35	0·3	0·25	0·2	0·15	0·1	0·05
210	0·476	0·428	0·38	0·33	0·285	0·238	0·19	0·142	0·095	0·047
220	0·454	0·409	0·363	0·318	0·272	0·227	0·18	0·136	0·09	0·045
250	0·4	0·36	0·32	0·28	0·24	0·2	0·16	0·12	0·08	0·04
300	0·33	0·3	0·266	0·233	0·2	0·166	0·133	0·1	0·066	0·033
400	0·25	0·225	0·2	0·175	0·15	0·122	0·1	0·075	0·05	0·022
500	0·2	0·18	0·16	0·14	0·12	0·1	0·08	0·06	0·04	0·02
800	0·125	0·111	0·1	0·087	0·075	0·062	0·05	0·037	0·025	0·012

Appendix 2

SUPPLIERS OF SCREEN PRINTING EQUIPMENT IN THE
UNITED KINGDOM

1. Screens

These may be purchased from:

Screen Process Supplies Ltd. (a member of the Sericol Group),
    24, Parson's Green Lane, London, SW6 4HS
Screentex Ltd., Penlake Works, Reginald Road, St. Helens, Lancs.
Pronk Davis & Rusby Ltd., 90–96, Brewery Road, London, N7 9PD
A. J. Purdy & Co. Ltd., 248, Lea Bridge Road, Leyton, London, E10
George Hall (Sales) Ltd., Hardman Street, Chestergate, Stockport,
    SK3 0HA
Langley Manufacturing Co. (Screens) Ltd., Langley, Nr. Macclesfield,
    Cheshire

2. Tables and General Screen-printing Equipment

The Macclesfield Engineering and Sheet Metal Co. Ltd., Windmill
    Street, Macclesfield, Cheshire, SK11 7HS
Tecnic Gali Ltd., 2, Pendennis Road, Streatham, London, SW16
Screen Process Supplies Ltd., address as in (1)
Pronk Davis & Rusby Ltd., address as in (1)
A. J. Purdy & Co. Ltd. (screen-making equipment), address as in (1)
George Hall (Sales) Ltd., address as in (1)

3. Table Coverings

Macclesfield Engineering & Sheet Metal Co. Ltd., address as in (2)
Sykes & Oliver Ltd., Drydock Mills, Littleborough, Lancs., OL15 8LX

4. Perforated-beam Washing Machines

Sir James Farmer Norton & Co. Ltd., Adelphi Street, Salford,
    Manchester, M60 9HH

5. Screen Gauze

Brocklehurst Fabrics Ltd., Hurdsfield Mills, Macclesfield, Cheshire, SK10 2QY
Screen Process Supplies Ltd., address as in (1)
Pronk Davis & Rusby Ltd. ('Monyl' nylon gauze, 'Monden' polyester gauze), address as in (1)
A. J. Purdy & Co. Ltd., address as in (1)
George Hall (Sales) Ltd., address as in (1)

6. Photographic Gelatine, PVA Emulsions or Other Screen Sensitisers

Screen Process Supplies Ltd., address as in (1)
A. J. Purdy & Co. Ltd., address as in (1)
George Hall (Sales) Ltd., address as in (1)

7. Small-scale Steaming Equipment

Macclesfield Engineering & Sheet Metal Co. Ltd., address as in (1)
Ellis Jones & Co. (Stockport) Ltd. (Arioli laboratory *A-HT* steamer), Tiviot Colour Works, Stockport, SK4 1UR
John Godrich (Werner Mathis *HT* laboratory steamer), Ludford Mill, Ludlow, Shropshire

8. Opaque Inks

Screen Process Supplies Ltd., address as in (1)
Pronk Davis & Rusby Ltd., address as in (1)
A. J. Purdy & Co. Ltd., address as in (1)

9. Lacquers

Screen Process Supplies Ltd., address as in (1)
Pronk Davis & Rusby Ltd., address as in (1)
A. J. Purdy & Co. Ltd., address as in (1)

10. Tracing Film

Screen Process Supplies Ltd., address as in (1)
Pronk Davis & Rusby Ltd., address as in (1)
George Hall (Sales) Ltd., address as in (1)

11. Screen Table Adhesive

Screen Process Supplies Ltd., address as in (1)
Lankro Chemicals Ltd., Eccles, Manchester, M30 0BH
George Hall (Sales) Ltd., address as in (1)
Ellis Jones & Co. (Stockport) Ltd., ('Adex' *W*), address as in (7)
Royal Scholten-Honig (Trading) Ltd., Moss Lane Trading Estate,
    Moss Lane, Whitefield, Manchester, M25 6FH
EGK Textile Machinery and Accessories Ltd. (Kiwotex range of
    products), 256, Park Lane, Macclesfield, SK11 8AB

12. High-speed Stirring Equipment

Joshua Greaves & Sons Ltd., P.O. Box No. 2, Ramsbottom, Bury,
    Lancs., BL0 9BA

13. Doctor Blades for Roller Printing

William Pinder & Sons Ltd., Haigh Avenue, Whitehill, Stockport,
    Cheshire, SK4 1PG

14. Block Printing Equipment, Lino Blocks and Lino Cutting Tools

A. J. Purdy & Co. Ltd., address as in (1)

15. Transfer Printing Presses (Intermittent Type)

Phipps-Faire Ltd. ('Double *A*' press), P.O. Box No. 1, Guildhall
    Road, Northampton, NN1 1DT
Ibis Engineers Ltd., P.O. Box No. 23, Ibis Works, Kendal
Labap (Huddersfield), 31—33, Lord Street, Huddersfield, HD1 1RU
Dyeing Services Ltd., Upper Hulme, Leek, Staffs., ST13 8TY
The B & W Machine Co. Ltd., 13, Hanway Works, Hanway Place,
    Oxford Street, London, W1P 9DL
Adamson & Co. (Machines) Ltd. (Kannegiesser machines), Prospect
    Works, Upper Accommodation Road, Leeds, LS9 8LP
B. L. Engineering Co. (Lemaire machines), 159, Oldham Road,
    Ashton under Lyne, Lancs.

16. 'Formosul' and 'Redusol' Reducing Agents, and Dichromates

Albright & Wilson Ltd., Industrial Chemicals Division, P.O. Box No. 3, Oldbury, Warley, Worcs., B69

17. General Chemical Products

Lankro Chemicals Ltd., address as in (11)
May & Baker Ltd., Dagenham, Essex, RM10 7XS
Albright & Wilson Ltd., Industrial Chemicals Division, address as in (16)
BDH Chemicals Ltd., Broome Road, Poole, BH12 4NN
T. Saville Whittle Ltd., Albion Bridge Works, Hulme Hall Lane, Manchester, M10 8HA

18. Shirlastain and Shirley Multifibre Fabric

Shirley Developments Ltd., P.O. Box No. 6, 856, Wilmslow Road, Didsbury, Manchester, M20 8SA

19. Thickening Agents

CPC (United Kingdom) Ltd. (British Gums), Industrial Division, Trafford Park, Manchester, 19
T. M. Duché & Sons (UK) Ltd. ('Lamitex' sodium alginate), 50, Mark Lane, London, EC3R 7QJ
Ellis Jones & Co. (Stockport) Ltd. ('Indalca' brands *S, S60D, PA3R* and *SRC 60*), address as in (7)
Royal Scholten-Honig (Trading) Ltd. ('Nafka' Crystal Gum, 'Solvitose' *C5*), address as in (11)
Tragasol Products Ltd. ('Galaxy' thickeners, formerly Gum Tragon and Gum Tragasol), Hooton, Wirral, Cheshire, L66 7NE
Alginate Industries Ltd. ('Manutex' *RS* and 'Manutex' *F*), 22, Henrietta Street, London, WC2E 8NB
T. Saville Whittle Ltd., address as in (17)
Rohm and Haas Company, European Operations, Chesterfield House, Barter Street, London, WC1A 2TP

20. Dyestuffs

'Procion' dyes and the reagents used in their application can be purchased in small quantities from:

269

Dylon International Ltd. (a subsidiary of Mayborn Products Ltd.) ('Dylon' cold dyes), Worsley Bridge Road, Lower Sydenham, London, SE26 5HD

Keegan Brico Tetley Chemicals Ltd., 55–57, Glengall Road, London SE15 6NQ. (This company also supplies 'Helizarin' pigments (BASF) as well as all ICI dyes)

T. Saville Whittle Ltd., Albion Bridge Works, Hulme Hall Lane, Manchester, M10 8HA. (This company does not usually supply in less than 1 kg lots; they also supply 'Naphthanilide', 'Ronagen' and 'Sinagen' azoic dyes)

Other suppliers of dyestuffs in small quantities include:

Pronk Davis & Rusby Ltd., address as in (1)

Albright and Wilson, Industrial Chemicals Division, address as in (16)

SUPPLIERS OF SCREEN-PRINTING EQUIPMENT IN THE USA

21. Screens

Print Tables and Equipment Corp., 340, Elmwood Terrace, Linden, NJ 07036

22. Tables and General Screen-printing Equipment

Print Tables and Equipment Corp., address as in (21)

23. Tables Coverings

Print Tables and Equipment Corp., address as in (21)

Dewey and Almy Chemical Co., 62, Whittmore Avenue, Cambridge 40, Mass.

24. Screen Gauze

Tobler, Ernst & Traber Inc. ('Nitex' nylon monofil gauze, '*PE* Polyester' polyester monofil gauze), 420, Saw Mill River Road, Elmsford, New York 10523

25. Photographic Gelatine

J. T. Baker Chemical Co., 222, Red School Lane, Phillipsburg, NJ 08865 (outlets in many major cities in USA)

26. Small-scale Steaming Equipment

Print Tables and Equipment Corp., address as in (21)

27. Opaque Inks and Lacquers

Ace Lacquer and Chemical Co. Inc., 11–18, 33rd Avenue, Long Island City, NY

28. Tracing Film

Celuton Plastics, 276, Park Avenue South, New York 10010

29. Screen Table Adhesive

Print Tables and Equipment Corp., address as in (21)
Stein, Hall & Co. (a division of Celanese Corporation), 605, Third Avenue, New York, NY 10016

30. High-speed Stirring Equipment

Lee J. Joyal Co. Inc. (Greaves mixers), P.O. Box No. 117, Lyman, South Carolina 29365

31. Doctor Blades for Roller Printing, Squeegees for Screen Printing, Block-printing Equipment Lino Block and Lino-cutting Tools

William Pinder & Sons Ltd. (Doctor blades). No. US agents; enquiries to UK address as in (13)
Print Tables and Equipment Corp. (squeegees), address as in (21)

American Crayon Co. (Division of the Joseph Dixon Crucible Co.) (Block-printing equipment and lino blocks) 2002, Hayes Avenue, Sandusky, Ohio

SUPPLIERS OF CHEMICALS, ETC. IN THE USA

32. 'Formosul'- and 'Redusol'-type Reducing Agents, and Dichromates

'Formapon' (chemical equivalent to 'Formosul') sold in the USA by Rohm and Haas Co., Independence Mall West, Philadelphia, PA 19105

'Decrolin' D (chemical equivalent to 'Reduzol' Z) sold in USA by GAF Corporation, Dyes and Chemicals Division, 140, West 51st Street, New York, NY 10020

Dichromates and the above reducing agents are probably available from J. T. Baker Chemical Co., address as in (25)

33. General Chemical Products

J. T. Baker Chemical Co., address as in (25)
Rohm and Haas Co., address as in (32)

34. 'Shirlastain' and Shirley Multifibre Fabric

Schmidt Manufacturing Co., Box 2484, Greenville, SC 29602

35. Transfer Printing Presses (Intermittent Type)

David Gessner Co., Worcester, Mass. Refer to first five manufacturers listed in (15) for details of any agency representation in the USA

36. Thickening Agents

'Manutex' F is sold in the USA under the trademark 'Viscobond'. All other 'Manutex' grades are sold under the trademark 'Halltex'. Both types are available from Stein Hall & Co. Inc., address as in (29

Rohm and Haas Co. (including pigment binders for pigment printing),
    address as in (33)
Dycol Chemicals Inc. ('Indalca' brands), 666, Albany Avenue,
    Amityville, NY 11701
Scroll Chemical Corporation (a division of W. A. Scholten's Chemische
    Fabrieken NV) ('Nafka' Crystal Gum, 'Solvitose' and 'Solvitex'
    brands; 'Lamitex' sodium alginate), 1375, Linden Avenue East,
    Linden, NJ 07036

37. 'Procion' Dyes and the Reagents Used in Their Application

These may be purchased in small quantities from:

ICI America Inc., 151, South Street, Stamford, Conn.
Dylon International Ltd. (a subsidiary of Mayborn Products Ltd.),
    refer to first company mentioned in (20) for nearest USA supplier
American Aniline Products Inc. (insoluble azoic dyes), Box 3063,
    Paterson, NJ 07509

Appendix 3

REGISTERED TRADEMARKS

Trademarks Registered by ICI that are Referred to in the Text

Trademark	Classification	Trademark	Classification
Acronol	D	Limbux	M
Albavar	M	Lissamine	D
Alcian	D	Lissapol	A
Alkathene	M	Lissolamine	A
Alloprene	M	Matexil	A
Azoguard	A	Metabol	A
Bedacryl	M	Monastral	D
Bedafin	M	Monolite	D
Brentamine	D	Nylomine	D
Brenthol	D	Perminal	A
Bri-nylon	F	Procion	D
Caledon	D	Procilan	D
Calsolene	A	Procinyl	D
Carbolan	D	Rexine	M
Chlorazol	D	Silcolapse	A
Chromazol	D	Soledon	D
Coomassie	D	Solochrome	D
Crimplene	F	Soloxan	D
Dispersol	D	Solway	D
Disulphine	D	Synacril	D
Duranol	D	Synperonic	A
Durazol	D	Tanninol	A
Durindone	D	Terylene	F
Fixanol	A	Tumescal	A
Fluolite	A	Ultralan	D
Glydote	A		

Classification Key: A = Print paste additive or processing auxiliary product
D = Dye (including pigments)
F = Fibre
M = Miscellaneous

Notes:
1. 'Procion' and 'Procinyl' dyestuffs and their application to textile materials are the subject of patents and pending patent applications in the main industrial countries.
2. 'Alcian' dyestuffs and their application to textile materials are the subjects of patents in the main industrial countries.

Trademarks Registered by other Companies that are Referred to in the Text

Trademark	Name of Firm	Classification
Acramin	Farbenfabrik Bayer AG, Leverkusen, W. Germany	D
Acrilan	Chemstrand Corp., USA	F
Actibon	Clydesdale Chemical Co., Glasgow, Scotland	A
Aljaba	Aljaba Ltd., Manchester, England	M
Amichrome	Francaise des Matièrès Colorantes S.A., Paris, France	D
Aminosol	Farbenfabrik Bayer AG, Leverkusen, W. Germany	D
Aquaprint	Inmont Corp., Hawthorn, NJ, USA	D
Aridye	Inmont Corp., Hawthorn, NJ, USA	D
Arnel	Celanese Corp. of America, Charlotte, NC, USA	F
Astrazone	Farbenfabrik Bayer AG, Leverskusen, W. Germany	D
Avilon	CIBA Ltd., Basle, Switzerland	D
Banlon	J. T. Bancroft & Sons Inc., USA	F
Bemberg	J. P. Bemberg AG, W. Germany	F
Blandola	The Blandola Co. Ltd., Whaley Bridge, England	T
Brotasul	Associated Chemical Companies Ltd., Harrogate, England	A
Calgon	Albright & Wilson Ltd., London, England	A
Celacol	Coutaulds Ltd., London, England	T
Celliton	General Aniline & Film Corp., New York, USA	D
Celon	Courtaulds Ltd., London, England	F
Cellosolve	Union Carbide Corp., New York, USA	A
Cesalpinia	Cesalpinia SpA, Milan, Italy	T
Cibalan	CIBA Ltd., Basle, Switzerland	D
Cibacet	CIBA Ltd., Basle, Switzerland	D
Coprantine	CIBA Ltd., Basle, Switzerland	D
Courtelle	Courtaulds Ltd., London, England	F
Creslan	American Cyanamid Co. Inc., New York, USA	F
Cuprofix	Sandoz AG, Basle, Switzerland	D
Cuprophenyl	J. R. Geigy AG, Basle, Switzerland	D
Dacron	Du Pont de Nemours & Co., Wilmington, Delaware, USA	F
Dedeko	D. Dupuis & Co., Münchengladbach, W. Germany	M
Dicel	Courtaulds Ltd., London, England	F
Dralon	Farbenfabrik Bayer AG, Leverkusen, W. Germany	F
Dynel	Carbide & Carbon Chemicals Corp., USA	F
Enkalon	American Enka Corp., Enka, NC, USA	F
Erio	J. R. Geigy AG, Basle, Switzerland	D
Estero-quinone	Francaise des Matièrès Colorantes SA, Paris, France	D
Ethulon	M & B Plastics Ltd., London, England	M
Formosul	Associated Chemical Companies, Harrogate, England	A
Fortrel	Fibre Industries Inc., Charlotte, N.C. 28209, USA	F
Gatto	Ellis Jones Ltd., Stockport, Cheshire, England	T
Glyezin	Badische Anilin und Soda Fabrik AG, Ludwigshafen, W. Germany	A
Halltex	Stein Hall & Co. Inc., New York, USA	T
Helizarin	Badische Anilin und Soda Fabrik AG, Ludwigshafen, W. Germany	D
Hifast	Inmont Corp., Hawthorne, NJ, USA	D

Continued

Trademark	Name of Firm	Classification
Imperon	Farbwerke Hoechst AG, Frankfurt (M), W. Germany	D
Indalca	Cesalpinia SpA, Milan, Italy	T
Indocarbon	Casella Farbwerke Mainkur AG, Frankfurt, W. Germany	D
Irgalan	J. R. Geigy AG, Basle, Switzerland	D
Irganol	Farbenfabrik Bayer AG, Leverkusen, W. Germany	D
Kiton	CIBA Ltd., Basle, Switzerland	D
Kodatrace	Kodak Ltd., London, England	M
Lamitex	Protan & Fagertun AS, Dramman, Norway	T
Lankro	Lankro Chemicals Ltd., Eccles, Manchester, England	A
Leucotrope	Badische Anilin und Soda Fabrik AG, Ludwigshafen, W. Germany	A
Lifebond	Hilton Davis Chemical Co., Cincinnati, Ohio, USA	D
Lurex	Dow Chemical Co., Midland, Michigan, USA	F
Lycra	Du Pont de Nemours & Co., Wilmington, Del., USA	F
Manofast	Hardman & Holden Ltd., Manchester, England	A
Manutex	Alginate Industries Ltd., London, England	T
Maxilon	J. R. Geigy AG, Basle, Switzerland	D
Meypro	Meyhall AG, Kreuzlingen, Switzerland	T
Minerprint	Industria Chimica Minerva, Milan, Italy	D
Mobilcer	Mobil Oil Co. Ltd., London, England	M
Monyl	Zurich Bolting Cloth Mfg. Co. Ltd., Rüschlikon, Switzerland	M
Nafka	W.A. Scholtens Chemische Fabrieken NV, Gronigen, Holland	T
Neopralac	Francaise des Matières Colorantes SA, Paris, France	D
Neutrogen	Francaise des Matières Colorantes SA, Paris, France	D
Nigranilina	ACNA (Aziende Colori Nationali Affini), Milan, Italy	D
Nylo-quinone	Francaise des Matières Colorantes SA, Paris, France	D
Nytal	Swiss Bolting Cloth Mfg. Co. Ltd., Thal S.G., Switzerland	M
Orafix	CIBA Ltd., Basle, Switzerland	A
Orlon	Du Pont de Nemours & Co., Wilmington, Del., USA	F
Ortalion	Badische Anilin und Soda Fabrik AG, Ludwigshafen, W. Germany	D
Perlon	Fabwerke Hoechst AG, Frankfurt (M), W. Germany	F
Photopake	Vanguard Manufacturing Co. Ltd., Maidenhead, England	M
Phthalogen	Farbenfabrik Bayer AG, Leverkusen, W. Germany	D
Polyestren	Cassella Fabwerke Mainkur AG, Frankfurt (M), W. Germany	D
Polyprint	Polygal AG, Maerstatten, Switzerland	T
Ponsol	Du Pont de Nemours & Co. Inc., Wilmington 99, Del., USA	D
Printofix	Sandoz AG, Basle, Switzerland	D
Profilm	Selectasine Silk Screens Ltd., London, England	M
Questral	Roma Chem. Div., United Merchants & Manufacturers Inc., New York, USA	D

Continued

Trademark	Name of Firm	Classification
Rapidogen	Farbenfabrik Bayer AG, Leverkusen, W. Germany	D
Remazol	Farbwerke Hoechst AG, Frankfurt (M), W. Germany	D
Redusol	Associated Chemical Companies (Sales), England	A
Rilsan	Organico SA, France	F
Rongal	Badische Anilin und Soda Fabrik AG, Ludwigshafen, W. Germany	A
Rongalite	Badische Anilin und Soda Fabrik AG, Ludwigshafen, W. Germany	A
Seabond	Hilton Davis Chemical Co., Cincinnati, Ohio, USA	D
Sevron	Du Pont de Nemours & Co, Wilmington, Del., USA	D
Shirlestain	Shirley Institute, Manchester	M
Solanile	Francaise des Matièrès Colorantes SA, Paris, France	D
Solvocine	Francaise des Matièrès Colorantes SA, Paris, France	A
Solvitex	W. A. Scholtens Chemische Fabricken NV, Groningen, Holland	T
Solvitose	W. A. Scholtens Chemische Fabricken NV, Groningen, Holland	T
Solutene	Francaise des Matièrès Colorantes SA, Paris, France	A
Sublistatic	Soc. des Procedes Sublistatic, Tourcoing, France	M
Syngum	Stein Hall & Co. Inc., New York, USA	T
Teklan	Courtaulds Ltd., London, England	F
Tergal	Société Rhodiaceta SA, Paris, France	F
Terital	Montecatini SA, Milan, Italy	F
Telenka	Algemene Kunstzijde Unie NV, Holland	F
Tetoron	Toyo Rayon Co. Ltd., Japan	F
Trevira	Farbwerke Hoescht AG, Frankfurt (M), W. Germany	F
Tricel	Courtaulds Ltd., London, England	F
Tricelon	Courtaulds Ltd., London, England	F
Tylose	Farbwerke Hoechst AG, Frankfurt (M), W. Germany	T
Velesta	ACNA (Aziendi Colori Nationali Affini), Milan, Italy	D
Verel	Tennessee Eastman & Co., USA	F
Vialon	Badische Anilin und Soda Fabrik AG, Ludwigshafen, W. Germany	D
Vincel	Courtaulds Ltd., London, England	F
Viscobond	Stein Hall & Co. Inc., New York, USA	T

Classification Key: A = Print paste additive or processing auxiliary product
   D = Dye (including pigments)
   F = Fibre
   M = Miscellaneous
   T = Thickening agent

Note.
   The trademarks listed belong to the companies indicated, or to their
   subsidiaries.

Appendix 4

REVISED NOMENCLATURE FOR ICI DYES

Since the publication of the 3rd edition in 1971, ICI have carried out a major revision in nomenclature covering both dyes and auxiliary products, and ICI Dyestuffs Division has been renamed ICI Organics Division.

The publication of this 4th edition provides the opportunity of presentin lists which relate the old names in the text with the new names which are now in current use. Where a product mentioned in the text has been withdrawn from the Selling Range, this fact is also recorded.

The new names appear in all the Technical Information Notes, Pattern Cards, etc. issued by ICI Organics Division. Thus to relate new nomenclature used in such publications back to that used in the text of this book, the present lists are to be read right-hand column and compared with the left-hand column. Conversely, when enquiring about or ordering material that is described in the text of this book, it is advisable to transform the old names to the new names. This will not only ensure the correct material is received but avoid any disappointments due to ordering material which has been withdrawn from the Selling Range.

New additions to the Selling Range have not been included since application properties may differ. Information will be provided on request provided details of the end-use are given. Similarly, alternatives to be offered against products no longer on the Selling Range cannot be correctly made unless the end-use is described in any query.

In addition to giving the old and new selling names for ICI dyes the lists now include the Colour Index (C.I.) numbers for all dyes for which such numbers have been allocated. The C.I. number will be of assistance in determining whether there is an alternative supplier when an ICI dyestuff has been withdrawn from the range or is not immediately available for some other reason.

The abbreviations used in these lists are:
Generic Dye Types: A = Acid, B = Basic, D = Direct, Ds = Disperse, M = Mordant, Re = Reactive, Vt = Vat, Sv = Solubilised vat.
Colours: Y = Yellow, O = Orange, R = Red, V = Violet, B = Blue, G = Green, Br = Brown, Bl = Black.

Examples
(1) Colour Index Disperse Blue 35 is abbreviated to 'C.I. Ds. B.35' or further to 'B.35' (under the column headed *C.I. Disperse*). The dye

involved is available from ICI as Dispersol Navy B–T in either Grain or Liquid form.

(2) The abbreviation R.11 under the column headed *C.I. Reactive* becomes Colour Index Reactive Red 11, which is Procion Red MX-8B.

(3) Further examples are given under some of the lists of dyes. It is important to remember that the phrase 'Colour Index Red 60' has no meaning until the Generic Type is inserted. This corresponds, in general, to that given in the lists but is in any case given exactly in the column heading above the various numbers; hence the Dispersol range is composed of C.I. disperse dyes.

ACID DYES

Old Name	*C.I. Acid*	*New Name*
Carbolan Yellow 3GS	Y.72	Carbolan Yellow 3G
Carbolan Yellow 4GS	Y.70	Carbolan Yellow 4G 100
Carbolan Yellow RS	Y.71	(withdrawn from range)
Coomassie Yellow R 200	Y.42	Coomassie Yellow R
Lissamine Fast Yellow 2G 125	Y.17	Lissamine Yellow 2G 100
Lissamine Flavine FFS	Y.7	Lissamine Yellow FF
Tartrazine N 200	Y.23	Lissamine Yellow N
Coomassie Fast Orange G 150	O.33	Coomassie Orange G
Naphthalene Fast Orange 2GS	O.10	Lissamine Orange 2G
Naphthalene Orange GS	O.7	Lissamine Orange G 100
Coomassie Fast Brown RS	O.51	Coomassie Brown R
Azo Geranine 2G 200	R.1	Carbolan Red B
Carbolan Crimson 3BS	R.138	(withdrawn from range)
Carmoisine LS	R.12	(withdrawn from range)
Coomassie Red PG 150	R.85	(withdrawn from range)
Coomassie Milling Scarlet G 150	R.97	(withdrawn from range)
Lissamine Fast Red B 200	R.37	Lissamine Red B
Naphthalene Red JS	R.88	Lissamine Red J
Naphthalene Scarlet BS	R.102	(withdrawn from range)
Naphthalene Scarlet 4RS	R.18	Lissamine Scarlet 4R 100
Carbolan Violet 2RS	V.51	(withdrawn from range)
Coomassie Violet R 150	V.17	Coomassie Violet R 200
Carbolan Blue BS	B.138	Carbolan Blue B
Carbolan Brilliant Blue 2R 140	B.140	Carbolan Blue 2R 140
Coomassie Brilliant Blue FF 200	B.15	Coomassie Blue FF
Coomassie Brilliant Blue G 250	B.90	(withdrawn from range)
Coomassie Brilliant Blue R 250	B.83	(withdrawn from range)

AZOIC DYES

The 'Brenthol' and 'Brentamine' ranges of azoic dyes have been withdrawn from the ICI Selling Range. The products, together with acid-steaming and neutral-steaming stabilised azoics, are made by Rohner in Switzerland. In the UK, enquiries for supplies should be made to T. Saville Whittle (address as in Index of Suppliers, Section 17).

Old ICI Name	C.I. Azoic Coupling Component Number
Brenthol AS	2
Brenthol AT	5
Brenthol CT	8

The Rohner trademark corresponding to the above 'Brenthol' types is 'Naphthanilide' dyes. The Colour Index does not give a colour classification to either the Azoic Coupling Components or the Azoic Diazo Components since the colour produced on the fibre depends on the particular combination of coupling component and diazo component

Old ICI Name	C.I. Azoic Diazo Component Number
Brentamine Fast	
Yellow GC Base and Salt	44
Orange GC Base and Salt	2
Orange GR Base and Salt	6
Bordeaux GP Base and Salt	1
Red B Base and Salt	5
Red 3GL Base and Salt	9
Red TR Base and Salt	11
Scarlet GG Base and Salt	3
Scarlet R Base and Salt	13
Blue BB Salt	20
Blue VB Salt	35
Violet B Salt	41
Black K Salt	38

Rohner sell equivalents to the majority of the above as Fast Bases and/or Fast Colour Salts. The last four in the 'Brentamine' list are normally supplied only as the Fast Colour Salt owing to the difficulty of diazotising the Base.

The former acid-steaming 'Brentogen' dyes are marketed by Rohner as 'Ronagen' dyes. They also sell a range of neutral-steaming 'Sinagen' dyes.

ALIZARINE DYES

Old Name	C.I. Mordant	New Name
Alizarine Orange AS Paste	O.14	(withdrawn from range)

Example   O.14 in the *C.I. Mordant* column represents Colour Index Mordant Orange 14. Any equivalent to this product may be used in place of Alizarine Orange AS Paste.

BASIC DYES

Old Name	C.I. Basic	New Name
Acronol Sky Blue 3G	B.3	Synacril Blue 5G
Acronol Brilliant Lake Blue A220	B.5	(withdrawn from range)
Auramine ON 150	Y.2	Auramine O
Bismarck Brown RLNS	Br.1	Bismarck Brown RN
Magenta Large Crystals	V.14	(withdrawn from range)
Magenta PN 140	V.14	(withdrawn from range)
Methyl Violet 2BN 200	V.1	(withdrawn from range)
Rhodamine B 200 Liquid	V.10	Rhodamine B Liquid
Rhodamine BN 450	V.10	(withdrawn from range)
Rhodamine 6GBN 500	R.1	(withdrawn from range)
SS Rhodamine Red 6GDN	R.1	(withdrawn from range)
Safranine TN 125	R.2	(withdrawn from range)
Victoria Pure Blue BON 110	B.7	(withdrawn from range)

Example B.7 in the *C.I. Basic* column represents Colour Index *Basic* Blue 7. Any product listed in the Colour Index under this number may be used as a replacement for the former ICI product Victoria Pure Blue BON 110

MODIFIED BASIC ('SYNACRIL') DYES

Old Name	C.I. Basic	New Name
Synacril		**Synacril**
Yellow G	Y.28	Yellow G
Yellow G Liquid	Y.28	Yellow G Liquid
Fast Yellow 8G	Y.13	Yellow 8G
Fast Yellow R	O.48	Yellow R
Fast Yellow Brown G	O.30.1	Brown G
Brilliant Red 4G	R.14	Red 4G
Brilliant Red 4G 200 Liquid	R.14	Red 4G Liquid
Fast Red 5B	R.56	Red 5B
Fast Red 2G	R.18.1	Red 2G
Fast Scarlet G	R.55	(withdrawn from range)
Blue 2G	B.101	Blue 2G
Blue 5G	B.3	Blue 5G
Fast Blue R	B.22	Blue R
Black A	None	Black A
Fast Black R	None	Black R

Example R.55 in the *C.I. Basic* column represents Colour Index Basic Red 55. Any product listed in the Colour Index under this number may be used as a replacement for the former ICI product Synacril Fast Scarlet G.

CHROME DYES

Old Name	C.I. Mordant	New Name
Fast Printing Green S	G.4	(withdrawn from range)

281

DIRECT DYES

Old Name	C.I. Direct	New Name
Chlorazol		**Chlorazol**
Chrysophenine G 300	Y.12	Yellow CG
Orange PO 150	O.1	(withdrawn from range)
Bordeaux BS	R.13	(withdrawn from range)
Fast Pink BK 200	R.75	(withdrawn from range)
Fast Red F 125	R.1	(withdrawn from range)
Fast Scarlet 4B 150	R.23	Scarlet 4B Liquid
Fast Helio 2RK200	V.7	Violet 2RK
Diazo Blue BR 175	B.120A	(withdrawn from range)
Sky Blue FF 250	B.1	(withdrawn from range)
Dark Green PL 125	G.1	(withdrawn from range)
Diazo Green BD 150	G.47	(withdrawn from range)
Green BN 125	G.6	(withdrawn from range)
Black E 300	Bl.4	(withdrawn from range)
Black GF 400	Bl.22	Black GF
Durazol		**Durazol**
Flavine RS	Y.50	Yellow FR
Yellow GR 200	Y.28	(withdrawn from range)
Yellow 4GS	Y.44	(withdrawn from range)
Yellow 6G 150	Y.46	(withdrawn from range)
Orange 2G 125	O.34	Orange 2GN
Orange 4R 150	O.37	Orange 4R
Brown BR 150	Br.95	(withdrawn from range)
Brilliant Red BS	R.80	Red B
Red 2B 150	R.81	Red 2B
Red 6BS	R.79	Red 6B
Helio B200	V.51	Violet R
Blue G 200	B.78	(withdrawn from range)
Blue 2GN 200	B.76	(withdrawn from range)
Blue 8G 150	B.86	Blue 8G Grains
Blue 2R 150	B.71	(withdrawn from range)
Blue 3R 200	B.258	(withdrawn from range)
Blue 4R 200	B.67	(withdrawn from range)
Grey RG 125	B.51	(withdrawn from range)
Grey VG 150	B.71	(withdrawn from range)

DISPERSE DYES

Note Only the 'Dispersol' trademark is now used for ICI disperse dyes. This involved reclassifying 'Duranol' dyes as 'Dispersol' brands.

Old Name	C.I. Disperse	New Name
Duranol		**Dispersol**
Printing Brown G Paste	None	(withdrawn from range)
Red X3B Liquid	R.11	Red B-3B Liquid
Brilliant Violet B300 Pdr. Fine	V.4	(withdrawn from range)
Brilliant Violet BR 300 Pdr. Fine	V.8	(withdrawn from range)
Blue G Liquid	B.26	Blue B-G Liquid
Dark Blue T Liquid	B.35	Navy B-T Liquid
Fast Blue T2R Grains RD	B.83	Blue D-2R Grains

Old Name	C.I. Disperse	New Name
Duranol		**Dispersol**
Fast Blue T2R Liquid	B.83	Blue D-2R Liquid
Turquoise TG Liquid	B.87	Turquoise C-G Liquid
Printing Blue B200 Paste	B.3	Blue BN Liquid
Blue Green B Liquid	B.7	Blue 7G Liquid
Direct Black T Liquid	None	Black B-T Liquid
Printing Black R Paste	None	(withdrawn from range)
Dispersol		**Dispersol**
Fast Yellow A Liquid	Y.1	Yellow B-A Liquid
Fast Yellow G Liquid	Y.3	Yellow A-G 50 Liquid
Fast Yellow GR Grains RD	Y.39	Yellow B-GR Grains
Fast Yellow T Liquid	Y.42	Yellow C-T Liquid
Fast Yellow T3R Liquid	O.60	Yellow D-3R Liquid
Fast Yellow T4R Liquid	O.54	Yellow C-4R Liquid
Printing Yellow 3GS Paste	Y.4	(withdrawn from range)
Fast Orange A Liquid	O.1	Orange B-A Liquid
Fast Orange B Grains	O.13	Orange C-B Grains
Fast Brown T3R Liquid	Br.4	Brown D-3R Liquid
Fast Orange Brown RN 150 Powder Fine	O.5	Brown B-RN Powder
Fast Crimson B 150 Pdr. Fine	R.13	Rubine B Grains
Fast Red R Liquid	R.19	(withdrawn from range)
Fast Red TB Grains RD	R.131	Red D-B Grains
Fast Red TB Liquid	R.131	Red D-B Liquid
Fast Red T3B Grains RD	R.82	Red C-3B Grains
Fast Red TR 300 Pdr. Fine	R.103	Red C-R Powder
Fast Rubine BT Liquid	V.33	Rubine C-B Liquid
Fast Scarlet B Liquid	R.1	Scarlet B Grains
Fast Scarlet TR Liquid	R.158	Scarlet B-RN 50 Liquid
Fast Blue GFD 300 Pdr. Fine	B.82	Blue GFD Powder
Fast Navy TG	None	(withdrawn from range)
Fast Navy T2G Liquid	B.122	Navy D-2G Liquid
Printing Blue B200	B.3	(withdrawn from range)
Navy P-R Paste	None	(withdrawn from range)
Fast Blue T2R Grains RD	B.83	Blue D-2R Grains
Black P-MF Paste	None	Black P-MF Paste
Fast Black T2B Liquid	None	Black D-2B 133 Liquid

INDIGO DYES

Old Name	C.I. Vat	New Name
Indigo N Lumps	B.1	Indigo N Lumps
Indigo 20% Paste	B.1	Indigo 20% Paste
Indigo Powder	B.1	Indigo Powder
Indigo Vat 1	(Reduced) B.1A	Indigo Vat 1
Indigo Vat 60% Grains (XQ1)	(Reduced) B.1A	Indigo Vat 60% Grains (XQ1)
Indigo White 50% Paste (XQ1)	(Reduced) B.1A	Indigo White 50% Paste (XQ1)

Note The Colour Index distinguishes between Indigo available in the normal oxidised form and the specially reduced (i.e. vatted) form, since the two differ in chemical structure.

'NYLOMINE' DYES

Old Name		C.I. Acid	New Name
Nylomine			**Nylomine**
Acid Yellow P-4GS		Y.17	(withdrawn from range)
Acid Yellow P-3R 200	R*	Y.34	Yellow P-3R
Acid Yellow P-5RS		None	(withdrawn from range)
Acid Orange P-RS		O.116	Orange P-R
Acid Orange P-2RS		O.33	Orange P-2R
Acid Brown P-2BS	R*	Br.12	Brown P-2B
Acid Brown P-3BS		Br.78	(withdrawn from range)
Acid Brown P-3RS	R*	O.26	Brown P-3R
Acid Red P-4BS		R.114	Red C-2R
Acid Scarlet P-RS		R.85	(withdrawn from range)
Acid Scarlet P-2RS		R.73	Scarlet P-2R
Acid Blue P-BS		B.127:1	Blue P-B
Acid Blue P-2GS		B.175	Blue P-2G
Acid Blue P-RS		B.112	Blue P-R
Acid Navy P-RS	R*	B.60	(withdrawn from range)
Acid Green P-3G 150		G.28	Green P-3G
		(= C.3G)	
Acid Black P-RS		Bl.172	Black P-R

*R Some Nylomine dyes are classified in the Colour Index under Reactive
dyes; these are designated *R.

ONIUM ('ALCIAN') DYES

Old Name

Alcian Yellow GXS
Alcian Blue 2GX
Alcian Blue 5GX
Alcian Blue 7GX 300
Alcian Green 3BX
Alcian Green 2GX

All the 'Alcian' dyes have been withdrawn from the
range. For direct printing styles on cotton 'Procion'
dyes are replacements. No alternative offer is
possible for printing alongside vat dyes or Fast
Colour Salts.

OXIDATION DYES

Old Name	C.I. Identity	New Name
Soloxan Black	Oxidation Base 3	(withdrawn from range; see p. 113 for equivalent and related products).

ORGANIC PIGMENTS AND CARBON BLACK

Old Name	C.I. Pigment	New Name
Monastral		**Monastral**
Fast Blue BVS Paste	B.15	Blue BV Paste
Monolite		**Monolite**
Fast Green BNS Paste	G.8	Green B Paste
Fast Red 2RVS Paste	R.2	Red 2RV Paste
Fast Yellow GNVS Paste	Y.1	Yellow GN V Paste
Fast Yellow 10GVS Paste	Y.3	Yellow 10G V Paste
Carbon		**Carbon**
Black VS Paste	Bl.7	Black V Paste

'PROCILAN' DYES

Old Name	C.I. Reactive	New Name
Procilan		**Procilan**
Yellow 2G 200	Y.34	Yellow 2G
Orange RS	O.26	Orange R
Dark Brown B.175	Br.12	Brown B
Red G	R.72	Red G
Grey BR 200	Bl.12	Grey BR
Black RS	Bl.11	Black R

'PROCINYL' DYES

Old Name	C.I. Reactive	New Name
PQ Procinyl		**Procinyl**
Yellow G Paste	Y.5	(withdrawn from range)
Yellow GS	Y.5	Yellow G Grains
Orange GS	O.3	Orange G*
Red GS	R.44	Red G*
Rubine BS	R.30	(withdrawn from range)
Scarlet GS	R.10	Scarlet G*
Blue R Paste	B.6	Blue R*

* Only Powder Brand now available.

'PROCION' DYES

MX brands are high-reactivity dyes, for dyeing and selected printing applications. H brands are of moderate reactivity, for dyeing. P brands are 'Procion' dyes recommended for printing, and show the best fixation and wash-off properties.

Old Name	C.I. Reactive	New Name
Procion		
Brilliant Yellow H-4G	Y.18	Yellow H-4G / Yellow P-4G
Brilliant Yellow H-5G	Y.2	Yellow H-5G / Yellow P-5G
Golden Yellow H-R	O.12	Yellow H-3R / Yellow P-3R
Supra Yellow H-4GP	Y.51	(withdrawn from range)
Supra Yellow H-8GP	Y.85	Yellow SP-8G
Supra Yellow H-2RP	O.40	(withdrawn from range)
Yellow H-A	Y.3	Yellow H-A
Yellow H-G	Y.80	Yellow H-G / Yellow P-G
Brilliant Orange H-GR	O.2	(withdrawn from range)
Brilliant Orange H-2R	O.13	Orange H-2R / Orange P-2R
Orange H-4R	O.35	Brown H-GR / Brown P-GR
Dark Brown H-B	Br. 8	Brown H-BD / Brown P-BD
Dark Brown H-6R	Br.17	Brown H-4RD / Brown P-4RD
Printing Brown H-G	None	Brown P-2R
Red Brown H-4R	Br.9	Brown H-5BR / Brown P-5BR
Brilliant Red H-3B	R.3	(withdrawn from range)
Brilliant Red H-8B	R.31	Red P-8B
Brilliant Red H-3BN	R.29	Red P-3BN
Red H-B	None	(withdrawn from range)
Rubine H-BN	R.32	Rubine H-BN / Rubine P-BN
Scarlet H-RN	R.33	Scarlet H-RN / Scarlet P-RN
Supra Red H-4BP	R.79	(withdrawn from range)
Brilliant Purple H-3R	V.1	Violet H-3R / Violet P-3R
Blue H-B	B.2	Blue H-B
Blue H-3G		(withdrawn from range)
Blue H-5R	B.13	Blue H-5R / Blue P-5R
Brilliant Blue H-5G	B.25	Turquoise H-5G
Brilliant Blue H-7G	B.3	Turquoise H-7G
Brilliant Blue H-GR	B.5	Blue H-GR / Blue P-GR
Brilliant Blue H-3R	B.49	(withdrawn from range)
Brilliant Blue H-4R	B.74	Blue H-4R / Blue P-4R
Navy Blue H-3R	B.26	Navy H-3R / Navy P-3R
Supra Blue H-3RP	B.99	Blue SP-3R
Supra Turquoise H-2GP	B.63	Turquoise SP-2G
Turquoise H-A	B.71	Turquoise H-A / Turquoise P-A
Olive Green H-7G	G.8	Olive H-7G / Olive P-7G
Printing Green H-5G	None	(withdrawn from range)
Black H-N	Bl.8	Black H-N / Black P-N

Old Name	C.I. Reactive	New Name
Procion		
Supra Black H-LP	Bl.8	Black SP-L
Brilliant Yellow M-4G	Y.22	Yellow MX-4G
Brilliant Yellow M-6G	Y.1	Yellow MX-6G
Yellow M-GR	Y.7	Yellow MX-GR
Yellow M-R	Y.4	Yellow MX-R
Yellow M-4R	O.14	Yellow MX-4R
Brilliant Orange M-G	O.1	Oiange MX-G
Brilliant Orange M-2R	O.4	Orange MX-2R
Brilliant Red M-2B	R.1	(withdrawn from range)
Brilliant Red M-5B	R.2	Red MX-5B
Brilliant Red M-8B	R.11	Red MX-8B
Red M-G	R.5	Red MX-G
Rubine M-B	R.6	(withdrawn from range)
Scarlet M-G	R.8	Scarlet MX-G
Blue M-3G	B.1	Blue MX-3G
Brilliant Blue M-R	B.4	Blue MX-R
Green M-2B	G.7	(withdrawn from range)
Olive Green M-3G	G.6	Olive MX-3G
New dye of novel shade	B.161	*Blue MX-7RX
New dye of novel shade	B.162	*Blue P-7RX

* Applicable by normal methods, both dyes give very similar shades but differ
in reactivity. They represent a significant advance in this shade area.

'SOLEDON' DYES

Old Name	C.I. Solubi-lised Vat	New Name
Soledon		**Soledon**
Golden Yellow GKS	Y.4	Yellow GK
Golden Yellow RKS	O.1	Yellow RK
Yellow 3RS	O.11	Yellow 3R
Brown RS	Br.3	(withdrawn from range)
Dark Brown 3RS	Br.1	Brown 3RD
Pink FFS	R.1	(withdrawn from range)
Red 2BS	R.10	Red 2B
Blue 4BC 125	B.5	(withdrawn from range)
Blue 2RCX	B.6	Blue 2RC
Indigo LLS	B.1	Blue LL
Green GS	G.3	Green G
Jade Green XS	G.1	Green X
Olive DS	Bl.25	(withdrawn from range)
Grey BS	Bl.1	(withdrawn from range)

VAT DYES

QF pastes are for 'all-in' printing and FA pastes are for 'flash-age'
printing.

Old Name	C.I. Vat	New Name
Caledon		**Caledon**
Golden Yellow RK-FA Paste	O.1	Yellow RK-FA Paste
(QF) Printing Yellow 5G Paste	Y.2	Yellow 5G-QF Paste
(QF) Printing Yellow GK Paste	Y.4	Yellow GK-QF Paste
(QF) Printing Yellow GN Paste	Y.1	Yellow GN-QF Paste
Brilliant Orange 6R Grains	O.3	Orange 6R Grains
(QF) Printing Orange 6R Paste	O.3	Orange 6R Liquid
Brown R Grains	Br.3	Brown R Grains
(QF) Printing Red 3B Paste	R.10	Red 3B Liquid
(FDN) Brilliant Violet 3R Grains	V.12	Violet 3R Grains
(QF) Printing Purple 4R Paste	V.1	Violet 4R Liquid
Blue GCP-FA Paste	B.14	Blue GCP-FA Paste
Blue XRC-FA Paste	B.6	Blue XRC Liquid
(FDN) Brilliant Blue 3G Grains	B.12	Blue 3G Grains
(QF) Printing Blue 3G Paste	B.12	Blue 3G-QF Paste
(QF) Printing Blue GCP Paste	B.14	Blue GCP-QF Paste
(QF) Printing Navy Blue AR Paste	B.18	Navy AR-QF Paste
Jade Green XBN Grains	G.1	Green XBN Grains
Olive R Grains	Bl.27	Olive R Grains
(QF) Printing Jade Green 2G Paste	G.2	Green 2G Liquid
(QF) Printing Jade Green XBN Paste	G.1	Green XBN-QF Paste
(QF) Printing Olive Green B Paste	G.3	Olive B Liquid

Old Name	C.I. Vat	New Name
Durindone		**Durindone**
(QF) Printing Orange RS Paste	O.5	(withdrawn from range)
(QF) Printing Orange RN Paste	O.5	(withdrawn from range)
(QF) Printing Brown G Paste	Br.5	(withdrawn from range)
(QF) Printing Pink FF Paste	R.1	(withdrawn from range)
(QF) Printing Red 3B Paste	V.2	(withdrawn from range)
(QF) Printing Scarlet 2B Paste	None	(withdrawn from range)
(QF) Printing Magenta B Paste	V.3	(withdrawn from range)
(QF) Printing Blue 4BC Paste	B.5	(withdrawn from range)
(OF) Printing Black TL Paste	None	(withdrawn from range)

AUXILIARY PRODUCTS

Old Name	New Name
Alcian Developer X	(withdrawn from range)
Azoguard 35% Solution	(withdrawn from range)
Bedacryl L	(withdrawn from range)
Bedafin 2001	(withdrawn from range)
Bedafin 2101	(withdrawn from range)
Caledon Developer AQ Paste	Caledon Developer AQ Paste
Direct Developer Z	(withdrawn from range)
Dispersol PR	Matexil PN-PR
Dispersol VL	Matexil DN-VL
Dispersol VP	Matexil PN-VP
Fluolite BW	(withdrawn from range)
Fixanol PN	Matexil FC-PN
Fluolite C	(withdrawn from range)

288

Old Name	New Name
Fluolite XMF Paste	Fluolite XMF Paste
Fluolite XNR	(withdrawn from range)
Glydote BN	Matexil PN-BN
Lissapol D	(withdrawn, see note 1)
Lissapol ND	(withdrawn, see note 1)
Lissapol NX	(see note 2)
Metabol W	(withdrawn, see note 3)
Perminal KB	Matexil WA-KB
Proxel PM	Proxel PM
Resist Salt L	Matexil PA-L
Silcolapse 5000	Silcolapse 5000
Solution Salt BN 200	(withdrawn from range)
Solution Salt SV	(withdrawn from range)
Tumescal D	(withdrawn from range)
Tumescal PCA	(withdrawn from range)
Tumescal PH	(withdrawn from range)
Turkey Red Oil PO	Turkey Red Oil PO

Note 1. 'Synperonic' *BD* is recommended as a replacement for 'Lissapol' *ND*. 'Lissapol' *D* may be replaced by 'Perlankrol' *C* Paste (Lankro Chemicals).

Note 2. The manufacture and sale of 'Lissapol' *NX* has been transferred to ICI Petrochemicals Division who also manufacture 'Synperonic' *BD*. This ICI Division is also responsible for Technical Service on both products.

Note 3. 'Leucotrope' *W* (B.A.S.F.) is chemically equivalent to 'Metabol' *W*.

Further reading from

Newnes
Butterworth

MAN-MADE FIBRES — 6th Edition
R. W. Moncrieff, BSc

1975 · 1068 pages · 216 x 138mm · 0 408 00,129 1 · Illustrated

Man-Made Fibres describes all the fibres that have been produced commercially and shows how their chemical structure determines their uses. Dyeing, finishing and chemical processing are dealt with, and recent advances in this field are summarised. The text is supplemented with many well chosen photographs and informative drawings. In this sixth edition, new chapters have been added and a general updating of the complete text has been undertaken.

The book fully maintains its high reputation as one of the finest compilations covering the most important factors associated with the steadily expanding science and technology of fibres. Well set out and printed it is a treat to read and is an indispensible source of reference to all connected with natural or man-made fibres.
Textile Manufacturer

Mr. Moncrieff is to be congratulated on doing such a magnificent job. His personality is projected in his writing and his personal views and comments enliven and add interest to a purely factual matter which he has so painstakingly compiled, revised and augmented. Like all the fore-runners of this sixth edition, this volume can be thoroughly recommended and is well worth the price.
Wool Record

CONTENTS
Part 1: The Structure and Properties of Fibres. Fundamental Conceptions. The Structure of Fibres. The Synthesis of Fibres. Orientation and Crystallinity. The Influence of Orientation on Fibre Properties. Stereoregular Fibrous Polymers. Chemical Constitution and Fibre Properties.
Part 2: Fibres Made from Natural Polymers. The First Rayons: Chardonnet Silk. Viscose Rayon. Cuprammonium Rayon. Cellulose Acetate. Cellulose Triacetate: Tricel, Arnel. High-tenacity Cellulosic Fibres: Tenasco, Cordura, Durafil, Fortisan. Polynosic Rayons: Vincel, Zantrel. Chemically Modified Cellulosic Fibres. Alginate Fibres. Casein Fibres:

Lanital, Aralac, Fibrolane, Merinova. Ardil, Vicara, Soybean. **Part 3: Synthetic Fibres.** Nylon, Nylon 6, Nylon 7, Nylon 11: Perlon, Caprolan, Kapron, Enant, Rilsan. Aromatic Polyamides: Nylon 6-T, Nomex. Qiana. Polyureas. Polyesters: Terylene, Dacron, Kodel, Vycron. Polyesterethers: A-Tell. Snap-back Fibres: Lycra, Vyrene, Spanzelle. Vinyon and Vinyon HH. Dynel. Saran: Velon, Permalon, Tygan. Polyvinyl Chloride: Pe Ce, PCU, Rhovyl. Vinylon and Kuralon. Verel, Teklan, Orlon, Pan, Dralon. Acrilan and Courtelle. Creslan. Zefran. Dervan or Travis. Polyethylene: Courlene, Marlex. Polypropylene: Meraklon, Ulstron. Teflon. Glass. Carbon Fibres: Hyfil, Thornel. Metallic Yarns. Fibres of the Future. **Part 4: Processing.** The Control of Static. Textured Yarns. Staple Fibre. Non-woven Fabrics. Felts and Papers. Dyeing and Finishing. Identification and Estimation of Man-made Fibres. Economic and Social Aspects of Man-made Fibres. List of Commercial Man-made Fibres. Bibliography. Index.

THE STANDARD HANDBOOK OF TEXTILES — 8th Edition
A.J. Hall, BSc, FRIC, FTI, FSDC

Consulting Chemist to the Textile and Allied Industries and Gold Medallist for Research (The Worshipful Co. of Dyers), sometime Examiner to the City & Guilds of London Institute in the Dyeing and Finishing of Textiles.

1976 · 448 pages · 216 x 138mm · Illustrated
0 408 70458 6 Cased

A completely revised and up-dated edition of a book which has firmly established itself as a standard work for over 20 years. It incorporates all of the main developments in the production and use of textiles, and in allied processes, which have occurred since the previous edition. The author, who has spent a lifetime in 'textiles' is well qualified to write knowledgeably and with interest about the present state of the industry.

This standard handbook will continue to be of great value to students and to all who need a general knowledge of textiles
Textile Times

A.J. Hall has won a place of distinction with this book, and it is of such a wide scope that it can safely be purchased as a general reference.
Textile Institute & Industry

As a reliable standby which will serve as a guide to the multitudinous aspects of the textile trade there is nothing better.
Textile Manufacturer

CONTENTS
The Natural and Man-made Textile Fibres. The Properties of Textile Fibres. The Conversion of Fibres into Yarns and Fabrics. Bleaching. Dyeing. Printing and Finishing: Methods and Machinery. Colour and Finish from the Viewpoints of Manufacturers and User. The Care of Clothes and Simple Identification Tests. Bibliography. Index.

WATSON'S ADVANCED TEXTILE DESIGN —
4th Edition
Z.J. Grosicki
Department of Fibre Science, University of Strathclyde

1977 · 448 pages · 234 x 156mm · 0 408 00250 6 · Illustrated

An established work of reference on compound woven structures and the only comprehensive English language book in
this field. The present edition has been almost completely re-
written to bring it into line with modern practice and to provide a more logical approach to the subject. There is a new
chapter on modern methods of designing and card-cutting and
there are rational and logical explanations of compound structures and simple explanations of very complex constructional
systems; these are illustrated by clear cross-sectional diagrams.

CONTENTS
Designing and Card-Cutting Systems. Figuring with Extra Threads.
Backed Cloths. Figured Pique Fabrics. Stitched Figuring. Weft Con-
structions. Damasks and Compound Brocades. Stitched Double Cloths.
Interchanging Double Cloths. Multi-layer Fabrics. Figured Double and
Treble Cloths. Tapestry Structures. Gauze and Leno Structures. Weft
Pile Fabrics. Terry Pile Structures. Warp Pile Fabrics Produced with the
aid of Wires. Warp Pile Fabrics Produced on the Face-to-Face Principle.
Spool and Gripper Axminster Carpets. Appendix 1: Traditional Loom
Mountings and Special Jacquards. Appendix 2: Uncommon Woven
Structures.

WATSON'S TEXTILE DESIGN AND COLOUR
Elementary Weaves & Figured Fabrics — 7th Edition
Z.J. Grosicki
Department of Fibre Science, University of Strathclyde

1975 · 416 pages · 234 x 156mm · 0 408 70515 9
290 illustrations

Since the first edition of this book was written more than
sixty years ago by William Watson it has become an accepted
work of reference. The seventh edition has been thoroughly
revised by Mr. Grosicki, and now brings out the basic principles involved immediately before describing the various classes
of weave.

This book is necessary reading for textile students in universities and
technical colleges, and for textile manufacturers with design and setting
departments: it will also be valuable for art school students.
Textile Times

It continues to offer a most valuable service and provides the industry
with an excellent source of information . . . may fairly be described as
'The weavers' Bible', for there is no question but that Mr. Grosicki has

performed his task extremely well . . . a major work that is,a practical
source of standard references for fabric designers concerned with man's
oldest cloth-making machine, the loom.
Textile Manufacturer

CONTENTS

Elements of Woven Design. Construction of Elementary Weaves. Development of Weaves from Elementary Bases. Fancy Twill, Diamond and
Diaper Designs. Miscellaneous Elementary Structures. Special Rib and
Cord Structures. Stripe and Check Weave Combinations. Elements of
Colour. Simple Colour and Weave Effects. Compound Colour and
Weave Effects. Elements of Jacquard Shedding. Construction and Development of Jacquard Designs. Arrangement of Figures. Construction
of Designs from Incomplete Repeats. Appendix I: Standard Yarns and
Standard Woven Fabrics. Appendix II: Man-made Textile Materials.
Appendix III: Basic Yarn and Cloth Relationship in Simple Woven
Fabrics. Index.

PRINCIPLES OF TEXTILE TESTING — 3rd Edition
J.E. Booth, BSc, FTI
1976 · 564 pages · 222 x 141mm · 0 592 06325 9 · £7.50

This well known book is aimed at students studying for the
HND in textiles or degrees and diplomas in textile technology,
candidates for the Associateship of the Textile Institute, and
anyone connected with physical textile testing. This edition
has been updated to include a special chapter on the elements
of statistics, to enable the reader to obtain the maximum
amount of information from the numerical results of the
testing methods discussed.

The author has used his wide industrial and educational
experience and enabled the textile student to learn to appreciate the value of objective assessment of textile structures and
their various characteristics.

'a most necessary book for anyone concerned with quality control in
the mill, in the distribution chain, or for students of textiles'.
Textile Weekly

"this edition, like its predecessor, is highly recommended to all
connected with physical textile testing'.
Wool Review

. . . so good that it merits a companion volume on chemical testing
written in the same clear and attractive style'.
The Textile Institute

CONTENTS

Introduction to Testing. The Elements of Statistics. The Selection of
Samples for Testing. Moisture Relations and Testing. Fibre Dimensions
and Quality. Yarn Dimensions. Fabric Dimensions and Properties. The
Tensile Testing of Textiles. Evenness Testing. Miscellaneous Testing
Instruments. Conclusion. Appendix. Subject Index. Name Index.